BOOKS BY MAX WILK

Don't Raise the Bridge, Lower the River
Rich is Better
Help! Help! Help!
The Beard
The Yellow Submarine
Every Day's a Matinee
Memory Lane
Eliminate the Middleman
The Wit and Wisdom of Hollywood
One of Our Brains Is Draining
A Dirty Mind Never Sleeps
My Masterpiece
They're Playing Our Song
The Golden Age of Television
The Moving Picture Boys
Get Out and Get Under

WITH AUDREY WOOD

Represented by Audrey Wood

REPRESENTED BY
AUDREY WOOD

Represented by Audrey Wood

AUDREY WOOD
with MAX WILK

1981
DOUBLEDAY & COMPANY, INC.
GARDEN CITY, NEW YORK

The speech from "Camino Real" Copyright 1948, 1953 by Tennessee
Williams is reprinted here by permission of New Directions Publishing
Company.

ISBN: 0-385-15201-9
Library of Congress Catalog Card Number 81–43129

In memory of my father, William H. Wood, who encouraged me to read unproduced plays sent to him as a producer;

In memory of my mother, Ida May Wood, who took me to see everything in the New York theater since she and I enjoyed "professional courtesy";

In memory of my husband, William Liebling, who believed for thirty-two years I could move mountains and for him I continue to try.

AUDREY WOOD

ACKNOWLEDGMENTS

As with any theatrical production, no venture such as an autobiography can reach an audience without considerable assistance from a willing cadre of fellow workers, interested friends and contributors behind the scenes. Instead of relegating their names to the small type at the back of the program, I should like to cite their credits "up front."

Thanks and acknowledgments, then, to a long list, including (in no order of billing, please) my good friends and confreres Lewis Funke, Robert Anderson, Sidney Sheldon, Arthur Kopit, John Murray, Jerome Chodorov, Irving Brecher, Ben Benjamin, Kay Brown, Edward Colton, Milton Goldman, Morris Schrier, Maurice Valency, Elia Kazan, David Berry, George White, Roberta Pryor, Mitch Douglas, Eva Le Gallienne, all of whom have been generous with their time and recollections. Some of their contributions have been used in the text, some not, but all were equally valuable.

To the Humanities Research Center of the University of Texas, for permission to quote from correspondence.

To Ken McCormick, who initially suggested this project and for nearly three years has had faith in its completion, and to Mary Trone, the editor, who has spent weeks editing and preparing the book for publication.

To Lois Porro, who diligently spent long hours transcribing taped history, and to Louise Webb and Zelda Davidow, who later typed the book.

And last, but far from least, to Max Wilk, whose perpetual tenacity and devotion forced me to remember the details of a long life.

CONTENTS

INTRODUCTION

by Richard L. Coe

As tradition's actor-playwright-managers knew—Shakespeare and Molière, Irving and Booth—art needs commerce. In the last century such producers as Daly, the Frohmans and Belasco used their own taste and money to make their play choices. But the twentieth century has complicated all that—more expensive paper money, more crafts people, more audiences, more potential profits, more spin-offs and more dead-end playwrights.

Enter the play, or literary, agent. So effective has Audrey Wood been for over forty years in spotting the true gifts—in such hitherto unknown playwrights as Tennessee Williams, Robert Anderson, Preston Jones, Arthur Kopit, Carson McCullers and Brian Friel—that she truly has no peer.

Hers have been the first professional eyes to recognize that certain words of our major playwrights could be transferred effectively into three dimensions. She is the one who chose for these individual creators the equally individual producers she sensed would do the most for them, a little-considered aspect of agentry. She has drawn up the contracts best designed, from her experiences, to protect her discoveries in the way of directors, players, credits and highly remunerative rights, domestic, foreign and spatial. When the word seeps around that "Audrey Wood is interested" in some new script, she is as importuned as the goddess Ceres by canny impresarios bearing divine moneybags.

So, one expects Audrey Wood to be larger than life, a physical fusion of Gertrude Stein, Lady Macbeth and Margaret Dumont

—perceptive, peremptory, unassailable and with a club in her hand. She's no such thing. Barely taller than that tiniest of geniuses, Anita Loos, Audrey has the vocal calm of Lillian Gish, and she can make the most startling statements sound sensibly matter-of-fact. Audrey's is a flaming spirit embodied in a teddy bear.

What is this gift of discerning what will, or will not, "work" on a stage?

A theater manager's daughter, she began her theatergoing as an infant and seventy years later remains, as she admits, "hopelessly, constantly, on a twenty-four-hour daily basis, stagestruck." At her father's death she tried acting, halfheartedly you feel, but gave it up, you know, because she was too honest. She can kid neither herself nor others.

Audrey's unblinking realism hit me after the New York opening of Arthur Kopit's *Indians*. Having admired its previous Arena Stage production in Washington, I'd decided to report on its future fate from the angle of the Blaine Thompson ad agency on Sardi's tenth floor. A handful of people intimately involved with the production were in the rooms, while public relations master Harvey Sabinson clicked the TV dials and culled the notices from his newspaper composing-room sources.

"Grimly fascinating," "our theater has come alive again," "magnificently played," "intelligent and provocative," "superbly arresting" and "marathon dimensions," ran the heady gamut. Audrey, first to read the words that had inspired such hosannahs, cautioned: "Very nice. But wait until tomorrow morning. If there's not a line in the Brooks Atkinson lobby at ten o'clock, we're sunk." I got there at ten and found three people. *Indians* got only ninety-six New York performances, a fiscal disaster. It would have a movie future but, *oy vey*, what a future!

How things can go wrong forms some of the dramatic scenes of Audrey Wood's career. How they might be right has been her vision throughout. She has seen them go this way or that, Saturday closings and Pulitzers. But in all of the plays she has represented, she has had a faith, the serenity which comes after the ringing of a bell that only she can hear. That serenity is marvelously matched with that of her writers who know the mood, the inspiration they were trying to capture. In plays from *Room Service* to *Battle of Angels* to *Wings* and *Sarah in America*, she has empathized with the spirit of those scripts she has read in Fifty-seventh Street or Westport loneliness. She has withheld productions and conceivably even has been wrong about her choices. But who else has influenced so doggedly the transference to the world's imaginations such vivid characters and scenes as her authors have created?

Though she was born just off Times Square—"Nine thousand plays ago . . . the year was 1905"—and though her memorable husband-partner, William Liebling, was as compleat a New Yorker, she has had a vital awareness of the whole of the United States, the South of Williams, the Midwest of Inge, the Texas of Preston Jones.

Yes, this other part of the theatrical forest records the sunshine and shade of how plays get from page to stage. No one knows the hidden glade more intimately, or could tell about it so honestly. And still admit, in her final, zesty sentence, that she remains "stagestruck."

When you sit in your stall at the theatre and see a play moving across the stage, it all seems so easy and so natural, you feel as though the author had improvised it. The characters, being, let us hope, ordinary human beings, say nothing very remarkable, nothing, you think (thereby paying the author the highest possible compliment) that might not quite well have occurred to you. When you take up a playbook (if you ever do take one up) it strikes you as being a very trifling thing—a mere insubstantial pamphlet beside the imposing bulk of the latest six-shilling novel. Little do you guess that every page of the play has cost more care, severer mental tension, if not more actual manual labor, than any chapter of a novel, though it be fifty pages long.

SIR ARTHUR PINERO

Petersburg, October 15, 1896

. . . My *Sea Gull* comes on the seventeenth of October. Madame Komissarzhevskaya acts amazingly.

October 18, 1896

. . . Stop the printing of the play. I shall never forget yesterday evening, but still I slept well, and am setting off in a very tolerable good humor. I am not going to produce the play in Moscow. I shall *never* either write plays or have them acted.

October 18, 1896

. . . The play has fallen flat, and come down with a crash. There was an oppressive strained feeling of disgrace and bewilderment in the theatre. The actors played more than stupidly. The moral of it is, one ought not to write plays.

The Personal Papers of Anton Chekhov
Lear Publishers, Inc., New York, 1948

REPRESENTED BY
AUDREY WOOD

1

Flashback

Always take phone calls.

You never know where your next hit is coming from.

My secretary announced that there was a Mr. McGuire calling, a Mr. Mitch McGuire, one of the directors of an organization known as the Manhattan Punch Line company.

Although I pride myself in keeping in touch with my field, the legitimate theater, I'd never heard of this group. But its name appealed to my sense of humor. I picked up the phone.

Mr. McGuire, who seemed young and enthusiastic, got directly to the point. Yes, his group was an off-off-Broadway company, one of many such small theater ventures which have in the past decade proliferated like mushrooms in basements, lofts and other such converted premises on side streets all over New York and, for that matter, across the country. From their hard work have emerged all sorts of interesting theater, sometimes wildly experimental, often unsuccessful, but always sparked by energy and suffused with hope. Most importantly, these "showcase" theaters offer young playwrights, directors and actors and actresses a toehold, a crack in the door, a place in the spotlight where they can work and be seen.

Mr. McGuire's new group had been organized to present American comedy. "We've been looking at scripts," he explained, "comedies and farces, plays we might be able to revive, and we've found one we think could work. It was produced on Broadway a while back, and we've checked around to see who represents the authors of this play, and it seems to be you, Miss Wood, so that's why I'm calling. I'd like to know if it's available."

. . . And what was the name of this play?

"*Room Service*, by John Murray and Allen Boretz," said Mr. McGuire. "You *are* the agent, aren't you, Miss Wood?"

"Yes, I certainly am," I told him. "And I have been since the first night the play opened, which was in May nineteen thirty-seven."

"*Nineteen thirty-seven?*" said Mr. McGuire.

"Didn't you know it was that long ago?" I asked.

There was an audible sigh from Mr. McGuire. "Miss Wood," he said, finally, "that was the year I was *born*."

It was also the year in which my late husband, William Liebling, and I, Audrey Wood, hitherto a struggling literary and theatrical agent, formed a partnership, Liebling-Wood, Inc. We both agreed that April 23, 1937—Shakespeare's probable birthday—would be a fitting date on which to open the new agency's doors in our offices at 30 Rockefeller Plaza.

Forty-two years ago.

I couldn't blame Mr. McGuire for his consternation.

Could it really have been that long? Forty-two theatrical seasons ago?

. . . And within a month of opening Liebling-Wood, we had our first smash hit play. *Room Service*, at the Cort Theatre.

I cannot take bows for having discovered it. Liebling had brought it with him when we joined forces. It was a script he'd found and liked—his first, in fact. Up till then, he'd been solely an actors' agent, one of the best on Broadway. Among the clients whose careers he'd further would be such future stars as Marlon Brando, Tony Randall, Lorne Greene, Karl Malden, Lee Grant, Yul Brynner, David Wayne and Cloris Leachman. Liebling had a reputation even then as one of the shrewdest judges of talent in the theater district; producers trusted his opinion and relied on his suggestions.

He had faith in *Room Service*, but so far his faith was being tested. Earlier that season, the play had tried out in Philadelphia under the auspices of the late producer Sam H. Harris. It closed in Philadelphia.

But Liebling was certain the play would work if it were properly rewritten, and he brought the authors, Murray and Boretz, to his hotel room at the Piccadilly, on West Forty-fifth Street, where he installed them so that they might go to work. The two young playwrights were earnest, eager, willing and hungry, not only for another chance at the jackpot, but for food. (Later, Liebling would say of their stay in his hotel room, "*That's* when I first learned about room service!")

The parallel between fact and drama was ironic. *Room Service* is a wild farce in which a penniless producer installs himself in his brother's hotel suite, along with his director, an equally penniless playwright and a batch of starving actors; there he proceeds, through three hilarious acts, to produce the play, sustaining the entire troupe through various adversities, avoiding the hotel manager and his spies and finally attaining success.

Liebling's faith in *Room Service* was to be more than justified. A shrewd diagnostician, once he had a rewritten script he was certain the next step was to find the right director to get the play properly staged.

At the time, the most successful practitioner of comedy-farce on Broadway was George Abbott. In 1935 Abbott had taken on an unsuccessful farce called *Hobby Horses* by John Cecil Holm, which had also failed out of town. Abbott had recast the play, spurred Holm on to revisions, redirected the work and, as its producer, reopened the newly named *Three Men on a Horse* at the Playhouse. It instantly became a smash hit, and remained so for many years.

Since that triumph, Abbott had performed his magic on another comedy, *Boy Meets Girl*, by Sam and Bella Spewack, a slam-bang satire on the foibles of Hollywood and its mores; it, too, would be a hugely successful hit, earning stacks of profit from audiences depressed by the Depression. Abbott then went on to produce *What a Life*, by F. Hugh Herbert, a comedy that engendered the character of Henry Aldrich as well as bookings everywhere; and he followed that with another comedy hit which dealt with life at a military academy, *Brother Rat*, by John Monks and Fred Finklehoffe, Jr.

With such a track record, with his touring companies here and abroad sending back fat royalties for all concerned, Abbott was the reigning king of comedy on Broadway, the man with the magic. The "Abbott touch" was the best medicine any producer or playwright could lie awake nights and dream about for his own particular project.

For the rewritten *Room Service*, none other than Abbott would do. So decided William Liebling, and he was determined to secure the king for our clients, Messrs. Murray and Boretz. This was the first play he'd ever represented as an agent, and even after its out-of-town failure he felt it deserved the best.

How to accomplish such a feat?

Sam Harris still had first call on the rewritten script—and yet it was obvious to Liebling the source of the play's future salvation would be, had to be, Abbott.

The problem was to get them together, and it was a tough one.

Both Harris and Abbott were eminently famous theatrical men, sovereigns in their own right. Such panjandrums did not merely pick up a telephone to call on each other, no indeed. There was a certain ritual, as befits royalty, involved. Who would make the first move? Certainly not Harris, a producer of major hit plays, a powerful force since World War I. Certainly not Abbott, currently the most sought-after success in the business.

In order to break the logjam, Liebling went to work. He was a determined man, not to be stopped by mere protocol.

One weekend, having discovered that Abbott was staying in New York instead of going to his country home on Long Island, Liebling called Abbott's house and left a message: Sam Harris had phoned and wished to discuss *Room Service* with Abbott.

Promptly Abbott called Harris, ready to discuss *Room Service*. When Harris responded, it was to report that while he had read the revised script—the product of all those days spent by Murray and Boretz at the Piccadilly Hotel—he still did not feel that the play was right for him. He declined to continue; the play was now available.

Abbott quickly read the revision; a man known for his prompt judgments, he decided the play *was* right for him. He would produce and direct *Room Service*.

There was a jackpot in sight. I drew up a production contract for Murray and Boretz—the first out of our new firm.

Abbott was also famous for his speed.

In mid-May, a few weeks after Liebling-Wood had gone into business, *Room Service*, with a cast that included Eddie Albert, Betty Field, Teddy Hart, Philip Loeb and Donald MacBride, expert farceurs all, opened at the Cort Theatre on West Forty-eighth Street.

Opening night, Liebling and I watched as the performers on-stage went through their rapid-fire paces. The audience roared with laughter and the final curtain descended to waves of applause. The play had come a long way from Philadelphia. Abbott had done it again—or had he? Now it was up to those notoriously difficult fellows, the New York drama critics, to say yea or to turn thumbs down.

Nowadays, after a theatrical opening, it's traditional to go to Sardi's Restaurant on Forty-fourth Street and wait for the reviews to be brought in by an out-of-breath press agent who's been upstairs at the *Times* office and gotten it hot out of Frank Rich's typewriter, or who has a spy over at the *Post*, where he can pick up Clive Barnes's opinion. Meanwhile everyone concerned can watch an upstairs TV set and listen as the various network critics come on to give their instant verdicts.

But back in 1937, there was no such elegant ritual. (There also were many more newspapers in business in New York than the three which survive today.) That night in May, Liebling and I left the Cort Theatre and went to have something to eat; and then nervously we made our way over to the basement of the Times Building, on Times Square, where an all-night newsstand would be getting in the early editions of the morning papers.

The first to arrive was the *Herald Tribune,* and its review was a rave. If I remember correctly, its critic said something wonder-

ful, to the effect that *Room Service* was five times as funny as
Three Men on a Horse.

Then the *News* arrived. We snatched one off the stack and
shuffled through to the drama page, to find that *Room Service*
had been given three stars—almost a perfect rating. Wonderful!

I then asked the newspaper dealer, "What time does the New
York *Times* come in?"

He looked me in the eye and said, "Lady, you *got* three stars.
Why don't you go home and go to bed?"

Less than sixty days after we'd formed our partnership, the
firm of Liebling-Wood had a hit play running on Broadway.

Room Service would go on to earn huge profits for all concerned. Abbott promptly began to cast actors for touring companies, the play was successfully produced in London and then
came the sale of rights for a motion-picture version.

There was spirited bidding for this new Abbott hit. Warner
Bros., which had a business relationship with Abbott on his prior
ventures, assumed that they had an inside track and that he
would prefer to sell the play to them. But Liebling, who with
me represented the authors, was determined to secure the best
possible price for them. He took their case to the Dramatists
Guild and insisted that any negotiation for screen rights be
handled at an open auction, with the bidding to be handled by
the official Dramatists Guild negotiator.

When the dust had cleared away, the screen rights to *Room
Service* had been sold to RKO for a sum which set a new record
—$250,000.

The film was subsequently made with the Marx Brothers as
stars; Liebling also saw to it that part of the deal included the
hiring of Murray and Boretz at fat salaries, to write the screenplay.

(*Room Service* as a film was not one of the Marx Brothers
classics. Shortly after it was released, RKO went into bankruptcy. Upon hearing the news, Liebling remarked, "We drove
them into bankruptcy.")

In subsequent years, this rapid-fire farce about the shoestring
producer with his ingenious, desperate campaign to get his play
onto a stage would continue to evoke laughter from audiences.

As a film, it would be made three times. In stock companies and little theaters, it became a standby, a reliable crowd pleaser. Every year, somewhere, someplace, you could be certain that there would be audiences chortling over *Room Service*.

. . . And now, in 1979, Mitch McGuire of the Manhattan Punch Line company had discovered the play as if it were a brand-new work, and was enthusiastically proposing a new production.

Well, why not?

If the play had been a sturdy vehicle for all these years, was it not possible it could make New York audiences laugh again—four decades later?

The theater is a venture (one hesitates to call it a business) built on equal parts faith, energy and hard work—all tied together with massive injections of nerve.

But to revive a forty-two-year-old comedy?

Lately there have been other such revivals, and rarely have they succeeded. Comedy is a fragile medium, one which does not age well. Audience tastes change. *Boy Meets Girl,* for example. Back in 1936 it convulsed theatergoers. When it was revived several years ago, it met with stony silence.

Why should *Room Service*, in the hands of a group of hitherto unproven young people, have a better chance at success?

And yet, if Mr. McGuire and his enthusiastic associates were willing to invest their time and energy (in a tiny upstairs theater on West Forty-first Street, one that they'd actually constructed themselves), to give them *Room Service* to revive was a gamble, surely, but somehow my intuition suggested it might be a worthwhile one.

After all these years in and around the theater, I've learned to rely on my intuition. It's helped me to recognize the enormous talent of young Tennessee Williams when his first one-act plays arrived in an envelope on my desk, so many years ago, at Liebling-Wood. It also served me well when I encountered the first work of young William Inge, of Robert Anderson; or when I read Carson McCullers' first play, *Member of the Wedding*. Somewhere, deep down inside, there always comes that reaction, that green light, the signal to *go*.

. . . And when it came to *Room Service*, and this proposed
gamble on an unproven theatrical company on West Forty-first
Street—hadn't my late husband William Liebling been a gam-
bler, all those years ago, when he took a failed comedy after its
out-of-town disaster, installed its authors in his own hotel room,
set them to work and sustained them, and helped them to turn a
flop into a Cinderella-type smash hit?

Indeed he had.

It seemed only correct to carry on where he'd left off.

Luckily, Messrs. Murray and Boretz, now gentlemen in their
seventies, were intrigued, as I'd become, with the possibilities
offered by such a revival.

Certainly it was not the money offered by Mr. McGuire. As
their agent, I eventually drew a contract for this proposed production by which they were to be paid one hundred dollars'
royalties weekly—said sum to be divided equally. By agreeing to
such terms, they proved they, too, are dedicated gamblers.

Thus it was, in the fall of 1979, Manhattan Punch Line went
into rehearsal with *Room Service*, and in November, seven
blocks south and two blocks west, three flights up from its original home at the Cort Theatre, the play reopened.

Up the stairs came the audience, in they filed—the tiny theater seats only seventy-six—the house lights went down, the curtains parted, and the first scene began.

Yes, Virginia, there are miracles on off-off-Broadway.

The laughs began very early on, and continued through all
three acts. Roars greeted forty-two-year-old jokes and pieces of
comic business. Time had done nothing to wither the humor of
Room Service. The curtain went down to waves of applause.

The reviewer of the august New York *Times*, John Corry, had
himself a marvelous time. "Hooray!" he said in print. "This is
what live theatre is all about!" "Fast, frenzied and funny!" said
the man from the *News*, and the other notices were equally enthusiastic.

Room Service was originally scheduled for a limited engagement, but business at the Manhattan Punch Line company's box
office was so brisk the run was extended. A seventy-six-seat thea-

ter on West Forty-first Street? No matter. The audiences, hungry for comedy, didn't mind climbing stairs to get to the jokes.

In company with John Murray and Allen Boretz, I climbed the stairs as well. What a pleasant evening we had. Basking in the warmth of the laughter, we three enjoyed ourselves, somewhat like fond relatives at a recital. The laughs were all fresh; the play was as funny as it had ever seemed to be; truly, it was a proper rebirth!

The gamble will continue.

Back in 1937, Abbott's original production of *Room Service* raised its opening-night curtain at the Cort Theatre for a total investment of eight thousand dollars.

To bring this 1979 production to a midtown Broadway theater, as a first-class Equity production, would require a total investment of three hundred thousand.

Same exact play. Slightly different economics. Does anyone have any further questions about inflation?

So far, so good, but no one could possibly guarantee Mr. McGuire and his associates any further success. Compared to investing your cash in a Broadway play, tossing your funds onto a blackjack table is a safe investment. At Vegas, you have at least a chance of breaking even. On Broadway, a bad notice from the *Times* and next morning you're the owner of a nifty tax loss.

Room Service thrived on West Forty-first Street, my office daily receives inquiries as to a possible London production and/or further revivals, and we may go forward with another off Broadway producer. With luck, sometime soon, the Murray-Boretz farce, a healthy forty-two years old, will make it back to Broadway.

I am sure William Liebling would approve.

After all, he paid for room service at the Piccadilly, didn't he?

2

Curtains Going Up and Curtains Going Down

This is no business for anyone who cannot remain calm. In the theater, you have to have good nerves. If I had been at all on the hysterical side, I'd have been dead years ago.

Five mornings a week I leave my hotel on West Forty-fourth Street and go uptown to 40 West Fifty-seventh Street. I ride up to my office on the sixth floor.

On the second floor of this gleaming new building is the famous Marlborough Gallery, where there are always shows of art and sculpture. On the fifth floor is the equally prestigious Kennedy Galleries, and there are many days when I wish I might get off at either one of those two establishments and spend the morning looking at paintings and sculpture. But that is a luxury which will have to be, for now, at least, postponed.

And so, as I have been doing for many years, I go directly to my office. The art galleries will have to wait a while longer.

I will not blame you for asking me right here, as so many people do when I'm introduced to them, exactly what it is I do up on the sixth floor. I am, and have been for more than forty years, an authors' agent.

And if that doesn't clarify my job precisely enough, it is because being an author's agent has no precise definition. Broadly put, my work involves locating talented playwrights, wherever and whenever their ability manifests itself, to encourage them to write, either in their earliest stages or as they emerge from the cocoon to create for the professional theater. If they accept me as their representative, I will attempt to guide their careers and see to their business affairs. Hopefully, together we will both enjoy a long and rewarding future.

In order to find playable scripts, I read. And read. You may curl up each night with the latest best seller, or to watch TV. Not me. I always have a stack of scripts waiting for me, either from my established clients or from hopeful tyros who are waiting for me to tell them they are the next New York Critics' Circle Award winner. On nights when I am not at the theater somewhere on or off Broadway, I'm reading. Weekends, when you are tending your garden or jogging, I am still reading. The stack of scripts on my desk never shrinks; they descend on me like a steady Irish rainstorm. I am convinced there are more playwrights than people.

One night I attended a dinner party in Westport, Connecticut, where I have long had a home. To this affair came two Jesuit priests, one of whom had been a close friend of my late husband. When the evening ended they proceeded to deliver me home in a well-worn jeep. Since both of them had imbibed rather heavily during the affair, the driving was a bit erratic. But we arrived safely. I was escorted to my front door and then the smaller of the two priests drew me aside. He opened his coat, rummaged beneath his cloth and produced an envelope. "Miss Wood," he said, "I have written a play. I wonder if you'd read it and give me your opinion." It was after two in the morning, the moon shone down and somewhere William Liebling was laughing, I'm sure.

Once I have in hand a manuscript that seems playable and provides me with hope it will succeed—ours is a business that has hope for its cornerstone—then it becomes my job to locate the producer who will give that play a proper production. To negotiate terms for the playwright. To see that contracts are

drawn. To consult with the producer and the author on an endless series of decisions. Who will direct? Who will (hopefully)
play the leading roles? Can financial backing be secured for the
production, and which theater, here or somewhere out of town,
can be booked? Long months will pass while such matters are
dealt with. Then, once the play actually goes into rehearsal, I
will be a party to all the attendant arguments, crises and daily
eruptions which inevitably ensue when talented people are pro-
jected into a pressure-cooker situation.

Later on, when the play opens, wherever that birthing takes
place, I will be there while the problems multiply and prolif-
erate. There will be clashes of personality, struggles for power,
arguments and temper tantrums. More often than not, there will
be a late night conference, discussions of rewrites and more arguments. (I believe it was Larry Gelbart, the writer, who once
said, "Hitler should have had to go out of town with a musical
show that was in trouble.")

The birthing process will continue and, finally, the opening
night in New York arrives. Fingers crossed, teeth clenched, we
will arrive at the theater and sit there while the play is presented. When it is all over and the curtain has fallen my client
and I will repair to a wateringhole and wait for the reviews from
the TV and newspaper critics. If Mr. Rich of the New York
Times has seen fit to smile down upon the end result we will all
go home to sleep in a euphoric state. If not—well, regardless, tomorrow morning I will be back at my office, ready to start on
the next one.

In return for this work, I am entitled to charge 10 per cent of
the revenues I can secure for my clients. Since under our tax
laws an agent's 10 per cent off the top is considered a deductible
expense from their incomes, I can modestly claim I am worth
every penny.

For the most part, I represent theatrical playwrights. Most of
them also try their considerable talents at writing screenplays
and television scripts. Others often write novels, and when they
do I am responsible for negotiating those deals as well. Every so
often I also deal on behalf of a very small group of actors and

actresses, although that particular line of work was much more the province, in our family, of my late husband.

It is traditional in show business to provide those whom you encounter with a list of your credits. On my list you will find, at one time or another, clients such as Tennessee Williams, Carson McCullers, William Inge, Robert Anderson, Studs Terkel, Arthur Kopit, Brian Friel and Preston Jones. And in doing this job, my life is filled with meetings and luncheons with lawyers, film executives, producers, accountants and many other such high-powered types.

It is a peculiar line of work, precarious, filled with a certain amount of success, many disappointments and often disaster. I am really not sure how it is I am able to keep at it; dealing with such tensions is far from easy. But I have been an agent for a long time now and I intend to continue for as long as my sense of humor stays with me.

I really do not need to consult with a psychiatrist to find out why I choose each morning, instead of a pleasant retirement somewhere in a sunny condominium, to continue coping with the problems that are waiting for me upstairs on the sixth floor. After working with gifted playwrights all these years, I instinctively understand my own motivations as clearly as I should recognize them in any of the characters in a well-crafted play.

I enjoy what I am doing.

All of it. Nearly every day.

3

Supporting Cast

Nine thousand plays ago, I was born on the dining-room table in a New York apartment on West Fifty-first Street.

The year was 1905—February 28—a Tuesday.

My father, William H. Wood, was at the time the business manager of the Broadway Theatre on Broadway at Fortieth Street. My mother, Ida Wood, decided to have a child a few years after her marriage to my father and, finally having had me, showed no desire to try again. I would be their only child.

From the start, I was a cut-rate baby.

Dr. Shoales, who delivered me, was the doctor on twenty-four-hour call at the Broadway; he was what is known in the profession as the "house doctor" and he quite rightly sent a bill for his services. My mother was shocked at his audacity. "What —*pay* doctors?" she complained. Her indignation paid off because his bill was immediately reduced from a respectable twenty-five dollars to a puny fifteen.

My parents decided to name me Audrey as a result of their admiration for a dramatization of a novel by one Mary Johnston, produced on Broadway before I was born. Perhaps it was a bad choice but, happily, it was not an omen. That play closed with unusual rapidity. I, however, have stayed around quite a while.

As a middle name for me they chose Violet. When I grew older my father proudly had visiting cards printed for me to use, using the full billing of Audrey Violet Wood. On the left-hand corner, with old-world politesse, he added, "Saturdays at Home."

The first moment I began to develop a small mind of my own, I managed to rid myself of Violet. Since neither parent took any position in the matter, I breathed with more ease and was considerably less self-conscious.

People reach the theatrical profession in ways that are usually stranger than any playwright's fiction. My father began his lifelong infatuation with the American theater by way of a Milwaukee bookstore, out of London, England.

In the eighteen-seventies the Wood family lived in Finsbury Park, a genteel suburb of London. My grandfather was a bookkeeper. When my father was a child of seven, the Wood family decided to immigrate to America. Why this small English family chose to leave the tranquil British life for the new world of the colonies I have never been able to discover.

Bag and baggage, the Woods arrived in New York City with only one tangible connection in this vast country. A family of English friends had previously migrated to that city with the strange name of Milwaukee. After another journey, my grandfather brought them all to the largely German-populated Middle Western city. There my grandfather continued to earn his living as a bookkeeper and his children were sent to the local public schools.

My mother, whose maiden name was Ida May Gaubatz, was a native-born Milwaukean. Her family had come to America from Germany. They had migrated here some years before the Civil War. When that terrible conflict began, my maternal grandfather, Philip Gaubatz, enlisted and became a teenage drummer-boy in Company F, 6th Regiment, of the Wisconsin Volunteer Infantry on July 16, 1861. He served for three years and participated in numerous battles. Ultimately promoted to corporal, he was taken prisoner at Gettysburg in 1863 and confined in the infamous Libby Prison in Richmond, Virginia.

He was honorably discharged "on account of the closing of the war in July 1865," returned home, married a lady, my grandmother, whose lovely name was Ottilie, and fathered ten children, five of whom survived, among them, happily, my mother.

During his postwar life, Grandfather Gaubatz traveled on the road, selling baking powder and tobacco. His business Christmas card portrays him in a frock coat wearing a high silk hat. Years later, when she described his attire, my mother, with a great deal of pride, always commented, "In my father's time, *all* commercial travelers wore high silk hats."

When he died, at forty-eight in 1892, my grandmother was left with five children to raise, of whom my mother was the eldest. I still have photographs of the family, taken after my grandfather's death. They are in mourning, the children with their hands clasped together, sad but strong because they are together. My grandmother was a lady with firmly controlled emotions. A new widow, she staunchly managed to keep her flock in order. She took over the management of the real estate her husband had left her, coped with all the family finances and saw to it that all five of her children graduated from grade school.

My mother attended the same public school as did my father and, oddly enough, the same Baptist Sunday school. Even though my mother was a whole twelve months older than my father, the two began "keeping company" while still young teenagers.

Since she was that full year older than father, she graduated from grade school a year ahead of him. He was unfazed by the gap in their ages. According to my mother, he attended her graduation and, as she went through the ceremony, made frightening faces at her from his seat in the audience. It was obviously love.

Ida May Gaubatz pretended grim displeasure at William Wood's antics but from the beginning of their friendship she was totally beguiled by this adventurous blue-eyed blond boy from that island far across the Atlantic. The following year father managed to get through the eighth grade. That was the end of formal education for both my parents. Each of them was now ready to get a job and to get on with the serious business of "Life."

At seventeen, my father went to work as a clerk for a lawyer and seemed headed straight ahead to a career in the law. But somehow he became attracted to the world of literature and took a job as a salesman for a local book emporium. After a time he cannily secured a job for my mother with the same store, and with the training she'd secured from her mother, she became its bookkeeper.

In Milwaukee the Bijou Theatre, a thriving legitimate playhouse, was owned by an impresario named Jacob Litt. He also owned and managed other theaters in the Midwest, produced touring attractions and was doing quite well. He met my father and obviously became impressed with young William Wood's personality and his ability to put in a good day's work.

One day Litt said, "Willie, you are not meant to be a lawyer or a book salesman. You must come into the theater. That's where you belong." My father, always the adventurer, answered the call.

In that period, circa 1898, Litt also had shows on tour and in New York. They included productions of such spectacles as *The Sporting Life, Shenandoah, In Old Kentucky,* as well as that reliable old standby of a tearjerker, *East Lynne.*

When Litt offered my father his new way of life, he gave him a choice of locations in which to start: Chicago or New York. Father quickly opted for the big town, New York. Chicago was, after all, merely a thriving road company town whereas New York was, like today, the theatrical capital of the United States.

He and my mother were not yet married but hoping to be. Prudently, they agreed he would go alone to the far-off metropolis and she would wait in Milwaukee until he found out whether or not the theater was indeed to be his future way of life.

Father came to New York on a train which took twenty-nine hours from Chicago on the Nickel Plate Railroad. The train's last stop was Jersey City. From there he crossed the Hudson by ferry, the same river he remembered crossing seventeen years earlier when his family arrived from England.

I still have some letters which the young husband-to-be sent off to his intended, which evoke so well the metropolitan world of eighty years ago as seen through the eyes of a hopeful Wisconsin youth bent on making his name on Broadway. In his first, he wrote her, "Our offices are right in the center of the theatrical district, theatres on all sides, and at this time, 10 P.M., the places remind me of a fairyland, so brilliant are the illuminations. I'm sure if I spend a year here it will make a man of me, but I'd awfully like to have you here with me. . . ."

He took to the business like the proverbial duck to water and in a very short time young William Wood of Milwaukee had established himself as an up-and-coming theater man assigned to Mr. Litt's various touring shows.

January 1899: "My duties are not so heavy now and I have a little time for myself and I am taking advantage of it—a different theatre every night. *Shenandoah* is here for two weeks at the Grand Opera House. BIG BUSINESS. *Sporting Life* is turning them away in Philadelphia. Don't know where I'll be next season, might be West and maybe stay here. I guess I'm through with Milwaukee as long as I stick to this business and I don't know any other business I can make as much money as I do now. Have made myself useful down here and they like me. I move from the Aulic tomorrow to 104 West 38th Street—hall room—third floor—$3.00 a week (am paying $5.00 at Aulic). I am going to buy an aquarium for my room—they are selling them here for fifty cents complete—one gold fish, sea weed and coral and shells—cheap, eh? Have purchased a trunk and there is room for the clothes of a little girl I know. Hug yourself for your bad New York boy. Will."

April 1899: "New York's beginning to look like a real battleground. The *Shenandoah* pictures are all over the place. The show will open May 1st with Joseph Haworth in the leading role. He was the leading man in *The Christian* and is a splendid actor and an immense favorite down here. The only member of the old company who will be retained is Mary Hampton. All the rest of the people will be new and the best money can buy. *Cyrano* was so rotten that the show busted."

July 1899: "It's just this way—if they put me in the box office and make me assistant treasurer I'll stick it out to give you a chance to see New York and then ask them to be switched to the Northwest next season. If I'm going to work in a box office I want to be the WHOLE THING. See? And I'd rather be in the Northwest anyway. I'll know more about it in the next couple of weeks. I don't think any job down here is too good for me and I'm out for all I can get." This letter is signed "Love from New York Bill, your man."

In a year or so he was made part of the staff at the Broadway Theatre at Fortieth Street, which was under Litt's management. Soon he was able to send for his intended. My mother arrived from Milwaukee, they were married and, in time, I also arrived in New York.

My earliest memory of the theater is of being taken to the Broadway Theatre on Sunday mornings when my father would sequester himself in his office to catch up on the box-office statements for the previous week's performances. I was allowed to keep myself busy running up and down the aisles of the darkened theater, no one to stop me from pushing seats up and down in that large orchestra floor for endless periods of time. To wander totally free about that vast darkened space provided me with a sense of great delight and I may well have become infected with the show business bug right then and there.

Father kept his job at the Broadway until 1913 and across that stage came many great stars, ranging from E. H. Sothern and Julia Marlowe—they were known as the King and Queen of Shakespeare; Marie Dressler, who was later to become a great film star; Vernon and Irene Castle, the dancers; Anna Held, who was one of Florenz Ziegfeld's earliest attractions and who drew great attention in the press because of her penchant for taking her bath in milk; and the singer Elsie Janis.

As the manager's daughter, I got to see all the shows, usually from a good seat. I may have been on the scene a little too late to see some of the other stars but I do remember seeing such great performers as Weber and Fields, who did a great double Dutch act in mock-Germanic accents, and Fay Templeton, who sang with them in their shows, and the famous Lillian Russell, the beloved of the prizefighter John L. Sullivan.

My mother, who saw everything before I was born (and after-

ward, as well), told me of the opening performance at the
Broadway when an admirer of the buxom Lillian Russell ordered a curtain made entirely of American Beauty roses to be
hung behind that living beauty as she sang her songs onstage.
For years afterward, I could almost smell the sweet scent of "a
million flowers," as the little boy used to say, in Carson
McCullers' lovely play—which I was to represent—*Member of
the Wedding*.

The Broadway housed many great spectacles, plays in which
the vast stage was filled with such rousing sights as a real
prizefight and a thrilling horse race, a reenactment of the English Derby in *The Sporting Life*. In the fall of 1899 there opened
at the Broadway the first theatrical production of *Ben-Hur*, a
dramatization of General Lew Wallace's romance of ancient
Rome which starred William S. Hart and Grace George. Both of
them would go on to become major attractions, although in
vastly different areas of the business.

In *Ben-Hur* the climax was the realistically staged chariot
race; later it would be made by MGM into a spectacular film,
both silent and sound. At the Broadway, it would run to packed
houses for an entire year.

However, before the play actually opened, advance business
at the box office was not brisk and one day my father took home
a sheaf of free tickets to my mother and asked her to distribute
them as she could.

The day after the opening the glowing newspaper notices
brought a long line to the Broadway box office and my father
promptly called home to ask my mother to return those now-
precious tickets.

"They're not here," my mother told him.

"Where *are* they?" he demanded.

"Well, some went to the vegetable man," she said, "and some
to the iceman, and some to the man who just fixed our kitchen
sink a few minutes ago."

According to family legend, my mother thus became the only
person on record who was ever capable of getting anyone in to
see *Ben-Hur* for free.

Far from being the glamorous business which today's nostalgia specialists fondly depict, show business in those days was, for those behind the scenes, a treadmill of constant hard work, low pay and tough conditions of living and travel, often with rascally small-time managers who exploited the hapless performers.

I have another letter from my father to my mother in which he tells her of the enormous work involved for all concerned in the staging of *The Sporting Life*. "Talk about rehearsals," he writes, "I never experienced a good one until yesterday. The company commenced at 9:30 Sunday morning and were still rehearsing at 6 o'clock this morning—*19-½ hours*. I left the theatre at 4 A.M. and slept until 8, and didn't feel overstrong. . . . First public performance tonight at 8:15."

Since I was permitted the run of the theater, one of my earliest memories is of watching a rehearsal of a musical show, one which involved large dance sequences. The director-choreographer was a man named Ned Wayburn and he supervised the work onstage from high above, in a box. In my mind I can still see this corpulent man, perched on his chair, eating a large piece of roast beef with his fingers as he watched his tired chorus girls dance on and on below, with no break for their food. In those pre-Actors Equity days, anyone who complained faced a simple answer: *Quit and be replaced*. To me he seemed like some Roman aristocrat, gorging himself from his banquet, as his slaves toiled on for his amusement.

In 1912 the Broadway closed as a home for the legitimate theater; it was decided the house would reopen its doors as a home for the purpose of showing that latest novelty, silent movies.

My father's disdain at this decision was vocal—"Five-and-ten-cent entertainment." He was a theater man and would have no part in such a demeaning enterprise. Word of his availability reached the office of B. F. Keith, a powerful producer who specialized in vaudeville shows all over the country. Keith and Martin Beck were building a new theater at West Forty-seventh Street and Broadway. It was to be called the Palace.

The Palace was scheduled to open in the spring of 1913 and it was designed to be the ultimate showplace for vaudeville stars. Vaudeville was a thriving field. Comedians, singers, dancers, actors and actresses in one-act playlets, magicians, acrobats, acts featuring talented animals—all of them worked in theaters throughout the United States. To play a week of two shows a day at the Palace on the bill of the seven acts, to be seen by the Palace's audience and perhaps, if your act scored, to be held over for a longer run—that would be every vaudevillian's fondest dream. The Palace would become the flagship of bookings, the big time; and to get there, appear on its stage, would be the ambition which lured performers on as they toiled through the weeks and months of touring across the land in day-coach "jumps" from small towns to smaller, in dingy backstage dressing rooms or at night on lumpy boardinghouse beds.

But it took some time before the New York audiences began to make ticket buying at the Palace box office a regular habit. In fact, when the theater first opened the location was considered by show business prophets to be "too far uptown—five whole blocks from Forty-second Street."

The vaudeville impresario Martin Beck had a considerable financial interest in the Palace and for those first few shaky weeks he and my father were both very concerned about the lack of business at the box office.

One Monday morning, before the matinee, which was the most important opening performance since it was attended not only by theatergoers but also by talent agents and producers scouting the bill, one of the acts had not yet appeared. It was a family of elephants which would be the opening act on the bill, a spot usually reserved for jugglers, acrobats or animals.

All preparations had been made for the elephants, including, most importantly, the reinforcing of the Palace stage. Everything was ready but by noon the elephants were nowhere to be found. To lose a troupe of full-grown elephants is not an easy feat.

Martin Beck and my father stood in front of the Palace, searching up and down Broadway, looking for this missing act. Mr. Beck kept questioning my father nervously, "Willie, where are the elephants?"

My father shrugged his shoulders in despair. The Palace audience was already beginning to file into the theater, in a few minutes now the overture would strike up in the orchestra pit and the show would begin.

But no elephants!

Five or six minutes before curtain time, a strange sight appeared a block or so down Broadway. A family of elephants, guided by their trainer, lumbering trunk to trunk through the busy Manhattan traffic, headed for the Palace!

They had, it seemed, had to walk from the Forty-second Street Ferry.

The overture began. Up went the curtain, on went the errant elephants, and it was another opening of another show at the Palace.

After its first few uncertain months, a brilliant casting coup by Martin Beck finally established the theater. In May, Beck proudly presented to the New York audience the greatest star he could find for his Palace—Madame Sarah Bernhardt. She was not only the leading actress of her day, the reigning queen of the French theater, she was also well known here in America as the Divine Sarah, the biggest theatrical attraction of her time.

Bringing with her several members of her Paris company, Bernhardt opened at the Palace. As her leading man she had a dashing young actor named Lou Tellegen, who would later become a matinee idol in his own right. For Palace audiences, she performed scenes from her dramatic repertoire, ending with her particular *pièce de résistance*, the final scene from Dumas' play *The Lady of the Camellias*, later to be immortalized on the screen not only by Sarah, but also by Garbo in the film *Camille*.

That scene, in which the aging Parisian cocotte, once the toast of Paris society, dies a desperate cough-racked death, was a tried and true piece of powerful dramaturgy and the Divine Sarah knew how to wring out of it every dramatic nuance. Her audiences were fascinated, and moved to tears and loud bravos. Business at the Palace box office was fantastic.

Bernhardt had been booked to play two weeks only, but so great was the response that she was extended, first for another week and then half of the next, leaving New York only because she had prior commitments in Paris. The one thousand dollars cash per day—a huge sum in those days—which Miss Bernhardt, a shrewd bargainer, demanded and received, induced enormous dividends for the Palace management.

A grateful Martin Beck arranged a tribute to the Divine Sarah. One afternoon, after her matinee, a group of the leading actors and actresses then appearing in New York gathered at the Palace to crown the great French star with a golden wreath. Needless to say, the theater was sold out to the lobby doors.

My father permitted me to stand in the back of the auditorium. To me, as a child, the ceremony was a magical moment, the crowning of an ancient legendary queen. Madame Sarah sat on a high-backed chair center stage; her leonine head rested against the chair for support, a fur wrap thrown over her lap. On either side of her chair the assembled stars stood to pay homage.

At the proper moment, two great American theatrical producers, Daniel Frohman and David Belasco, both of them royalty in their own worlds, stepped forward. The appropriate words of adulation were spoken and then the golden wreath was placed on Madame Sarah's head.

The audience stood and cheered. In the rear, overwhelmed by the moment, I stood and cried.

Many years later, when I talked with Laurette Taylor, an equally great actress, who starred in Tennessee Williams' successful play *The Glass Menagerie*, Miss Taylor told me she was one of the young stars chosen to pay homage to the great lady at this memorable afternoon at the Palace and that it was a day she had never forgotten either.

The headliners at the Palace came and went; it was my weekly treat to attend a matinee. Each week brought some new discovery. Miss Ethel Barrymore, playing in Sir James M. Barrie's one-act play *The Twelve Pound Look*. Toto the Clown. Alla Nazimova, another great actress, in *War Brides*. W. C. Fields doing his juggling act. Douglas Fairbanks, Sophie Tucker, "The Last of the Red Hot Mamas," Bert Williams, the great black comedian . . . they all headlined at the Palace in those early days of its—and my—youth.

Almost half a century later, after a period in which the Palace was reduced to a motion-picture "grind" house, it was reopened as a vaudeville house. The star attraction was Judy Garland; the remaining acts on the bill were the best money could buy.

On opening night of Miss Garland's appearance at the Palace, I went back to the theater with my husband. Sitting in the orchestra with him I felt as if I had returned home. The conductor lifted his baton; the house lights went down and the orchestra began to play the notes of the overture, Gershwin's *Strike Up the Band*.

In my mind I was seeing again a montage of all the acts I had applauded up there on the stage as a child. I was once again standing in the back of the Palace, watching Sarah Bernhardt become a queen of the theater. Instantly I was dissolved in tears. I continued my quiet sobbing during the opening act—animals, of course—and went on through the first team of comics. My husband, in alarm, whispered, "Audrey, control yourself. At this rate you'll never last until Garland appears!"

In between going to the Palace and attending all sorts of other theaters—my mother and I could get in without paying for our seats (in those days there was what was known as "professional courtesy," cheerfully extended to members of the profession)—I also attended Public School 84 on Fiftieth Street, in the heart of a section of Manhattan which was even then known for its rough denizens and dubbed Hell's Kitchen.

I suspect word must have gotten around school that young Audrey Wood had a theatrical background; surely that information could have come from no other source than me. On Sundays I also attended a Lutheran Sunday school at Sixty-fifth Street and Central Park West. Neither my mother nor my father felt any need for churchgoing. Indeed, my mother used to say she could pray in her closet just as easily but my neighborhood girlfriends dragged me along with them on Sundays, obviously feeling I needed to learn something about God and Jesus as well as who was headlining the bill at the Palace next week.

In 1916 my father was selected by B. F. Keith's executive

office to become the manager of a stock company housed in a theater that was part of the Keith-Albee circuit in a small town called Union Hill, across the Hudson in New Jersey.

Later, Union Hill became a thriving small metropolis and is now known as Union City. The theater to which my father was assigned was known as the Hudson. In it a permanent company of actors was hired, as was customary in those days, to work fifty-two weeks a year. The pay was far from munificent but the job represented security, a scarce commodity in a theatrical career, then as now.

In return for that security, the actors and actresses put in an incredible amount of hard work. The bill changed *each week*; this necessitated that the company play matinees and evening performances of one play while rehearsing during the days for the next week's attraction.

Working in such a stock company was superb basic training for the performers; if one could survive such a regimen he or she could tackle any future dramatic problem. But a stock company salary was, in show business parlance, a "tough dollar."

On Sundays, the Hudson played two performances of superior vaudeville. Very often the theater was used as a tryout for vaudevillians breaking in new acts; the agents would cross the Hudson to scout the talent for possible bookings on the rest of the vast Keith-Albee circuit, or even the Palace.

Under my father's shrewd management, the Hudson became one of the most successful stock companies in the country at the time and its presence added a new dimension to my already exciting young life. Every Friday evening my mother and I used to take the ferry from Forty-second Street across the river, then take a streetcar or bus and get to the theater in time to be ushered to the manager's box to see whatever play was then running.

Sundays were especially hectic. I would have my morning session at Sunday school, followed by a rush journey across the river in order to be on time for the vaudeville matinee. Often I was able to persuade my parents to allow me to stay for both Sunday performances, after which we would still have to make the long trip home to Fifty-first Street in Manhattan. We would

get back to our New York apartment long after the bedtime
hour customary for a "normal growing young girl."

I may have been young and impressionable but my father did
not try to censor what I should see. He felt I could be exposed
to any kind of play. Each season he selected plays for his audience that catered to every sort of entertainment taste and thus I
was permitted to sit in that box and watch an astonishing variety of the dramas of the day.

It was a smorgasbord which contained such melodrama as
The Traffic (described in the house billboards as "An Astound-
ing White Slave Play"); *Graustark* (later to be brought to the
movie screen as the rousing adventure *The Prisoner of Zenda*);
Rip Van Winkle; Madame Sherry (a gay musical show, "And a
Chorus of Blushing, Bewitching Beauties"); that redoubtable the-
atrical standard, *Uncle Tom's Cabin* with its climactic scene of
poor Eliza crossing the ice, clutching her infant in her arms; *The
Revolt* ("This play answers the question, 'Why should there be
one law for Women and another for Men?'"); *A Fool There
Was* (which was later to be made by William Fox into a smash
hit film starring the famous "vamp," Theda Bara); and *The
Fatal Wedding* ("Witnessed by over Twelve Million People.
Don't get married until you see *The Fatal Wedding*").

All of this—plus Sunday vaudeville matinees at which young
Miss Wood could sit and applaud such personalities as Clark
and Verdi ("Two Sons of Sunny Italy Who Come to Union Hill
Direct from The Palace!"), *The Primrose Four* ("A Thousand
Pounds of Harmony"), Belle Baker ("The Famous Singer of
'Eili, Eili!'"), Van & Schenck ("Favorites of the Ziegfeld
Follies"), The Petticoat Minstrels ("Nine Exceedingly Clever
Young Women Who Sing, Dance and Tell Gags in the Proper
Old Time Minstrel Manner") and Babe Ruth. (Yes, the Sultan
of Swat himself, making an extra paycheck with a vaudeville
personal appearance.)

For such magical hours in the theater, at popular prices circa
1916 (matinees 15¢, 25¢ and 35¢; evenings 15¢, 25¢, 60¢ and
75¢), the price was certainly right. Especially since I never had
to pay it.

Despite the constant and pleasant distraction of the theater

and the two-a-day vaudeville on weekends, I somehow managed
to pass out of grade school and go on to Washington Irving
High School down on Irving Place in Manhattan.

I was never a really good student. Mathematics was my particular bane. I am still convinced that my generous high school
math teacher raised my average one point above failing in order
to help me graduate and get my diploma, which enabled me to
leave Washington Irving before I became middle-aged.

When it came to English, however, I had no problems. My
proficiency was due partially to the fact that I had been exposed
to so many plays, classic and not so classic, and through some
osmotic process I'd become literate. I also had a marvelous
teacher, Alida Hamilton, who inspired me to try my hand at
writing for the school magazine, *The Sketch Book*.

There I went through the first doorway that was to lead to my
eventual career. Ultimately, I became the editor and forthwith
established a dramatic review department published in each
issue. I cleverly saw to it that no one besides myself wrote the
critiques, which guaranteed me access to all sorts of current attractions, a happy combination of business and pleasure. In my
own not-so-humble opinion, I already knew as much about the
theater as did such contemporary critics as Alexander Woollcott
of the *Times* or Heywood Broun of the *Morning World*, both of
whom I read every morning in the subway on my way to Irving
Place.

One of the plays I reviewed and remember most vividly was
Henrik Ibsen's *Ghosts* starring the great Italian actress Eleonora
Duse. She was playing at the Century Theatre, and I remember
sitting in the gallery watching her performance, not understanding what she was saying for she spoke in Italian, but still
awestruck by her talent. I still have the review I wrote, which
was a rave.

My father was putting on a play, *Seventeen*, by Booth Tar-
kington, at the Hudson Theatre in Union Hill, and I'd never
acted before in my life. But since he thought maybe I would
become an actress, he let me have a small part. I was sixteen.

It was just a bit part, but it paid twenty-five dollars a week. I still have that pay slip—signed by my father.

The actors all knew my father. They'd watched me grow up, so they took care of me: each day my part got bigger, because they'd add little bits of business, and give me more to do. I want you to know I played this bit as though I'd been playing on Broadway for years!

After that, I actually got a job, with the Brooklyn Stock Company; and Mary Frye, who was Clay Clements' wife, was the leading lady. It was again just a bit part, but I was assigned to play—can you believe it?—*the mistress to a French roué!* I was about a hot eighteen by now, and you could never think of worse casting than me. This little girl, a neophyte—playing such a worldly character!

I dressed with Mary Frye, and one night a man came in to interview her for the papers. He didn't speak to me because I was a mere bit player, but with the brashness of youth, I said, "What did you think of my performance?"

He looked at me and said, with absolutely no humor, "Miss Wood, all I could think of all evening was a little crushed dove."

That's the way I played the mistress to a French roué!

The next week, the same company gave me a small part—this time a seventy-year-old woman! I didn't even know how to use makeup. All the actors got together and helped me learn about character makeup. So the first night, when I came on, the audience began to laugh! They had just seen me the week before as a young mistress, and here I was an old crone!

But it didn't bother me—no stage fright, nothing. I had such belief in myself I was unafraid.

I finished high school and entered Hunter College but I did not remain there long. By the end of the third month I had decided to withdraw. My decision was based on a combination of reasons. Not only had I come to suspect college was not really for me but suddenly my father suffered a stroke. He recuperated at our apartment and he became emotionally concerned about my having to study so hard every night to keep up with college classes.

I decided to find myself a job. I saw an ad in the paper for a firm called the American Surety Company which needed secretaries. Even though I had never studied shorthand or typing, I applied. In some remarkable manner I was hired and I stayed with that firm until my father, alas, died.

At that point in my young life I decided (I was making all my decisions quickly) I had to support my mother. This was not strictly true but I felt the obligation, so I decided to try to become an actress. It was what my father had always hoped I would do and now it was the time to try life upon the stage.

My career as a theatrical performer was, to say the least, brief.

In the company of a wonderful theatrical agent of that time, a man named Max Hart, I was taken out to see producers. He had been a friend of my father's and he took my desire to embark on a career seriously, totally ignoring the fact that even though I had been around the theater all my young life, I had never done anything on a stage that could be called professional experience.

In retrospect, he sold me in much the same manner as a salesman might peddle a case of breakfast food. He would bring me in to someone as important as Sam H. Harris, who was George M. Cohan's partner and a very successful showman, and say, "Sam, this is Billy Wood's daughter. What are you going to do for her?"

Blunt though it was, his method brought, remarkably enough, results. A man named Richard Herndon, also a friend of my father's, said he was sending a company to Chicago and asked whether I would come and read. Very grandly (as befitted a young ingenue-to-be), I told him I would. Then he asked whether or not I could sing.

I had never had any vocal training and, in fact, years later my husband used to say I had without a doubt the worst singing voice he'd ever heard. Since he himself had been a professional singer in vaudeville and in the course of his forty years' career as an actor's agent had heard quite a few bad voices, his appraisal of my singing potential was valid.

But on that day with Mr. Herndon I said (again, very grandly), "Of course I can sing."

Off I went to a sympathetic girlfriend who could play the piano. She played several songs for me and I sang them. That was my entire preparation for the forthcoming audition.

I was scheduled to be heard at the Belmont Theatre on West Forty-eighth Street, next to the Bristol Hotel. In order to get ready for the audition I went into the ladies' room at the Bristol and sang at the top of my voice, much to the astonishment of the matron, who had no idea what could be wrong with me. Then I proceeded to the theater.

When it came to my turn, the stage manager asked me "Where is your accompanist?"

Accompanist? It had never dawned on me I would need one.

But I did have my music and some kind man volunteered to play it for me. I stepped out onstage, he played and I sang. When I finished I said quite seriously, "That's all there is," and Mr. Herndon said emphatically, "It's enough!"

Perhaps Mr. Herndon was tone-deaf, for he actually offered me the job.

But the company was going to Chicago.

Suddenly I had to face cold reality. On the salary he offered (seventy-five dollars a week), it would be impossible to take care of my mother in New York and support myself in Chicago. So I regretfully turned down what could have been the beginnings of a great career in the American theater.

In retrospect, my loss was the audience's gain.

4

There's No Business . . .

Now that I am upstairs in my office, I put down my briefcase (in which are the scripts which I read last night before I went to bed), sit down at my desk, and proceed to sort out the various items of business that have been waiting, some of them none too patiently, for me.

Phone calls to answer (urgent, please call immediately), letters to read (this demands your immediate attention), requests for meetings (can you possibly find half an hour in which to sit down and thrash this matter out?) and contracts to study (initial each page where indicated and promptly return to our legal department).

Let's go back a bit in time to dramatize what I do. Say we are in the midst of the theatrical season of 1978–79. At this moment I am representing five separate productions, plays which are in various stages of preparation for their eventual Broadway openings. (It is a far from typical situation: in recent years there have been less and less—alas—of the "serious" dramas to be seen by audiences in the so-called mainstream theaters of Times Square—Broadway. But that's what makes this season of

1978–79 so perfect for the purpose of illustrating the work of a play agent.)

Somehow, in this fall of 1978, there seems to be a resurgence; instead of being produced in the many off-Broadway theaters or finding their temporary homes in the many new "tributary" theaters across the country such as the Tyrone Guthrie in Minneapolis, Long Wharf in New Haven, the Hartford Stage Company, Los Angeles' Mark Taper, the Arena Stage in Washington, D.C., and all the rest of these thriving and creative companies, these five plays which I represent are all on their way to the West Forties.

It may be a trend, one which would indicate a renewed interest on the part of the audiences here, the big ticket buyers, in serious drama. And if so, that is very important news for the American theater, for all of us who are concerned with its future. But we will not know that until after these five plays have opened—and the audiences come to see them.

But in the fall of 1978, the returns are not yet in.

Waiting in the wings, then, are *Wings*, by Arthur Kopit; *The Faith Healer*, by the Irish playwright Brian Friel; *G.R. Point*, a first play by young David Berry; *A Meeting by the River*, by Christopher Isherwood and Don Bachardy; and *Knockout*, by Louis LaRusso.

Each one of these forthcoming productions has involved long months of preparation and planning, fund raising, casting and infinite hours of work. Each one of them has already accumulated a complex history, in which I have been involved.

Let's start with *A Meeting by the River*.

When I first saw the play it had been given an experimental production at a special performance here in New York at the Edison Theatre under the auspices of T. Edward Hambleton, the hardworking and dedicated producer who runs the Phoenix Theatre and who specializes in bringing talented new playwrights to the off-Broadway audiences. At that point, a year or so before, I was not officially involved with the play, but I was immediately interested in the subject matter. The story deals with a young Englishman who has opted to leave the material world behind and join a group of ascetic monks in India. His very sophisticated brother comes to India to discover, if possible, what it was that caused this abrupt change in his sibling's life.

The play was given another tryout production in California and, again, I was still not its representative. Eventually two New York producers, Harry Rigby and Terry Allen Kramer, who had already produced one hit musical, *I Love My Wife*, became interested in this rather exotic subject matter and asked to buy the play. At that point, the West Coast office of the firm with which I am affiliated, International Creative Management, asked me to take over all the negotiations on behalf of Christopher Isherwood and Don Bachardy, the authors, and from that point on I became the agent for *A Meeting by the River*.

The play took many months to cast. In preparation for its production the director, Albert Marre, actually went to India to absorb the subject matter in more depth; and spent days at a monastery, learning, witnessing the ceremonies at which neophyte monks are accepted into the brotherhood, before he felt he was capable of directing the play properly.

Eventually the producers hired Keith Baxter, a fine young English actor who had previously appeared here in America in *Sleuth*, and Simon Ward, another talented English performer; you may have seen him as young Winston Churchill in the film based on that great man's early years. Siobhan McKenna, from Ireland, Meg Wynn-Owen, whom you may remember from the television series *Upstairs, Downstairs*, and that marvelous veteran Sam Jaffe, who is now in his eighties, composed the rest of the cast.

This new production started out in Knoxville, Tennessee, which may sound like a long way out of town—and it is. But there is a good reason for taking a troupe of actors far away from Forty-fifth Street. In Knoxville there is a wonderful new theater endowed by the late Clarence Brown, the film director: a theater fully equipped to build scenery, where a producer can get a show mounted for much less cost than he would elsewhere. Costs being the name of the game in the theater—or, to put it another way, where there's no business there's no show—Mr. Rigby and Mrs. Kramer accepted an offer from Professor Ralph G. Allen and opened *A Meeting by the River* in Knoxville.

After the run in Knoxville, *A Meeting by the River* was scheduled to play a two-week engagement in Boston but a hitch developed in that plan. Nothing very new—an old familiar problem: costs.

The play's production has exceeded its budget and there are no more funds to cover the cost of the Boston run. Now the producers have no choice but to bring the play directly from Knoxville into New York, to a very large theater, the Palace, for a cold opening.

A Meeting by the River is not an easy play; it is not the sort of popular romantic comedy or mystery or farce one expects to open on Broadway in these days of thirty-dollar seats. In order to exist it will have to attract audiences to eight performances a week. If it does not receive good notices, well . . . I don't need to provide you with a short course in theatrical economics.

I have seen this production and it is a thoughtful, well-written drama, filled with provocative ideas and characters. The cast is splendid, the scenery and costumes are spectacular. When I saw it in Knoxville I was encouraged by the play's prospects. But from here on its future existence rests in the hands (and typewriters) of a very small group of critics, not in India, or in Knoxville, Tennessee, but here in New York, at a meeting, not by the river but by Times Square.

Incidentally, Dr. Ralph G. Allen, who is the director of the Clarence Brown Company as well as a professor at the University of Tennessee, is a student of a historic form of traditional American entertainment known to your parents as burlesque, or, as *Variety* long ago named it, "burley." For years he has been collecting the materials of that rowdy medium with an eye to reviving the art of burlesque and restoring it to the stage. In the fall of 1979 a show based on his researches in that exotic subject, starring Mickey Rooney and Ann Miller, opened at the Hellinger Theatre on Broadway. *Sugar Babies,* produced by the same partners, Rigby and Kramer, has become the hit of the 1979 season.

G.R. Point, by David Berry, is in rehearsal this autumn of 1978. It has been playing in a small theater in Baltimore, Maryland, and there are now plans to bring it to New York.

"G.R." is Army talk for Graves Registration, and this is a

highly dramatic work which has as its background the late terrible war in Vietnam. It has taken long months for this play to arrive at this stage of production. The author, David Berry, was a student in a class for aspiring playwrights which I conducted a few years ago sponsored by the Eugene O'Neill Foundation in Waterford, Connecticut.

It was in the late sixties when George White, the man who began the O'Neill Foundation, which has done so much to encourage and induce young talented playwrights, called me and asked me if I would take on a class in playwriting at Wesleyan.

When I first undertook the assignment I was asked how many such aspirants I would be willing to handle in my seminars and I suggested twelve.

I must say I accepted the assignment with a good deal of trepidation. I had never done any teaching, and as the time approached for me to go to Connecticut I became more and more nervous. One day I said to my husband, "Do you realize I can go up there in September and they will all come in the first day, but if those twelve young people are not interested in what I am saying in this period of permissive education, they don't have to come back for the second session? What happens under those circumstances?"

Liebling—I always used his last name; it means darling—who had been in the theater all his life, was truly a pragmatist. He was also a man of few words. "So what?" he told me. "You close in Middletown."

His reply was most reassuring because I felt—well, of course, I've had plays close in New Haven, Boston, Philadelphia—so what the hell is Middletown, Connecticut?

The seminars went well and for the next two years I had the satisfaction of working with my group, helping them and watching their various talents flower. Not all of them may end up as professional playwrights, but David Berry is one who has. Also Jeff Wanshel.

Berry went off to Vietnam, and when he returned he wrote this play based on his experiences.

It was given its first performance at the O'Neill Foundation;

subsequently, T. Edward Hambleton became interested in the play and gave it a production in New York at the Phoenix Theatre on East Seventy-first Street, as a result of which the critics judged it one of the best plays produced off-Broadway a year ago, and Berry received the off-Broadway award.

Now for a set of strange circumstances. About a year or so prior to this a young man came into my office. He was an actor named Donald Warfield. He'd appeared in *G.R. Point* in its original production, had become enormously involved with the play and decided to try to produce it. He had absolutely no prior experience as a producer, but what he did have was a great deal of enthusiasm and faith. Who knows, perhaps in the long run in this business those qualities mean more than anything else.

I responded to his faith with an act of faith of my own. I made a production contract on behalf of David Berry. Well, that was to some extent pure faith, but then, on the other hand, I had nobody else at the time who wanted to buy the rights to a play which dealt with the horrors of Vietnam.

Here I had a young man in his twenties who had come to my office and told me how much he believed in this play; I had to respond. I'll admit it is not the sort of reasoning which goes into a deal between, say, IBM and its bankers, but then nobody ever said the theater resembles any sort of traditional business, did they?

Time passed. Warfield couldn't get money together for backing, which was understandable in view of the fact he had an unknown author, he himself was unknown and the subject matter of *G.R. Point* could hardly be considered as commercial and as magnetic to ticket buyers as, say, *Same Time Next Year*.

Several years before, a man named Peter Culman had come into my life. Mr. Culman runs a theater in Baltimore called Center Stage and he had become interested in *G.R. Point*. Center Stage is a smaller operation than most tributary theaters, but Mr. Culman is young and energetic. He, too, demonstrated faith. He decided to put the play on at his theater, to build the scenery and to cast it, bring the actors down and underwrite the production with a certain amount of his money.

Another demonstration of faith. Culman was able to interest Michael Moriarty, who is one of our more outstanding young actors today and can, if he wishes, command a large salary in films or TV, to play the lead in his production of *G.R. Point*.

Which made Moriarty kindred to the rest of those involved: he is an actor who, when he believes in something, will take a chance on his own judgment. And so is William Devane, another actor who has played leads, most recently on TV in *From Here to Eternity* on NBC. He read the play and offered to try his hand at directing it. More miracles . . .

Finally *G.R. Point* opened in Baltimore. Richard Coe, one of Washington's most respected critics, now critic emeritus on the Washington *Post,* agreed to come to Baltimore, which is not strictly in his territory, to review the play.

After the opening a party was scheduled for the cast and crew. I asked Mr. Coe if he would like to join it but he shook his head. He then told me he had been so moved by what he had seen onstage that he could not possibly socialize that night.

Mr. Coe wrote a rave review of *G.R. Point* in the Washington *Post,* and since the New York theatrical community is one big radar listening post, it did not take too much time before the word began to spread about this young man's play. From then on the problems narrowed down to a very familiar one: money, sufficient sums of it to enable *G.R. Point* to move to a New York theater. Not an easy task for a group of young people. Vietnam can hardly be called a popular subject, not even for Francis Ford Coppola, who spent millions of his own dollars on a film, *Apocalypse Now.*

But if faith can move mountains, it can also open checkbooks. By this time Warfield has acquired partners, Robert Fishko and Rick Hobard, and between them they have managed to lure some backing. And now, if all goes well, over two years since that first experimental production at the O'Neill Foundation, Berry's first play, *G.R. Point,* starring Michael Moriarty, directed by William Devane, is scheduled to open here in New York.

. . . And *if* the critics respond to it Berry will have been   .

launched on a career as a playwright. The theater needs all the talented playwrights it can possibly handle.

Late morning—1978.

An urgent call from Boston from producer Morton Gottlieb, one that involves *The Faith Healer,* Brian Friel's new play, which is trying out there prior to its Broadway opening.

One of the actors, Ed Flanders, has given his notice. Ordinarily, replacing an actor out of town is not such a major problem; it happens all the time. But when a play has a cast of only three, it is a major problem.

Brian Friel has been a client of mine for some years now and I have represented him in the production of such plays as *Philadelphia, Here I Come, Lovers* and *Freedom of the City.* About a year ago he sent me this new play, *The Faith Healer,* and I found it fascinating. It was in a new form, totally unlike anything Brian had written previously. As a matter of fact, I have never seen a play written quite like *The Faith Healer.*

It deals with only three characters: an itinerant Irish faith healer who travels from town to village, working his minor miracles on those who are willing to place their physical ills into his sometimes healing hands; his wife, who has traveled with him for many years now; and his manager, whose job it is to arrange the nightly appearances on their endless travels. But its form is highly experimental: *none* of these three characters ever has a scene with the other two. In the four scenes, each of the actors must be on stage solo and essentially each scene becomes a long monologue, first by the faith healer, then by his wife, then by his manager and finally, in the last scene, by the faith healer again.

I admired the play enormously but I knew immediately that finding a Broadway producer for such a play and then casting it —the major part required an actor of stature who was a star— would not be easy.

This being a business where nothing ever happens according to plan, I managed to get the star before I found the producer. I hadn't shown it to many producers when I happened to read in the newspaper that James Mason was in New York saying he wanted to do a play here. I had never met Mason and, of course, had never worked with him. But it seemed like a brilliant piece of casting—*if* he would agree to play the faith healer.

I found out where Mason was staying, called him up and said I would appreciate it if he would read *The Faith Healer.* I had no way of knowing Mr. Mason's wife, Clarissa Kaye, an Australian, was an actress who had worked extensively in the theater in her home country. Mr. Mason agreed to read the play and when he had done so the three of us met for lunch. It seemed they had both read the play and had decided to do it together, playing the faith healer and his wife.

This was a lucky set of circumstances. It solved one problem and left me with only one more: to find a producer.

Now in my life there is a man named Morton Gottlieb, a most successful Broadway producer. *Sleuth, Same Time Next Year* and *Tribute* are his latest three productions, a rather good batting average in this most chancy profession. He had worked with Friel before, having produced *Lovers,* with Art Carney in the lead; *The Mundy Scheme;* and a California production of Friel's play *Crystal and Fox* at the Mark Taper in Los Angeles. Gottlieb seemed, therefore, a logical choice to produce the play —if he would be interested in raising the large sum of money necessary, if he would be willing to take on this highly experimental play, if . . .

Those are very large ifs.

Evidently the strength of Mr. Friel's play appealed to him as much as it had to me and to Mr. and Mrs. Mason, and Gottlieb agreed to produce the play. As its director, he secured José Quintero, a sensitive and talented man who has a long history of success with the plays of Eugene O'Neill; and in the part of the faith healer's manager he cast that fine actor, Ed Flanders. Gottlieb raised the money to produce the play, a not inconsiderable task, considering that *The Faith Healer* is not precisely what one would call "popular" entertainment.

I was in Boston on opening night of the out-of-town tryout of the play and the audience reaction was excellent. All three members of the cast, Mason, Clarissa Kaye and Ed Flanders, gave marvelous performances. The next day the Boston re-viewers were generally favorable.

This is all a good sign, but in the theater it is easy to be carried away on a wave of euphoria. It is also very dangerous, especially before a New York opening—a long distance away.

When I arrived back in my office I got a call from Morton Gottlieb informing me about Mr. Flanders' decision to withdraw from the cast. With over a quarter of a million dollars invested in this production, Gottlieb seemed remarkably calm. He assured me he would solve this problem.

Now he's proven he is a man of his word. He has solved the problem. Donal Donnelly, the talented Irish actor who played the lead several years back in Friel's play *Philadelphia, Here I Come,* seems to have miraculously become available just this week. Last Saturday Donnelly closed in a touring company of *The Last of Mrs. Cheyney,* playing opposite Deborah Kerr, and today he is flying to Boston to begin rehearsing Ed Flanders' role.

Another major crisis has come and gone. Now I must get word to Mr. Friel. He is currently in Ireland, having returned home to attend rehearsals of yet another play, a new one which is to open shortly at the Abbey Theatre in Dublin. In due time I will fly over there to see it but in the meantime we are totally out of touch. He hopes to return here in time for the New York open-ing of *The Faith Healer* but right now in Ireland there is not only a postal strike but also a strike of telephone workers.

We have previously improvised a method by which I call his London agent, who then calls a number in Londonderry, one of the Northern counties unaffected by the strike, to leave Friel a message to call me in New York. It is close to Friel's home and he has heretofore been able to go across the border, pick up his phone messages and then get in touch with me. So now we go through that process again and I wait to hear from him.

Very late in the day, his call comes through. But this time the operator in Ireland sternly warns me, "Unless this is an emer-gency, you cannot talk."

So I tell her, "This is definitely an emergency." Brian finally comes on the telephone and he says, "Audrey?" I reply, "Brian, I must tell you what is happening in Boston. We have been trying to find a replacement for Ed Flanders and Morty Gottlieb has just informed me he's hired—" At which point the operator says, "*This is not an emergency!*"

Brian cried, "Yes it is, it's *my play*—"

"No!" says the operator, and cuts us off.

The transatlantic call is over and who knows when and how I will be able to inform Brian of the latest developments with *The Faith Healer?*

In this era of huge production costs, getting a play produced on Broadway takes faith and patience and luck, and a good deal of time. If you should consider writing a play my advice to you is not to write one that deals with a subject out of today's newspaper. If it is that timely your play may find itself dated in six months, while you are still waiting for someone to produce it.

On the stack of unproduced plays I have here on my desk, here is one that is a prime example of what I mean. It is called *Bledsoe*, a play I admire very much, by a playwright named Arnaud d'Usseau. He is not exactly a stranger to the theater; he has to his credit such plays as *Tomorrow the World* and *Deep Are the Roots*, which he wrote with his late partner, James Gow. I have been trying to get a production of *Bledsoe* for over three years now. Since it needs a star for the lead, various producers have tried to cast it and it has been close to production several times. First George C. Scott was interested in playing the leading role but then that fell through. Richard Boone also was attracted to *Bledsoe* but that did not work out, nor did its possible production with Robert Shaw—both, alas, now dead. There have been other major stars interested but so far all the elements have not come together. I still believe firmly in *Bledsoe*, and eventually I will find a producer and a star who agree with me.

But in order to survive this endless obstacle course, a playwright must try to write something of lasting value.

Take the case of *Wings*, Arthur Kopit's new play, which in 1978 was on its way to an opening at the Lyceum Theatre starring Constance Cummings.

Although Arthur is far from a stranger to the professional theater—he is the author of *Oh Dad, Poor Dad, Mama's Hung You in the Closet and I'm Feeling So Sad* and *Indians,* both of which have been produced extensively here and in Europe—this new work of his has been almost three years in making the journey to Broadway.

It began life as an hour-long radio play, which is far from an accustomed form of drama in the nineteen-seventies. Years back, before television came into our lives and became the enormously important medium it is, many writers earned a good living writing for radio. But in the past two decades American radio has become primarily a method for disseminating news and music.

Several years ago, a group of young men decided to try to bring to American radio a series of original plays written directly for the medium. The name of the program was to be *Earplay* and such programs were to be produced here with the assistance of National Public Radio and sold to European stations at the same time. Their reasoning was that in England practically every established playwright has for years contributed such original work to the BBC. Why not here?

Two of these men—Howard Gelman and a young English director named John Madden—came to see me to discuss possible contributions from some of my clients. They were able to pay advances, the plays were to be produced in a radio studio in Minneapolis, they'd already secured a commitment from Edward Albee, and they wanted to know if I could help with other works by playwrights I represented.

It seemed like a very exciting idea and since I am always ready to encourage original writing by authors, especially when they can be paid for their labors, I agreed to help. Perhaps something vital and exciting might come from the project, who could tell?

It certainly did.

Just about this time, Arthur Kopit's father had suffered a stroke and died in a sanitarium of its effects. The impact of his father's loss was very severe. Arthur needed some healing of his own. For a writer, work is often the best therapy.

After I had talked to Gelman and Madden, I thought perhaps

they might meet Arthur. It was purely intuitive on my part; I had no idea if anything would come of it, nor did I know whether or not he would have any idea for such a radio play.

The timing was astonishing. Because of his intense feeling of love for his father and from his observations of the sad event, Arthur began to germinate an idea to transfer his emotions into a play. He had never written for radio before but he had a totally free hand to experiment; that was the whole idea behind *Earplay*. Eventually, this extraordinary one-hour radio play was written. It dealt with a middle-aged woman named Emily Stilson who, when young, had been an aviator, who has a stroke and then undergoes the frightening experience of attempting to recover from the effects of losing the use of her faculties, especially the loss of speech.

Wings was a superb piece of work, completely subjective, taking place in Emily's mind, something uniquely suited to the radio form. Arthur dealt with language that was not really language, some of it gibberish; he took us, the audience, through the tedious and painful stages of Emily's slow recovery and finally led us to the moment of her death. To describe *Wings* in this way makes it sound like a depressing work. It is not. The play is an affecting and often thrilling drama.

Wings had its first production in Minneapolis for *Earplay* with the fine actress Mildred Dunnock playing the part of Emily Stilson. The finished work was heard on radio, both here and abroad, and in May 1977 it received excellent reviews.

Which might have been the end of this work, for there are not too many markets for a radio play. But then a remarkable series of events took place. First, during the summer, Robert Brustein, then dean of the Yale Drama School, heard the audio tape of *Wings* and suggested to Arthur that his radio play might make a theatrical play which could be produced the following season at the Yale Repertory Theatre in New Haven.

At first, Arthur was somewhat baffled; he could not quite see how to transform this subjective work, dealing with the woman's internal reactions, into a stage play. But since he is a highly imaginative author, he rose to the challenge. He locked the door, went to work and managed to adapt his radio play into a full-blown visual theatrical work—no mean feat.

Then came casting. Unfortunately, Mildred Dunnock had been ill and felt she could not assume the part of Emily Stilson for a grueling onstage production, eight performances a week. There were many conferences and discussions involving a replacement for her. We had the task of finding an actress with great talent and the stamina to carry this play, practically solo, for an hour and a half onstage.

Once again, a miracle happened.

Young John Madden, the director, is English and he went home to London for the Christmas holidays. While he was there he showed the Kopit script to a friend, A. B. Gurney, another playwright, who was vacationing in London. Gurney promptly suggested Constance Cummings for the leading role.

It did not seem probable. Here was Cummings, an established star, who had played the leads in *Who's Afraid of Virginia Woolf* and O'Neill's *Long Day's Journey into Night* with Sir Laurence Olivier, who had been in the company at the Old Vic, who had been married to Benn W. Levy, the playwright, and who, although she is an American by birth, had lived in England for many years; why should she pull up stakes and come here? She had never heard of John Madden, she had never met Arthur Kopit, and yet, after reading the script she was so excited by the challenge it presented that she told Madden she would be willing to fly here, take up residence in New Haven and play Emily Stilson in *Wings*—for a very small salary, I may add— with a supporting cast of drama students at the Yale Repertory.

Remarkable. But the theater is replete with such happenings.

When it was finally produced at Yale, the play was received very well. Miss Cummings fulfilled all our hopes: she gave a marvelous performance and received a rave review in the prestigious New York *Times*. But the general consensus was that the subject matter of Emily Stilson's story, no matter how brilliantly written, staged and acted, was somewhat too offbeat and not commercial enough for the Broadway theater.

Somehow *Wings* began to develop a momentum of its own.

Joseph Papp, who runs the Public Theatre in lower Manhattan, decided to invite the Yale Repertory down for a limited run in the spring of 1978. *Wings* was then presented in his theater; once again it met with rave critical notices. And that might have been the end of it; its prospects for a commercial production were limited indeed.

Roger L. Stevens runs the Kennedy Center for the Performing Arts in Washington, D.C., and he is a thorough man of the theater. Over the years he has been responsible for the production of many important plays, both as a producer and as the guiding spirit at Kennedy. Some two years before he had made what I consider to be a very impressive act of faith regarding Arthur Kopit's talents: he had given Arthur a substantial advance to write a play, whatever the play might turn out to be.

I must say I do not know any other producer who would make such a deal, literally on pure faith. Arthur had written the play and Roger was holding it, attempting to cast it properly, but there had been delays and in the meantime Arthur had gone ahead to write *Wings*.

When I persuaded Roger to come to see *Wings* at the Public Theatre, it was with a good deal of trepidation. Even though all of us who had been involved with getting *Wings* this far were enthusiastic about the work, I had no idea what this pragmatic gentleman's response to the play might be.

He called me the next day and said, "I consider this to be some of Kopit's best writing. I will bring this play to Broadway."

Now we were presented with more problems.

The entire physical production had to be redone; it was not possible for Stevens to use the scenery and costumes that were the property of the Yale Repertory. Then the actors, other than Miss Cummings, had to be recast; the students who had performed in New Haven were not members of Actors Equity and Dean Brustein would not permit them to take leaves of absence from his school to appear on Broadway. As a result of all these difficulties, if and when *Wings* was prepared for a Broadway production to star Miss Cummings, the budget would come to three hundred thousand dollars!

None of us ever had any notion, back when this venture began as a fairly simple one-hour radio play, that it would eventually cost such a huge sum of money to produce this one-set play with its fairly small cast which runs for one hour and forty minutes; but those are today's economic facts of life in the commercial theater in New York City.

Roger went ahead, raised the money and put *Wings* into production. He had so much faith in the play he was even willing to forgo such items as a weekly office expense.

Wings has opened at the Wilbur Theatre in Boston where it has received yet another set of rapturous reviews. Miss Cummings' performance as Emily Stilson is remarkable, but so far the customers are not exactly flocking to buy tickets at the box office. From Boston the play will go to Washington, after which it will open, finally, at the Lyceum Theatre on West Forty-fifth Street.

It has been a long journey from the radio station in Minneapolis to opening night in New York, and even now though *Wings* has made the trip, with the rapturous out-of-town notices for Miss Cummings' performance in Kopit's play, with the excellent word of mouth from those who have already seen it, nobody can predict whether this remarkable play will become a commercial success. But then if one is looking for security, one does not seek it in the theater.

It has been a long time since I can remember reading anything for recreation. My literary diet consists of play-production contracts, the drama section of the New York *Times* and *Variety*, and manuscripts. The big trick for me these days is to budget my spare time between luncheons, meetings and going to the theater so there are hours left in which I can do justice to the new plays in my briefcase.

Tonight I have to go to a reading of a new play at St. Clement's, an off-Broadway theater. Since I am the author's representative, I must be there and afterward there will be a conference in which we will discuss the work we have just seen in its early stages. Later this week the Actors Studio is going to have a staged reading of a new play, also by one of my clients. And the night after that I have a date to go to the American Place

Theatre on West Forty-sixth Street. Julia Miles, one of the producers there, called to say they have a play running by a young woman she feels is extremely talented who's in need of an agent. That brings me to the weekend, when I will travel to Westport, carrying a filled briefcase, close the door, turn off the telephone and try to concentrate on scripts that have passed through my reader and my assistant, Adele Franz. They have screened out the plays they consider to be worth my time. After that it is my responsibility to pass judgment on the author's potential for production. Many, many scripts call, but few are chosen.

Over the years I have represented many plays which often continue to develop new theatrical life and I now have to deal with a composer who has written me suggesting a production of an opera based on *The Madwoman of Chaillot,* by Jean Giraudoux. My client, Maurice Valency, did the English adaptation of that play. In the past twenty years it has been made into a film, which was a failure, and then it was produced on Broadway as a musical, *Dear World,* which also failed. Will it make an opera? Who knows? Meanwhile, I must still attend to Mr. Valency's interests, now and in whatever the future brings, as well as assorted deals for stock performance rights, foreign productions and motion-picture and television sales for my clients.

What next in this 1978–79 season?
There's the production of *Knockout.*

About two years before, Louis LaRusso became one of my clients. I can't claim credit for having discovered his talent, which is considerable; he came to me when another agent in our offices resigned from the firm.

LaRusso is a young man from Hoboken, New Jersey, who is most prolific. He writes very strong and interesting dramas which deal mostly with his Italian-American background. So far he has had a Broadway production of his play called *Lamppost Reunion.* Now he has a play called *Vespers Eve,* which is scheduled to be performed in the West Fifties by another off-Broadway group, and still another melodrama called *Knockout,* which has been acquired by a man named William Sargent for a Broadway opening a month or so from now.

LaRusso is a tall and good-looking man in his early thirties. Lately he has been getting some film work but he assures me his only real love is the theater. He told me once his dream was to have perhaps two or three of his plays running at the same time on Broadway. He's quite serious about it; who knows?

Last year I went to London for a combined business and pleasure trip. Most of my time was spent at the theater, for me both business *and* pleasure. I checked in at the Savoy Hotel and soon after I arrived I had a call from LaRusso. He was in the same hotel and invited me to lunch. At that time we knew each other casually; it was a welcome chance to socialize.

He was in London with an actor pal of his and we all met at lunch. During the repast he proceeded to tell me what a wonderful time he and his friend were having in London; many young ladies, whom they encountered on Piccadilly of an evening, were accompanying them back to the Savoy. Evidently the Savoy management took a rather dim view of their social evenings and the manager told Mr. LaRusso in private that the hotel could not permit this sort of thing to take place any longer. Whereupon Mr. LaRusso threw back his broad shoulders and told the manager, "Look, I'll bring anybody I want to into this hotel at any time I want to; is that understood, pal?"

Which seemed to have closed that particular discussion.

As we left the restaurant, both he and his very tall actor friend walked me back to the Savoy. I am, to say the least, not very tall, and Mr. LaRusso had to lean down to talk to me. When he had finished the story of the manager's complaint he said, quite straight-faced, "Now, Miss Wood, if there's anything we can do for *you* . . ."

As far as I was concerned, this caused the biggest laugh of my entire British stay.

So this afternoon I am dealing with Bill Sargent, who is going to produce *Knockout*. He is a short, cheerful man with a small beard, whose flamboyant showmanship style of action reminds me of the late Mike Todd. Mr. Sargent thinks very big: his plan is to run *Knockout* at a Broadway theater and simultaneously to film the play. He would thereupon run the movie at theaters all over the country, not a bit concerned that it will hurt the Broadway grosses, but certain that they will be stimulated by the publicity.

This is certainly not an ordinary sort of arrangement. It usually takes years after a play has finished its run in the theater before it appears as a film. But Mr. Sargent has had great success in filming a live performance of Sammy Davis, Jr., in *Stop the World, I Want to Get Off,* and most recently he produced a film which stars Richard Pryor, the comedian, in concert at a theater. The Pryor film has been playing all over and doing tremendous business and Sargent is now ready to repeat the process with *Knockout.*

When we had our first meeting he told me he had faith in *Knockout* as a commercial venture. It is a melodrama about an aging prizefighter who is retired from the ring to run a gym in Hoboken, and the play ends with an actual prizefight staged in front of the audience. He is prepared to invest $750,000 of his money in advertising and promotion of the play and to sell it to the audience, both as a film and as a play.

After he had outlined his plans, I asked him, "Now, truly, seven hundred and fifty thousand?"

He said, "Absolutely!"

"That's an awful lot of cash, Mr. Sargent. Supposing the Broadway critics aren't kind to Mr. LaRusso's play? What then?"

He grinned. "To hell with the critics, Miss Wood," he said. "They don't bother me a bit. I'll spend my money on *Knockout* and I'll tell you something else: I expect to have a ball doing it!"

I expect he will.

I know the feeling. It's quite simple. I suffer from the same dread disease, one for which there is no known cure.

I am, you see, stagestruck.

Intermission

(In which the curtain is lowered to denote the passage of several months.)

When it rises again it will reveal a vista very much like the last scene of a disastrous Shakespearean tragedy, complete with corpses strewn across the stage.

A Meeting by the River opened at the Palace Theatre, where it was received with polite but unenthusiastic notices. Sans sufficient capital funds with which to keep their play running, the producers chose to close it after the one opening performance.

Starring Michael Moriarty, *G.R. Point* made it to New York from out of town. It opened at the Century Theatre on West Forty-seventh Street. The critical notices were fair. Audiences did not seem at all interested in a drama dealing with the war in Vietnam. After several weeks of playing to half houses, the play closed.

Brian Friel's *The Faith Healer* arrived at the Longacre Theatre. The performances of James Mason, Clarissa Kaye and Donal Donnelly were well reviewed, as was Friel's drama. But, alas, no amount of advertising, radio and TV interviews and publicity by the producer, Morton Gottlieb, seemed to engender the one basic ingredient which makes a play into a hit, i.e., word of mouth. Most regretfully, Gottlieb closed the play. Friel is at work on his next play and James Mason will continue to earn a substantial living in films, which is definitely the theater's loss.

The New York *Times,* December 30, 1979, "The Ten Best Plays of the Year":

> ". . . Shall we sneak in a total failure? You surely missed Brian Friel's 'Faith Healer' because it ran for no more than a skimpy 20 performances. For a clear enough reason. Each of three players— James Mason, Clarissa Kaye and Donal Donnelly—told his (her) side of the story in separate monologues, separate acts. The three never met on stage, there were no dramatic confrontations and the business of piecing the action together from hearsay proved an invitation the general audience chose not to accept. I found the exercise stimulating; it would seem that Mr. Friel cannot write badly, and it was fun (serious fun) sharing risks with a playwright entirely willing to go for broke."

> WALTER KERR

With a great deal of advance fanfare and hoopla, *Knockout* by Louis LaRusso opened at the Helen Hayes Theatre. The critics

were relatively unimpressed by the melodrama. Mr. Sargent, as
he had promised, continued to spend a great deal of cash advertising and promoting the play. Despite the fact that audiences
stayed away in droves, Mr. Sargent did not lose faith and, in
fact, kept the play running through most of the summer of 1979.
But eventually even Mr. Sargent had to throw in the towel.
Knockout went down for the count and closed. And no TV production occurred—during the run or after the play closed.

Finally, Arthur Kopit's *Wings*.

The night it opened at the Kennedy Center, in Washington, as
we were sitting in the audience, I happened to overhear two ladies seated next to me, who were discussing what they were
about to see. One of them said to her friend, "I understand this
play is a bit of a mishmash."

I couldn't let that stand, so I said, "Excuse me, but I must correct you. This is a very fine play by a most talented playwright,
and Miss Cummings, who is the star, is a great actress; she is
giving a marvelous performance."

There was silence. As the lights went down, I heard one of the
women hiss to the other, "She must be her *mother!*"

Wings opened in mid-January, as planned, at the Lyceum
Theatre. The play and Miss Cummings' remarkable performance
received rapturous raves. But box-office response was only respectable, never overwhelming. Despite valiant efforts on the
part of producer Roger Stevens to continue the run, *Wings*
finally closed in mid-April. Financially, the play must be considered a failure, but its life is far from ended. Ironically, after the
closing Miss Cummings won the Tony Award for the Best Performance by an Actress in 1978–79.

Subsequently she returned to her home in London, where she
has since starred there in a production of *Wings* at the National
Theatre. *Wings* was produced in Paris, where the leading role
was played by the great French actress Madeline Renaud. There
are other productions scheduled around the world.

Box score, then for 1978–79: five productions, five closings.
A great deal of work by all concerned has come to naught.

So what then does an agent do when she's had five plays by her clients close in one season?

In the words of another pragmatic lady, the late Miss Dorothy Fields—who was also involved all her life in the theater—"she picks herself up, dusts herself off and starts all over again."

It's something I learned to do a long time ago.

5

In Which I Make a Job for Myself

It throws men off when a small woman, with a quiet, well-bred voice, comes in to them to do big business deals.

Being a woman isn't something I work on. It's just something I am. It's hard for men to compete with this.

Actually, this is the perfect field for a woman. It takes patience—the kind of patience, really, that only a woman has.

I've never had children, but I suppose being an author's representative is a little like having a child. You decide to take on a writer and you take on a tremendous responsibility. You handle all the details of his business life—his contracts, his whole financial present—and, perhaps, his future.

For more years than it might care to admit, the theater has been primarily a man's game. Even back in Elizabethan days, when female parts were customarily assigned to young men whose voices had not yet changed, Shakespeare's Globe Theatre was male turf.

In time, room was made onstage for lady troupers, both in England and here. Especially attractive and talented females, whose charms could draw audiences. Since ticket buyers were mainly males—males handled the family funds—the male theatergoer's interests lay in obvious directions, and by the nineteenth century, even though actors and actresses might be second-class citizens offstage (subject to signs that read NO DOGS, NO THEATRICALS), up there, behind the footlights, when the curtain rose a talented lady had just as good a chance at becoming a star as did her male cohorts. Sometimes better.

But in the "front of the house," the seat of theatrical power, in the booking offices, the producer's inner sanctum, the author's library, the reins were almost exclusively held by male hands. Even in the mid-twenties, when a number of talented women, Rachel Crothers, Zoe Atkins, Rose Franken and others began to make their names as playwrights, there were precious few opportunities for a female to get her small foot into the manager's office door.

I was certainly aware of the obstacles that lay ahead of me because I was a young female when I went looking for a job in those years, but they did not stop me. If most of the women I encountered in and around theater and Broadway offices labored at such undistinguished and badly paid jobs as answering the telephone, typing letters and contracts and taking notes for their male bosses, well then that was a fact of life, something I would have to live with, while at the same time trying to forge ahead.

I never thought of myself as a modern-day heroine, breaking down doors to invade male territory. I was too busy looking for a way, any way, to get myself a job.

Looking back, I suppose I had never really wanted to be an actress; all that auditioning and running in and out of producers' offices had something to do with the memory of my father. Once it was over with I was ready to start at the lowest rung somewhere, anywhere that would lead onward and upward.

The anywhere consisted of the offices of the Century Play Company and my job truly was at the lowest rung.

The Century Play Company, at 1440 Broadway, acted as agents for playwrights and was run by a man named Tom Kane, whose partner was James Thatcher. Thatcher managed the Poli chain, a large New England group of theaters, and was a very famous man at the time. My father had been a friend of Tom Kane's and that is how I became a play reader there.

Century's mail was filled with an endless stream of manuscripts submitted by aspiring playwrights, and it became my job to take home a sheaf of plays, read them and write a report on each one's potential for the commercial stage. I read whatever the staff at Century gave me and, if memory serves, I received three dollars per report.

Century Play was hugely successful. This was the mid-nineteen-twenties and Tom Kane would advance playwrights large sums of money for their produced Broadway plays to secure the "stock rights" for his firm. His job would then be to secure productions for his clients' work all over the country. At this time there were literally hundreds of local stock companies in cities and towns, which made for a thriving market. Various impresarios, such as Poli in New England and Henry Duffy, who had companies in key cities all along the coast of California and northward, toured stock performances in their chains. If, say, you sold a play to Duffy, it could run eight or nine weeks in Los Angeles, then go to San Francisco, then north to Portland, Oregon, and Seattle, Washington. This local business, in which the stock company bill was changed weekly, generated enormous income for playwrights and Century. A playwright such as Harry Delf could write a simple family comedy called *The Family Upstairs* which may not have had much impact on Broadway but could go on to make him a fortune in royalties for years to come.

Since each theater contract had to be negotiated for fifty-odd times a year, the volume of business was huge and so was the daily paperwork and bookkeeping in those precomputer days.

Century's stock department was managed by a man named Gus Diehl. One morning, when I went in to deliver some of my reports, I found him rushing back and forth, in and out of his office, highly agitated and waist-deep in problems.

With no forethought I said, "You know, Mr. Diehl, it seems to me you need somebody to help you and I think I'm the one to do this job." He and I were not complete strangers: he knew me and he had known my father.

Startled, he looked at me. Then, after a moment, he said, "You're right."

I went to work for the Century Play Company the next morning.

I have been a play agent ever since.

I enjoyed the job from the first. Since I had grown up in and around theaters and seen plays each week, I had naturally acquired a great deal of information about the dramas and comedies of the past few years. So whenever there was a question about some dramatic property which nobody else at Century Play could answer, they began to say, "Get Audrey!" I could usually remember what the play was about and who had been in the cast and that sort of information made me valuable to the office staff.

Then one day the lady who was running the new play department told me in confidence she was going off on holiday but had no plans for returning. She hadn't told this to Mr. Kane. In her absence Mr. Kane put me in as a temporary fill-in. I knew she wasn't coming back but he didn't and I stayed on in that job. I am certain Kane was trying each day to find somebody else for it, someone more mature and with more experience, but happily he did not. Eventually I became the permanent head of the new play department.

It was at this time, in the late nineteen-twenties, that Professor George Pierce Baker was the dean of Yale University's School of Drama. Baker had created the "47 Workshop" at Harvard, where he had taught the principles of playwrighting. Eventually he had been lured down to New Haven to move his school to Yale, where it became the keystone of the Drama School.

Baker was a powerful influence on American playwrights in the twenties and thirties. Among his successful students were such major dramatists-to-be as Eugene O'Neill, Sidney Howard, Edward Sheldon, Philip Barry, S. N. Behrman and George Abbott.

It occurred to me there must be new playwrights working in New Haven at the Yale Drama School who would someday need an agent to represent their work, and why should I not offer my services? A simple enough thesis, one that could only come to someone as young and enthusiastic as I. Without so much as a formal introduction, I wrote directly to Professor Baker and asked whether I could come up and meet him and discuss young American playwrights and their problems.

My effrontery was amazing.

Baker had never heard of Audrey Wood of the Century Play Company, and if he had tossed my letter into his wastebasket I should not have been unduly surprised. Agents quickly become accustomed to turndowns.

Remarkably enough, however, this important gentleman not only replied but offered me an appointment to meet with him at eight-thirty of a weekday morning the following week.

There was only one way to keep such a date. I made my first trip the night before to New Haven and took a room at the Taft Hotel. Thus I spent my first night in that hostelry which adjoins the Shubert Theatre, a well-used tryout house in downtown New Haven. In years to come I would spend many restless nights there, sometimes totally without sleep, following opening night performances of plays whose authors I would represent.

At eight-thirty on the dot I was ushered into Professor Baker's office and I told him why I had come. In retrospect, his response to my bold query about my possible representation of his crop of tyro playwrights was also truly amazing. Instead of commenting on my boldness and demanding my credentials, Baker not only said he would put me on the Drama School mailing list so I could see which plays were being produced there, but he would also let me know whenever a new play was being done where the author had no agent.

It was much more than I had ever expected. Triumphantly, I returned to New York. I had begun my career as agent for new playwrights!

Professor Baker was as good as his word; shortly afterward he referred to me a young author named David Hertz. He had written a play called *Miles of Heaven*. I took it on and went searching for a producer. In due time I found one in California, where the play eventually opened. It was not a success but it attracted Hollywood film people to Hertz's abilities. He subsequently became a well-paid screenwriter. For the next two decades he worked at various studios, an economic pattern that was to involve a good many of my aspiring dramatists.

In 1929 two major events took place. The stock market crashed, causing an economic depression and, simultaneously, "talkies" became the most dominant field in entertainment. The Los Angeles studio chiefs began desperately to import trainloads of "word men," any and all dramatists who could supply those actors and actresses on the screen with dialogue. The steady employment, those lush weekly paychecks Messrs. Mayer and Warner and Zukor and Laemmle et al. were dangling in front of playwrights were hard to refuse, especially since Broadway, two-a-day vaudeville and "the road" had all collapsed, nay vanished, beneath the impact of Al Jolson acting and singing at popular prices, five times a day on the silver screen in *The Jazz Singer*.

However, I began to meet many other aspiring authors. One of them was DuBose Heyward, a Southerner, who had written his play, *Porgy*, the same work which became the basis for the opera he was to write with the Gershwins, *Porgy and Bess*. Years afterward, when I started my own business, DuBose and his wife Dorothy became my first clients.

I also represented a young playwright from Yale named Arnold Sundgaard, who had written a play called *Everywhere I Roam*. I arranged its production in New York and Marc Connelly coproduced and directed it. It achieved a set of respectable notices and managed a decent run. Arnold, I am pleased to report, has remained with the living theater ever since and is still thriving.

There was another young man I remember well, Joseph Kesselring. He didn't have a button in his pocket but in a few years he would write the hilarious hit comedy, *Arsenic and Old Lace*. Another talented young aspirant, Harry Segall, would write *Heaven Can Wait*, the comedy which would become a classic film—twice, in fact. Richard Flournoy and Lawrence Hazard, both of them writing plays, would also end up as expert and highly paid screenwriters.

None of these young men had made it yet, often they didn't

even have eating money. Across the street from our office at Fortieth Street and Broadway there was a Childs restaurant where
we used to have lunch. In those days, hard as it is to believe, a
meal cost a quarter. Very often I had to put up some of the
quarters for these friends of mine because they simply did not
have the price—yet.

They were all loyal. Years afterward I sold one of Hazard's
plays to a film company and he was so pleased he came back
East to reward me in person. Life had been good to Larry, he
was earning a very good salary and was living in a California
house with a pool and servants. He decided he wished to give
me five hundred dollars personally because I had done such a
good job for him.

My boss, Tom Kane, thought it was wrong. There ensued a
terrible row between Hazard and Kane. But Hazard insisted. "I
want to give this to Audrey because she has worked so hard!" he
told my boss. Finally, Hazard prevailed and I was permitted to
take the five hundred dollars, a staggering sum in those days,
home to my mother.

In truth, during those early years I was at Century, Tom Kane
did not really have much interest in what I was doing. The
talkies had not arrived, he was still euphorically paying close attention to the large revenues from stock and Broadway. As a result, I had complete freedom of action, which is a great blessing,
especially when one is young and ambitious. I can remember
Mr. Kane early in the morning, peering through the open door
to ask, "What's new?" I would give him a short, happy response
and he would nod, leave and that was it.

I remained at Century Play Company for seven years. I suppose I should have left there earlier but I didn't have enough
sense to do so. I was so busy working away for my aspiring playwrights that I paid little attention to the deadly effect on Kane's
business caused by the burgeoning talkies and the rapidly
shrinking legitimate theater throughout the country. Then one
day in the midst of those dark mid-thirties Depression years,
Tom Kane informed me he was going to have to close the new
play department. He gave me a year's notice, a very decent ges-

ture indeed in those dreadful times of bread lines, apple sellers on every corner and darkened, empty playhouses.

So I began to make the rounds, looking to find a new affiliation. Among the people who helped me was another young woman agent, Kay Brown. Kay must have had some sort of intuition about my possible ability; we certainly did not know each other that well yet. (I am pleased to report that today Kay's office is down the hall from mine here on West Fifty-seventh Street, nearly half a century later, and that she continues to thrive, representing, among others, Arthur Miller and Ingrid Bergman.)

Kay was later to serve as story editor for David O. Selznick and she was responsible for his purchase of the screen rights to *Gone with the Wind.* But at this time she was working in the New York offices of the legendary agent Leland Hayward.

Hayward had rapidly built up a formidable client list, both in New York and California. His was the Tiffany's of agencies. He represented such valuable and expensive talents as Katharine Hepburn, Fred Astaire, Ingrid Bergman, Henry Fonda and James Stewart, and his East Coast drama department handled the affairs of Ben Hecht and Charles MacArthur, Paul Osborne, Edna Ferber and many other successful authors.

At this time in my career, for me to have moved into such a powerful national agency would have been a giant step forward. Through Kay's good efforts, eventually I went to lunch at Sardi's with Mr. Hayward's New York drama man, Paul Streger. When he offered me a job in his department, I asked him, "If I work with you and if a play comes along and I like it but you don't, what happens?"

"We do not handle the play," he replied.

At that moment I realized I could not go to work at the Hayward office.

Even then I had always operated on my own intuition and instincts. If I liked a play, if some mysterious force at work inside me signaled to me that the author was talented—and such playwriting ability usually manifests itself in the first fifteen pages or so of a manuscript—then I would go to work for that

author and continue to work for his play until I had exhausted
every possible chance to get it produced. All these years later, I
am still at it.

I sent Mr. Hayward a polite wire, making up some excuse
why regretfully I could not accept a job with his very prestigious firm.

Hayward was unaccustomed to being turned down, especially
by a cheeky young agent. He called up Kay Brown and asked,
"Who the hell does Audrey Wood think she is?"

Kay replied, "She's good, and she knows it."

I had not heard this at the time but many years later Leland
himself reminded me of the incident. By that time he was a very
successful Broadway producer with such massive hits as *Mr.
Roberts, A Bell for Adano, South Pacific* and *The Sound of
Music* to his credit. Once again he wanted me to work for him
but this time in a different capacity. He would call regularly to
request that I find him a good script he could produce. Sadly
enough, one of his last productions, an ill-starred venture, would
be a musical version of *Picnic,* retitled *Hot September,* by my
client the late William Inge, which closed before it came to New
York.

I had interviews with other theatrical agencies but nothing
came of them. Then one day one of my clients, Doris Frankel,
whose plays I had been working on and who was married to
Philip Barber, confronted me with a remarkable suggestion. "My
father has some vacant office space in the Heckscher Building,"
she said. "Why don't we open our own office? You and I can be
partners and we'll call the agency Audrey Wood."

It was indeed a long-shot chance. Since Mr. Frankel would be
giving us the office rent-free, I could draw no salary. We could
certainly not afford a secretary, not even an office boy. The re-
wards would be, to begin with, negligible.

But there was that lovely empty office waiting for us at Fifty-
seventh Street and Fifth Avenue.

I went home and discussed it with my mother, who was, in
modern terminology, supportive. What she said was, "Go ahead,
I'll give you a year."

In months to come I can remember her even doling out bus

fare to me. Even though a bus ride was only a nickel, I did a great deal of walking.

So we opened the office of Audrey Wood.

We sent out cards to everyone we thought could possibly be interested and off we went into business.

On the day we opened the agency we had sent out invitations to a small party to properly launch the new firm. Doris and I sat in the office, nervously, hopefully, waiting for a guest, any guest, to arrive. There was a knock at the door and when I opened it there stood our first guest, a producer named Harry Moses. He was a very prominent Broadway producer; he was responsible for the hit play *Grand Hotel*. I was astonished anyone so important would deign to come and I told him so.

"But you *asked* me, Audrey, didn't you?" he insisted.

We were well and truly launched.

My client list was so tiny at first that one needed a magnifying glass to read it. It consisted of some of the authors I had represented at Century who were willing to leave and come along with me. Dorothy and DuBose Heyward were my first clients and would bring me a new play, *Mamba's Daughters*. But for the next eight or nine months the firm of Audrey Wood, with barely enough income to sustain us, merely struggled on.

One day the phone rang. The caller was a man I had never met but had heard of all over the theatrical district. His name was William Liebling and he was then established at 30 Rockefeller Plaza as one of the leading casting agents in the business. At the time he was casting agent for most of the major theatrical producers. For Sam H. Harris and Max Gordon he handled every production, reading the play, suggesting the proper actors or actresses and bringing them to audition. He had been involved in casting such major hits as *You Can't Take It with You, Junior Miss* and *Abe Lincoln in Illinois*.

When he said, "I don't know whether you've ever heard of me," I told him I certainly had. I knew that Liebling was "the King of Forty-fifth Street" (as he was fond of describing himself).

He said, "They tell me you are a bright young agent who has interesting plays to sell. I would like to read some of them."

Because I didn't have an office boy, I promptly delivered the scripts myself—on foot—to 30 Rockefeller Plaza.

Nowadays Actors Equity has rules which permit one agent to represent certain actors and actresses exclusively by means of a contract that is beneficial to both parties. In those days of the thirties, a theatrical agent such as Liebling could represent any actor or actress who came to his office and for whom he could find a job.

Thus, every day Liebling's outer office would be filled with a constant stream of anxious and hopeful Equity members looking for their next acting job.

Out there, in front of the receptionist's cubicle, was a small bench. It was much more than a piece of furniture. Just recently Karl Malden, one of Liebling's clients who went on to well-deserved success, and now warns us all to keep our funds safe in American Express traveler's checks, recalled that same bench. "When I was young and making the rounds of the offices," he said, "it meant a lot of long days spent in pounding the pavements, believe me. But I'll always remember Bill as a guy with a heart. He was the only agent in New York who had a place where a struggling young actor could sit down and rest his feet and even if he didn't have any work for you he would always come out and say, 'Sorry, kid, nothing today but you're welcome to sit for a while.' How could you ever forget a guy like that?"

There I sat, manuscripts in hand, on the same bench. Mr. Liebling came out. A small man, immaculately dressed with a high collar and elegant tie, very dapper. He sent away all those hopeful actors, he had nothing for them that day, but I couldn't fail to notice that he was polite and treated each of the aspirants as if he or she were a human being. In show business, it's not often one encounters such sensitivity.

Then he turned to me. I introduced myself. He ushered me into his office and I gave him the scripts I'd brought.

We talked and then, to my utter astonishment, Mr. Liebling asked, "What are you doing for dinner?"

As I had never seen this man before in my life, I promptly

thought to myself, "Who the hell does he think he is?" But to Liebling I lied and said I was busy. I was, of course, quite available. I left with my head held high.

A few weeks passed and I went back to pick up my scripts. I thought he had had them long enough to read them by now and I sat outside, once again, on Mr. Liebling's bench.

Once again he ushered me into his office. "I want to talk to you, Miss Wood," he said. "I have been thinking about you. I have decided I want to open a play department and I'd like you to run it."

Once again I was astonished by his abruptness.

I shook my head. "I can't do that," I told him. "I am already in business. I have responsibilities and I also have a partner."

"All right," replied this remarkable man. "I'll wait."

He did well to do so.

One day, my partner, Doris Frankel, suddenly announced that what is referred to in theatrical contracts as an "act of God" had taken place. She and her husband were going to become parents. Since Doris was pregnant and also still hard at work writing her own plays, she decided she couldn't continue as my partner and the firm of Audrey Wood would somehow have to continue on its somewhat shaky business course without her.

I am not a believer in coincidence in dramas; it is a tired device which good playwrights always avoid. But that very day Mr. William Liebling called me and once again asked me if I was free for dinner.

This time I accepted. After we sat down at Sardi's I threw away my news most casually. "Something very interesting happened today, Mr. Liebling," and I proceeded to tell him about my ex-partner's departure.

When I finished, Liebling nodded.

"Well," he said, "I've been waiting for months now. Come."

And that was the genesis of a firm, Liebling-Wood.

Looking back on it you could say we, too, were an "act of God."

6

Enter William Liebling

> One night in London Liebling and I attended the opening
> night performance of Tennessee's *The Glass Menagerie*, star-
> ring Helen Hayes. The audience response was not good. At the
> party afterward, the director, a very distinguished British actor,
> came up to us as we were leaving, and said, "I promise you, it
> will be better tomorrow night." On the way out Liebling turned
> to me and muttered, "You're only as good as the night they
> catch you."
>
> By "they," he meant the opening-night audience.

My new business partner, and my eventual husband, Mr. Liebling, had for the past twenty-odd years thrived as a Broadway
casting agent, but his origins were thousands of miles east of
that street. He had been born in a tiny Polish village called Constantine, on the outskirts of the city of Lodz.

It was a poor village indeed, one similar to those immortalized
by the humorist Sholom Aleichem, in his brilliant tales of Tevye,
the milkman, and his daughters. The Jews of Constantine,
scratching out their meager daily livings under the omnipresent

tyrannical Russian rule, all shared the same dream—to scrape together enough money to buy passage westward, out of those muddy streets, to the golden land of opportunity, America.

Liebling's father packed up and went first, to earn enough to pay the way for the rest of the family to make the journey, and eventually there was enough saved from his labors to enable Liebling's mother to secure the same passage for herself and the two young boys.

"I remember a bitter cold winter day," he told me, years later. "This must have been around nineteen oh two, I was only eight or so, we were huddled in a one-horse wagon, with all our possessions, being driven from Constantine to Lodz. We drove through bleak woods, and then, suddenly, Russian soldiers on horseback came dashing past us, firing their rifles into the trees. They probably wanted to frighten us. When some of those trees caught fire," he said, wryly, "we certainly were."

A train took the Liebling family to the German border, where a knowledgeable friend managed to convey them across the border, past the guards and into Germany, to a seaport. From there, a steamer took the mother and her sons, their worldly possessions bundled up in large feather-stuffed quilts, to the city of London.

But the journey to America would not be so easily accomplished. In England, young Liebling developed an eye infection. It was common knowledge among potential immigrants to America that should they arrive at Ellis Island, in New York harbor, with any sort of disease, medical authorities could and would refuse their admission to the United States. Because of that dire possibility, the ailing young Liebling had to be left behind in England with a kind family until he recovered.

Months later, the lad, clutching his ticket, was placed aboard another steamer, put into steerage, down in the hold, and, totally alone, made the eleven-day trip to America.

Ellis Island was a traumatic experience.

"There I stood, with a big tag on my coat lapel, holding on to my bundle," he said, "surrounded by thousands of other immigrants, waiting for somebody to arrive, to guide me through the formalities. For three whole days I waited, alone in the crowds.

Frightened was hardly the word. Had they forgotten me? Would they ever find me? Where were they? Finally, I heard somebody calling the name out—'Lovelane'—or 'Leybling'—they'd been looking for me all this time, but nobody had ever called for me by my real name! Thank God, it was my father, come to take me to our new home!"

That would be a tenement flat on Essex Street, on the lower East Side. Four flights up, not much of a palace, but to the young Polish immigrant boy who'd come so far, it was opulent indeed. "Coming through Manhattan, down those crowded streets, in the U.S. at last, I had a sudden exultant feeling of freedom," he recalled. "Even at that early age, it was overwhelming. It's never left me; I have it to this day."

Liebling's father, Morris, had secured a job as a weaver, the skill he'd learned in far-off Poland, and the New York factory wages were sufficient to support his family. But Morris Liebling was gifted in other arts as well: while still in Constantine, he had learned ballroom dancing. When he arrived in New York, he promptly put his terpsichorean skill to work to provide a secondary source of income. On weekends, he would regularly hire an East Side hall and advertise in the papers that he was operating a dancing school. At twenty-five cents per lesson, he attracted many satisfied customers, eager men and women who wished to become truly Americanized. Eventually there was enough income to enable the Liebling family to move uptown, to the more opulent surroundings of Harlem.

It was shortly afterward that young Liebling embarked on a career of his own. "I discovered I had a talent for singing," he said. "I became a boy soprano, singing in the choir in synagogues, especially during the High Holidays. Then, one morning, I was about eleven, I woke up and overnight I'd become a real bass, with a deep baritone!"

Following in his father's graceful footsteps, the diminutive singer decided to capitalize on his newfound vocal equipment and go into the field of entertainment. Soon he had acquired an agent.

"I did a single act," he recalled. "They taught me some typical baritone solos—'Many Brave Hearts Are Asleep on the Deep, So

Beware,' and 'Rocked in the Cradle of the Deep,' that sort of thing—and there I was, out onstage, a very small kid in short pants, singing in that exceptionally deep bass voice.

"Whether or not I was going to school didn't matter much— I'd gotten up to grade six—what was important was that I'd found a job—one at which I could make money. If I was what they called in the business a 'freak act,' I didn't know or care about that. When I stepped out in front of the curtain and opened my mouth to sing, the audience used to burst out laughing. Didn't bother me a bit. I kept right on singing; nothing stopped *me!*"

There would be various engagements with singing quartets, with boy-and-girl acts, and even a stint with the famous Gus Edwards, a songwriter who had parlayed his hit songs, "School Days" and "Sunbonnet Sue" into a thriving vaudeville career. Edwards' specialty was to assemble talented young hopeful kids into an act and to take them on tour. By working with him, young Liebling would be joining such future stars as Eddie Cantor, George Jessel, Lila Lee and Walter Winchell, all of whom were Gus Edwards "discoveries."

"In our local neighborhood," he said, "my career had transformed me into some sort of a local hero. The kids could see me performing at some local theater, such as the Star, at Lexington Avenue and a Hundred and Seventh Street, and they'd promptly organize impromptu singing quartets, in which I would be the star. In those days, in the various Manhattan neighborhoods, each bunch would have its own quartet, and there'd be intense rivalry over which quartet sang the best. Every night we'd meet at a certain corner, our gang would assemble, maybe a hundred of us, and they'd follow us through the park into a tunnel, where we'd run into some other quartet, from another section of Harlem, and then we'd challenge them to a singing contest. We'd sing all the popular hits of the day—'The Sheik of Araby,' 'Ja-Da,' 'Dardanella,' 'You Made Me Love You,' songs like that.

"If there were parties in neighborhood tenements, they'd drag me upstairs—Willie the Bass and his quartet—I'd be pushed forward and I'd sing. That meant we'd get to eat from the party refreshments. Some nights I'd be home in our apartment, and some kid from my gang downstairs would call up—'Hey, Mrs. Liebling, is Willie the Bass home? Send him down—there's a bunch challenging us and we want to show 'em!'

"I remember," he continued, "one time we were walking through a Hundred and Sixteenth Street, and there was a sign on a little picture house nearby, it read 'Amateur Night.' This gang of mine pushed me onto the stage there, and I sang, and I won the silver cup. That almost caused a riot; I wasn't from that neighborhood, and somebody from that neighborhood had been all fixed by the management to win that cup!

"Well, we dashed out of there in a hurry, went over to a pawn shop on Third Avenue, hocked the silver cup for three dollars cash, and everybody went with me and had a soda. And just in time, too. If we hadn't hocked it fast, there were guys coming after us to take it away, believe me!"

Eventually, one of Liebling's friends who had a relative who sailed on a steamer that made regular runs to South America, arranged for young Willie the Bass to sign on as a steward-singer. Buenos Aires, Bahia, Santos, all of those far-off ports were on the itinerary; the young man indulged his wanderlust. By day, he polished brass and served drinks; by night, he entertained the passengers in the lounge. "I was young and looking for far horizons," he said, "and it was as exciting as anything a young teenaged kid could want."

But events on land, thousands of miles to the east, were to intrude on young Willie the Bass's flourishing career as a singing sailor.

It was 1917, and America had declared war on Kaiser Wilhelm's Germany, in what was to be instantly (and hopefully) called "the war to end all wars." Liebling returned to New York from a cruise to Barbados to find the country in a state of mobilization. His patriotism for his new homeland stirred, he immediately made up his mind to join that most elitist of branches of the service, the U. S. Marines. "All my friends gave me a big send-off party," he recalled, "and I went down to Madison Square Garden to sign up. The tough Marine sergeant in charge looked at me, and he must have had the biggest laugh of his day; I didn't weigh enough *with* clothes on as I should have weighed without. No Marines for Willie the Bass!

"Needless to say, I was very disappointed. But I wasn't going to give up. I wanted to serve my country. My pals threw me another farewell party, and I then went over to the Army recruiting station, at a Hundred and Twenty-fifth Street and Third Avenue. In the recruiting posters, Uncle Sam was pointing a finger and said that he needed *me*. When he got a look at me, he changed his tune. Obviously he had somebody else in mind for the part."

The lad was determined to serve. "I wasn't giving up. I went down to the merchant marine office, on Nassau Street and Sixth Avenue," he said. "He wanted to know if I'd ever been to sea, and I told him that I'd just returned from Buenos Aires, from Rio, from all those places, that I was an experienced sailor. That seemed to click. He informed me they had a big job for me in the merchant marine! But God must have had his hand on my shoulder. When I asked him when I was to leave, the officer told me that after I was sworn in, in the next room, I'd leave that very night.

"Well, that disturbed me very much; I wanted to go back to Harlem again, and make a big to-do with my pals, have another party. So I made an excuse, went out, and never came back to that office. Lucky for me I did; those merchant marine freighters to which I'd have been assigned were the same boats that were sailing, that very night, to Murmansk, in Russia. If you read your history, you'll discover that more than half the freighters headed for Murmansk never made it; the German U-boats saw to that. If I hadn't gone home to Harlem that night, I wouldn't be here to remember very much."

Liebling decided to return to show business. A mere nineteen years old, he was by now a seasoned performer, and was promptly hired to become part of a touring vaudeville act known as the Noreen Carman Minstrels. "It was a big-time act, starring Miss Carman, a stately blond singer, who performed with a quartet and two end men, one of which was me. When I signed my contract, it was for a two-year route on the B. F.

Keith circuit, very much the classiest booking any act could expect in those days. Two years of steady salary—not bad. I felt great.

"But we didn't get very far—at least I didn't. We'd played about a week and a half, and were on the road, in Albany, when I got a wire from my mother informing me that the U. S. Army was on my trail. I'd finally been drafted!"

There was another big Saturday night send-off in Albany, with tearful farewells for young Willie from the rest of his fellow performers on the vaudeville bill that week at Proctor's Theatre, and then he departed on the sleeper for New York.

There he ran head on into bureaucratic wrath. "I got home and my mother, very upset, told me that the police were looking for me! I was to report to a station at a Hundred and Fourth Street. By that time, I'd become pretty well known in those neighborhoods, so when I went over to find out what this was all about, the desk sergeant at the station, a very sympathetic guy, told me that not only was there a fifty-dollar reward out for me, but that he was supposed to arrest me on the spot! For some reason, they'd figured out at the draft board that I was trying to duck being drafted, which couldn't have been further from the case!"

The sergeant's friendly advice was that Liebling go downtown the next morning, report to the armory at Thirty-third and Park, and immediately sign up.

Liebling hastened to oblige. The following morning, resplendent in his actor's overcoat, with the requisite velvet collar, carrying a bundle of his sheet music, a large sum of cash in his pocket—"I was already a rich man in those days," he said; "I had at least seventy-five dollars on me"—arrived at the armory to report.

Amid the Army bureaucracy, the eager young trouper was shunted from room to room, from officer to officer, and then, suddenly found himself flanked by two soldiers with rifles. He was under arrest!

"I started yelling. I protested at the top of my lungs—I told them nobody was more anxious to get into the Army than I was

—I'd pay my own fare out to the induction center—I was ready to go!"

Evidently the young patriot's protests fell on sympathetic ears. He was able to convince the authorities of his sincerity. But the Army was first, last and always the Army. He could not leave until his draft papers came through. Meanwhile, he must remain under custody.

That evening, Liebling managed to bribe one of his guards with a ten-dollar bill. His plan was to get back uptown to his draft board, to expedite the documents and bring them back personally; he was determined to establish himself with Uncle Sam, not as a draft dodger but as a willing doughboy-to-be.

Accompanied by his guard, the next day he traveled to Harlem, hurried to his draft board and explained his case. The papers were supplied. Later that day, he and the amiable guard went back downtown. "But I didn't figure on eating an Army supper as a prisoner," he said. "I still had some cash, so I suggested that we could celebrate before going back to the armory. My guard and I went to one of the sweetest restaurants in town, Reisenweber's, for a gala dinner, and then I persuaded him to tour a couple of the best nightclubs as well. By three A.M., I had to *carry* my soldier guard, drunk as a lord, into the armory!"

At noon the next day, he and a batch of other potential draftees were marched up Park Avenue to a nearby luncheonette. "The Army was allowing us twenty-five cents for lunch—nothing lavish, not even then. So whatever money I had left, I spread around. Everybody got more to eat; it was all on Willie the Bass. When we got back, my papers had arrived. A couple of hours later, after all those months of trying, I'd finally succeeded. I was off to defend my country, to fight for my Uncle Sam."

He was to see a lot of the war, and to fight in many battles. But before he was assigned to the 77th Infantry Division, out at Camp Upton, on Long Island, he ran into Irving Berlin, the songwriter, also now a doughboy. Berlin was assembling a soldier show at Upton, one that was to be called *Yip, Yip, Yaphank!*, in which there would be a chorus of soldiers singing

"Oh, How I Hate to Get Up in the Morning," and the rousing "We're on Our Way to France." Berlin promptly offered Liebling a place in the soldier cast, but the young man turned him down. He was anxious to get to where the fighting was.

As a machine gunner, he saw plenty of action. He was wounded by shrapnel and gassed as well. He was decorated for his bravery under fire, and because of his talent he was also chosen by his commanding officer to become a member of the Argonne Players, a batch of soldiers from the 77th who'd had professional experience in various branches of show business.

The Argonne Players were assigned to entertain the troops with concerts and impromptu shows; they also went through the wards of Army hospitals to cheer up the wounded. "I used the machine gun by day, and my voice at night," he told me. "I was sitting in a shell hole one day, with the shells landing all around me during an artillery barrage, and I remember thinking to myself, what a dope I was not to have gone with Irving Berlin and *Yip, Yip, Yaphank!*"

The World War came to an end on November 11, 1918. The Allies had won. The Kaiser was defeated. But the Argonne Players were not to return home triumphantly, not just yet. They remained in France, continuing to entertain. One night they were brought to Paris, to the famous Sarah Bernhardt Theatre, to perform at a concert honoring President Woodrow Wilson, now in France for the formal signing of the peace treaty.

"I could never forget that night," he told me. "In that historic theater, there we were out onstage, singing, for an audience that was packed with dignitaries—Wilson, Georges Clemenceau, the Tiger, the Prime Minister, the two great generals, Marshals Foch and Pétain—everyone you could think of was there."

Forty years later, when the two of us made a trip to Paris, Liebling took me on his own private pilgrimage, back to the Sarah Bernhardt Theatre.

Another world war had come and gone, Paris was still Paris, and thankfully, there it stood, the building untouched, flanked by the same trees beneath which the victorious doughboys of the Argonne Players had marched as they headed for the stage door.

We made our way down the side alley, and he managed to persuade the ancient French stage doorman to permit two American tourists to go inside for a look. Then he escorted me out on the stage, and we stood there, staring through the gloom at the shadowy rows of empty seats that were shrouded with sheets.

My husband shook his head. "I can still remember where they all sat," he told me, softly. "Pershing there, President Wilson there—Foch and Pétain in that row, next to Clemenceau . . ."

It had been a very big night for Willie the Bass.

Then it was good-bye France, hello Broadway, for the young returned veteran who had served his country so well.

He picked up where he'd left off, continuing his career as a singer. But even though he had a fine bass voice, Liebling was a pragmatist. He began to recognize the immutable fact of show business casting: because of his short stature, he would never get leading roles, either in vaudeville or on Broadway.

Added to which he found that he was always giving advice and counsel to his fellow performers. "One morning," he said, "I looked myself in the mirror and I said, 'All right, Willie, you're never going to be a star; you're handing out free advice to all your friends; why not get paid for it?'"

Shortly afterward, he became an agent.

And since his advice was first class, it was not long before he had been recognized as one of the best in the business.

By 1937, when we formed Liebling-Wood, Inc., he was one of the busiest casting agents in New York. Since it was well known around Times Square that Bill Liebling was constantly involved in casting plays for such solvent producers as Sam H. Harris, George Cohan and Max Gordon, and that advance copies of their proposed productions always went first to him for his suggestions, our outer office was daily jammed with throngs of actors and actresses, waiting expectantly for a chance at a job . . . some job . . . *any* job.

Not many were called, and even fewer were chosen.

In those years of the thirties, the legitimate theater, shrunken by the Depression, its audiences siphoned away to Hollywood's

double-feature bargains (25¢ to 1 P.M.—POPULAR PRICES THERE-
AFTER! FREE DISHES MONDAY! AMATEUR NITE TUESDAY!), was a
tiny oasis of desperation in a vast sea of troubles.

When and if a lucky actor did get a part in a show, it was a
pure gamble. If the producer had sufficient cash to raise the curtain on opening night, there still remained the obstacle course of
the critics. Theatrical employment was at its lowest ebb. Earlier,
some fortunates had been given jobs with the WPA Federal
Theatre and survived on twenty-three dollars per week, in New
York and in other major cities. But eventually that worthy institution would be attacked by legislators as a "Communist network," devoted to producing plays by such suspect playwrights
as Christopher Marlowe and Henrik Ibsen, and it was dis-
mantled.

Most Equity members were on the street, pounding pavements, wearing out what was left of their thinning shoe leather
in a desperate attempt to be seen and heard.

Nowadays, it is a vastly improved scene. All across the American landscape there are tributary theaters. Such institutions as
Long Wharf in New Haven, the Tyrone Guthrie in Minneapolis,
Washington's Arena Stage, the Mark Taper in Los Angeles, the
Hartford Theatre Company, to cite only a few, are full-season
operations, providing actors and actresses with many months of
employment. Such acting companies have become rich seedbeds
for much of our new talent, and so have the many dinner theaters, a relatively recent phenomenon, where local audiences flock
to eat and to see revivals of Broadway's best. If an actor can't
find work in New York today, there are many more towns to
which he can move his makeup kit.

But in that dark and dreary era, for every available part, large
or small, even a mere walk-on, there were literally hundreds of
desperate and hungry troupers, fighting through the doors to get
in for an interview. Come spring, some of the luckier ones might
get low-paid work in one of the strawhats, those small out-of-
town stock companies from Maine down to Virginia which
played during July and August.

But right after Labor Day weekend, they were all back, in
force, their quest begun again. And each year their ranks would

eft, my father, William H. Wood, very much the successful theatrical manager. Right, yself, attired for the beach.

Right, my mother and me.

The first evening dress from my new husband, William Liebling.

And the young marrieds.

ile I study manuscripts, Liebling instructs a potential client in how to win that precious
 on Broadway.

Liebling-Wood, Inc., enjoying a much-deserved day off.

Right, "Liebling,"
as I like to remember him.

be augmented by dozens of newcomers, those hopeful young men and women who'd made it to New York, each and every one convinced that one day he or she would be standing center stage, in the spotlight, a new star.

Every day, Liebling ministered to the flocks of the hopeful.

The weary veterans, many of whom he knew personally, some of whom had been well known and were now reduced to hunting for character parts, side by side with the new arrivals, who dashed in from part-time jobs as waiters or as department-store Christmas help, to check on whether or not lightning had struck today.

Liebling's was a sympathetic eye and ear. After all, he himself had been through the show business mill. He was well aware of the odds against most of these tyros ever getting through a stage door. But he never stopped trying to be helpful.

A few years ago I was at a party in California, and one of my fellow guests was the actress Lee Grant. "I want to tell you about your husband," she said. "When I first started making the rounds in New York, way back then, I came to your office. I was a complete amateur who hadn't a clue about the business. Liebling took me into his office and told me all the reasons why I shouldn't be an actress. He explained to me what difficult work this was, and how particularly tough it was for a young woman starting out. He did everything he could to talk me out of becoming an actress!

"A few weeks later, I returned to Liebling-Wood, and once again, he singled me out for a private chat. He did the whole routine again, telling me all the negatives he'd brought up about how tough this game was. Then, on my third visit, he started in with that lecture, and I'd had enough, so I interrupted him. I told him, 'Mr. Liebling, no matter what you say, *I* am going to be an actress!' Whereupon he said, 'In that case, Miss Grant, *I* will represent you.'"

Liebling's casting technique was simple and direct, largely intuitive. After studying a play, he made up a list of actors he felt were very right for each individual part. He would not deal in alternatives. His choice was his choice, and only if an actor or actress was unavailable would he offer substitutes.

I used to say to him, "This is wrong. It looks too easy. You walk in to George Kaufman, or to George Abbott, and you tell them that these are the people who are right for these parts—and that's it. They have no idea how much work and effort you've put into bringing them the exact right choices. Why don't you provide them with two or three alternatives—dress up your list so that the one actor you believe in, who's the perfect one, looks better in contrast to the others? That way you would *dramatize* your choices."

Liebling would have none of that. He did not wish to waste time, not his own, the producer's, the director's, and probably most importantly, not that of those actors whom he felt were wrong. In a way, he was being compassionate. Why should he needlessly build up some performer's hopes?

He did have his own flair for the dramatic, however. He told me that back in the days when he was casting the George Kaufman–Edna Ferber play *Dinner at Eight,* one role presented great problems. It was that of the aging matinee idol who cannot face up to his loss of stardom. In the eventual motion-picture version, John Barrymore played the part brilliantly, but on Broadway, finding the right actor was difficult. For days everyone connected with the proposed production argued over choices; there was agreement on nobody.

One Sunday morning, in Atlantic City to attend the tryout of another play, Liebling took a walk on the boardwalk, trying to forget his problems. He passed a store outside of which was a cigarette machine. In those days, some cigarette packages contained souvenir cards on which were photographs of famous actors and actresses. In the glass panel of the machine Liebling spotted the profile of an actor named Conway Tearle. Up to that moment, nobody had thought of Tearle for that role in *Dinner at Eight.* But Liebling did, then and there. He went into the store, persuaded the owner to open up the cigarette machine—he himself did not smoke—and paid for the tiny souvenir photo of Tearle.

Next morning, back in New York, he hurried to the office of Sam Harris's long-time general manager, Max Siegel. No one had yet arrived for work. Puckishly, Liebling placed the photo of Tearle on Siegel's desk, and then departed.

When Siegel arrived to find the card on his desk, he was promptly struck with the same notion: Tearle for *Dinner at Eight* as the matinee idol! "Who left this card here?" he demanded.

"Mr. Liebling," said the secretary.

"Call him," said Siegel. "Tell him he's had a great idea; let him find Tearle and see if he's available!"

As it turned out, there was an ironic parallel to this whole process. Tearle was in California, and in fact was not having very much luck with his own career. Later he told Liebling he had practically come to the end of his rope. But he came to New York and was hired; when the play opened, he received excellent notices. *Dinner at Eight* reestablished him as a leading man.*

Once, for a new comedy, George Kaufman and Moss Hart had supplied him with a cast of characters, with descriptions. One of the roles called for a man who would wear a sweater with patched elbows. Liebling sent his choice to their office for a reading, and instructed the actor to wear a sweater in that condition. A simple trick, but effective. Kaufman called back later to say, "Very interesting, Bill, the man is absolutely right—and you know, he even *looks* exactly the way the character is supposed to?"

One day, Liebling was crossing Times Square. When he reached the small island that separates Broadway and Seventh Avenue, he stood waiting for the light to change. A young actor whom he knew came across in the opposite direction; both of them stood waiting for the light to change. "Listen," asked Liebling, "can you play a xylophone?"

---

* Many years later, Liebling and I were invited to Edna Ferber's sister's home in Connecticut for a cocktail party. Miss Ferber, who was well known as a strong, outspoken personality, crossed the room to him. She took him by the hand and said, "You, without a doubt, gave more care, more thought and attention, to our casting problems than anyone I've had the pleasure of working with; nobody will ever do the job as well as you, Mr. Liebling!"

It was truly a magnificent moment in Liebling's life.

"No," said the surprised actor. "Never even thought of it."

"Well, think of it," said Liebling. "Go to Schirmer's, ask for a teacher, sign up for xylophone lessons, and when you're ready, I'll call you; there's a part coming up!"

The lights changed, and the two men parted in opposite directions.

The actor did as he was told. Several weeks later, after many sessions at the xylophone, he received Liebling's call. He was to report to Sam Harris's office to be seen for a part in *You Can't Take It with You,* one that called for skill on the xylophone. He read for Mr. Kaufman, and then demonstrated his new talent. He got the part, and was gainfully employed for several seasons thereafter, acting and playing the xylophone.

. . . Whether or not he was called upon in years to come to play that instrument is not known.

Day after day they filled his office, and he would go out to see them. His was the unenviable task of saying, over and over again, "Nothing for you today, sorry," "Come back tomorrow, try again," or "Call me next week and check." Scarcely had he finished this litany and the hopefuls departed than the office door would open and another group would crowd in, to be met with the same discouraging words.

Long years of dealing with aspiring performers who filed through his waiting room gave Liebling a somewhat pragmatic attitude toward them. "Everyone has talent," he would say, "*until you hear it.*"

But he never stopped looking at the new faces, or listening to their stories. In truth, he was as much of an optimist as any of the eager youngsters who crowded his days.

For years, Liebling and I went to preview performances, usually out of town—at tryouts in New Haven, at the Shubert, or in Boston, Philadelphia, Wilmington, Chicago—wherever one of the plays I was presenting, or in which he had acting clients he represented—would be opening.

The ritual was always the same. After the performance (which was, needless to report, always disorganized, hesitant, replete with disasters, missed cues, and various other crises), we would trudge backstage, through the stage door, off to visit Liebling's client, climb the stairs and knock on the dressing-room door. "Liebling, here," he'd announce.

"Oh, *no!*" would invariably come the voice from inside. "Not tonight! Oh, you weren't here, were you? *Nobody* should have seen tonight!"

In fact, one night, Agnes deMille, the great choreographer-director, carried this reaction to the ultimate. We arrived at the Shubert in New Haven for the first performance of a musical in which one of Liebling's clients, lovely Joan McCracken, the dancer, was involved. As we came across the lobby, Agnes emerged. At the sight of us, she stopped, astonished. "What are you doing here?" she asked.

"Why, we've come up from New York to see the show," Liebling explained.

"Oh, *no,*" said Agnes, firmly. "You cannot come tonight. We're not ready. It's out of the question. Please go home. Come *tomorrow* night."

No sense trying to explain to her we'd traveled seventy miles for this performance, not for tomorrow's—that we were due back in our busy office the following morning. She was so distraught, so rapt, she couldn't understand that; all she knew was that what she was involved in wasn't ready for us—or for any-one else—to see.

Somehow or other, the show survived that first performance.

They usually do. Recently I went to Stratford, Connecticut, to see the first performance of my client Ruth Wolff's new play, *Sarah in America,* starring Lili Palmer as Sarah Bernhardt. I received a call from Ruth late in the afternoon. She was very upset. "Don't come tonight," she pleaded. "We haven't had a technical rehearsal, the whole thing is in a very rough state, we haven't rehearsed the lighting cues, or anything—Lili has so many costume changes, she's going to need more time—please—come *tomorrow!*"

I explained I was already on my way. And I did go to the first performance.

Miraculously, everything went quite well. A minimum of missed cues; the technical people did a wonderful job; and so did Miss Palmer.

A Canadian actor, tall and good-looking, arrived in Manhattan and began making the rounds. Liebling spotted him, was interested in what he saw, took him inside for an interview and a reading and decided that the unknown Lorne Greene would be right for a part in a new play. It was far from an ordinary role; Leland Hayward, one of the best producers in the business, was searching for a leading man to play opposite the great Miss Katharine Cornell in a new drama called *The Prescott Proposals*.

A very long shot, indeed. But Liebling was not fazed by the odds. He sent Greene over. Greene got the part. He scored with the critics, although the play did not. The rest, as they say, is history.

Once Liebling had decided on his choice of an actor or actress he felt was right for a specific part, he stuck tenaciously to his decision. Nothing could sway him from his choice. Once, in Sardi's Restaurant, he demonstrated his tenacity in a truly dramatic manner.

It was in 1935, while the late great star Jane Cowl was starring in one of Sam Harris's productions, *First Lady*, by Katherine Dayton and George S. Kaufman. Liebling had been active in casting the play, and at the end of the season, when time came for the show to go out on tour, certain performers were replaced.

Liebling had a young talented client named Ann Mason, whom he wished to cast for the road tour. Playwright Kaufman advised him not to interfere, since it was generally the right of the star to decide what players would travel with her on a long, grueling theatrical tour.

That did not stop Liebling. He went to Miss Cowl and told her about Miss Mason. Miss Cowl, truly a theatrical grande dame, every inch a star, agreed to interview the young lady. The interview seemed to go well. The signs and omens were favorable.

However, a couple of days later, still in the grand manner,

Miss Cowl reconsidered. She turned thumbs down on Miss Mason. Liebling told me he suspected it was because Miss Mason was a bit too young and attractive, but he shrewdly avoided raising that subject with Miss Cowl.

Nothing he said would change Miss Cowl's decision. He kept on trying. Finally, with the deadline for the road-company casting coming closer, he decided to change his tactics. He invited Miss Cowl to take supper with him after her performance in *First Lady*. She agreed.

A clause in Miss Cowl's contract with Sam H. Harris stipulated a limousine and driver would take her to the theater and call for her afterward. But on this particular night, Liebling was taking her one block away, from Forty-fifth Street, through Shubert Alley, to Sardi's—a distance of several hundred feet at most. Nonetheless, Miss Cowl insisted on her prerogatives. "We shall take a taxi," she insisted.

Liebling hailed a cab. As the cab made its way down the block to Eighth Avenue and one block to Forty-forth Street—in those days, Eighth Avenue was not yet a one-way street—he seized the opportunity to serenade Miss Cowl. He hummed and then burst into song, regaling the star with romantic songs from his old days as Willie the Bass.

Minutes later, the cab pulled up in front of Sardi's, and he escorted her inside. Once at the table, he continued his campaign. Throughout supper, he paid Miss Cowl extravagant tributes on her past performances in her various dramatic roles. He told her that she had always been one of his favorites. "You have done a wonderful thing by starring in *First Lady*," he said. "By giving this great performance, you've not only provided continuous work for a cast of about thirty people, but you've also kept all the stagehands, the electricians, the ushers and the office personnel eating and supporting their families for nearly an entire year!" (No mean feat in those dismal Depression days.)

Miss Cowl beamed and continued eating.

Liebling kept on talking. The meal ended. Sardi's began to empty out. Liebling paid no attention. He pursued Miss Cowl with further blandishments. The clock showed 2 A.M., and still Liebling went on.

Finally, his throat dry, he paused to take a sip of water.

Miss Cowl, abstractedly, as if it were the last thing on her mind, said, "You know, Mr. Liebling, I've been thinking that perhaps Ann Mason might do for that part after all."

Liebling, exhausted, called for the check.

Later he told me, "*That* was the toughest sale I ever made."

There were many more.

In 1954, Herman Shumlin, the producer-director, was preparing a new play by Jerry Lawrence and Robert Lee entitled *Inherit the Wind*. It was a dramatic script based on the famous Scopes trial of the Twenties, in Tennessee, in which Paul Muni would play a part based on the lawyer Clarence Darrow, and Ed Begley would be his courtroom opponent, a character based on William Jennings Bryan. In the play was yet another major part, a newspaperman, based on the young H. L. Mencken, who had been sent down South to cover the courtroom trial for a Baltimore newspaper.

There was great discussion as to the right actor for that role. All sorts of suggestions had been raised and rejected. Liebling had decided for himself on the right casting. He sent over young Tony Randall, who had hitherto been seen on live TV, in a weekly comedy show called *Mr. Peepers*. The choice of Randall seemed improbable, but not to Liebling. "He's talented; he's the one to do it," insisted Liebling.

Mr. Shumlin was not impressed by young Randall, and for a time the playwrights also sided with his decision. But Liebling, as usual, was not prepared to take no for an answer. Since *he* had decided that Randall was absolutely the right choice, he continued to insist. He kept on insisting, day after day.

Finally, he wore down his opposition. Randall got the part. Along with Muni and Begley, he received rave critical notices, scored a great personal success in *Inherit the Wind* and went on to become a major star.

Years later, after Liebling died, I received a letter from Jerry Lawrence and Bob Lee which read, "Both Jerry and I have always wished that somewhere in *our* lives, we had an agent who believed in *us*, as much as Liebling believed in Tony!"

He demonstrated the same sort of faith in a young girl named

Diahann Carroll. Our office became the agent for a new musical comedy called *House of Flowers,* with a book by Truman Capote and a fine score by Harold Arlen, who did his own lyrics.

How Harold Arlen came to write the score for *House of Flowers* with Truman Capote is a remarkable story. While Saint Subber, the producer, was in the very early phases of preparing the show, Capote was living somewhere in Europe. At that point, no composer had been chosen. Liebling and I felt that Arlen, who was and is one of the most gifted composers of our time, was exactly the right choice. We sent him the manuscript of the show to read.

Without any sort of commitment from us or from Saint Subber, Harold, who had been so delighted with the script, sat down to his piano and began to sketch out possible melodies for the show. Then, still strictly on his own, he went to a recording studio and made an audition record of himself singing (he is a marvelous singer) and playing one of the melodies he'd written, along with what he called "possible" lyrics. It was a lovely, haunting song.

Along with Harold's own explanation of it, directed to Capote, the record ran about seven minutes. We immediately shipped it overseas to Capote. When he heard Harold's record, he was just as taken with the lovely melody as we were, and promptly let us all know that he would be delighted to have Arlen as the composer.

That song which Harold had sketched out, with its "possible" lyrics? It remained very much intact. In fact, later it would be a major and lasting part of the show's score. You will remember it as the lovely ballad, "A Sleeping Bee." Pearl Bailey was the star, and there was an ingenue role for a young girl who could sing.

One night Liebling saw Diahann Carroll performing on a TV show, decided she was right and called her the next day. He took her over to audition. The young aspirant sang. No one in the group who heard her seemed overly impressed. "Thank you —*next!*" came the depressing verdict.

Time passed; many other girls were auditioned. None seemed suitable. Once again, Liebling persisted. He brought Miss Carroll back, not only for a second audition, but for a third.

Finally, once again, at the fourth audition, his persistence paid off. Miss Carroll was hired. In the show she was given "A Sleeping Bee" to sing. The show has long since closed, but Arlen's score and Miss Carroll are still very much, fortunately, with us.

When one remembers that his earliest theatrical training was as Willie the Bass, it is no surprise that Liebling's judgment in the complex field of musical comedy was so astute.

One night in 1941, he left our office to go downtown to the New School, to check on the performance of an as yet unknown actress who was appearing in a revival of a comedy by Julian Thompson called *The Warrior's Husband.*

Years earlier, the play, a comedy based on the revolt of the Trojan women against their warrior men, had been produced on Broadway, and in that same female part a young Katharine Hepburn, fresh from college, had made her theatrical debut. Hopeful that lightning might strike twice, Liebling told me before he left that he would see the first act and then join me uptown for dinner.

I waited in our apartment. Eventually the phone rang. "I'm in a phone booth outside; this is the intermission," said Liebling. "This is an interesting play; you go have dinner without me. I'll pick up a sandwich. I want to see the rest of the show."

When he came home, it was to tell me that he had decided Thompson's play would make a marvelous musical comedy. The following day we checked into the rights situation and found that there were no entangling alliances: the play was available. Liebling promptly made a deal to option the musical comedy rights. Then he began looking around Broadway to find the best talent available to do such an adaptation.

The team of composer Richard Rodgers and lyricist Lorenz Hart, two of the very best, was at that time working on a musical project. But the Broadway grapevine, which functions on a twenty-four-hour basis, and is usually one step ahead of the working press, had it that their proposed show wasn't shaping up as well as it might.

Liebling phoned to arrange a meeting. He brought along a copy of the original play, and evidently his enthusiasm must have been contagious. Shortly afterward, Rodgers and Hart abandoned their other show, contracts were drawn, and they proceeded to tackle *The Warrior's Husband.*

In very short order, in June 1942, the show was produced on Broadway. It was renamed *By Jupiter!* and it starred the wonderful Ray Bolger. It pleased the critics and ran for 427 profitable performances. Alas, it was also to be the final collaboration of the talented team. Within a few months, Rodgers was to break up with Hart, to accept an offer from the Theatre Guild to work on a show that would become *Oklahoma!*

In 1949, when Rodgers and his new partner, Oscar Hammerstein II, had begun to prepare *The King and I* to star Gertrude Lawrence as the Welsh schoolmistress who journeys to far-off Siam to serve as tutor for the King of Siam's large family of small children, there arose another one of those thorny casting problems. Where was the performer talented and dynamic enough to essay the complex role of the King of Siam?

One day, Virginia Gillmore, an actress whom he'd represented, got in touch with Liebling. She was quite perturbed, and she needed his help. She'd read a copy of the book on which the new show (and the earlier Fox film) had been based, and she was certain her husband, the actor named Yul Brynner, would be perfect for the leading role opposite Miss Lawrence.

An interesting idea. What was the problem, then?

The problem was Brynner himself. Several years before, in 1946, he had appeared in a musical called *Lute Song*, playing opposite Mary Martin. The show had been well received, but it had ended up an artistic failure. Even though Brynner had received excellent notices, little had come of his work as an actor. Discouraged at his lack of success, Brynner had subsequently taken a job as a director in the newly opened studios of CBS Television. He was now involved in the earliest stages of live television drama, and was totally uninterested in leaving his new career.

"I'm sure my husband is making a very great mistake," said Miss Gillmore. "He shouldn't give up acting. I do wish you'd try to persuade him to change his mind; I think he should be in *The King and I.*"

Liebling read the book, and came to agree with Miss Gillmore. He hadn't been Brynner's agent before, but he'd seen him in *Lute Song* and knew his capabilities. He proceeded to get in touch with Brynner and suggested that he would arrange an audition for him with Messrs. Rodgers and Hammerstein.

Brynner was extremely cold and distant. He told Liebling he was sorry, but his proposal did not interest him in the slightest. He had no desire to give up his thriving new career at CBS. He was through with the theater as an actor.

Once again, Liebling would not be deterred. He literally refused to let Brynner turn down the suggestion. "I don't think you realize what I'm talking about," he said, with his typical candor. "You simply cannot respond in this negative fashion; we're discussing the *legitimate theatre!*"

Finally, his persistence won through. Several calls later, Brynner grudgingly agreed to attend an audition. He permitted Liebling as his agent to escort him to the theater where Rodgers and Hammerstein were conducting their casting calls. Brynner, of European gypsy background, loftily disdained to be accompanied by anyone as traditional as an audition pianist. He had brought with him a guitar. "I will accompany myself," he announced.

At the appointed time he strode onto the stage, sat down, cross-legged, like some happy peasant, and proceeded to play and sing a batch of wild gypsy songs, in the language he had learned as a youth.

When he finished his impromptu concert, up on that empty stage, there was absolutely no reaction from anyone in the darkened theater.

No one said a word.

Liebling came across to Brynner and said, "Okay, Yul, come on, let's get out of here."

Halfway up the aisle, headed out to the lobby, the pair encountered both Rodgers and Hammerstein, who had materialized out of the darkness and were blocking their path. "Could you come back this afternoon?" asked Mr. Hammerstein. "We'd like John Van Druten, who's going to direct the show, and who isn't here, to come over and hear you sing, Mr. Brynner."

That afternoon Brynner repeated his gypsy concert. Immediately afterward, he was hired to create the role of the King of Siam. It was the rebirth of an acting career that would take him out of CBS Television and back to the theater. Liebling's persistence of a quarter century ago was amply rewarded. As of this writing, Yul Brynner is still playing the lead in a revival of *The King and I* to packed houses.

Many other acting talents came into Liebling's outer office and were eventually launched on successful careers. As agent, he represented young Paul Newman, Montgomery Clift and Cliff Robertson. Julie Harris, Cloris Leachman, young Eli Wallach—all of them at one time or another sat on the waiting-room bench, not so patiently waiting for that first acting breakthrough.

The young Marlon Brando was a definite exception to the rule.

He did not sit there, waiting. Back in 1947, Liebling had to send for *him*, and wait until Brando showed up.

It was during the preparation phase of my then client Tennessee Williams' great drama *A Streetcar Named Desire*. The producer was Irene Selznick, and she had engaged Elia Kazan to direct. Casting the various roles had taken several months of discussion. Jessica Tandy, Kim Hunter and Karl Malden had been selected, but when it came to the major role of Stanley Kowalski, there were problems.

Originally, it had been agreed that John Garfield, the screen star, would be right for the part. But when the time came to draw up contracts, his agent insisted on what is known in the business as a "get-out" clause, one which permitted Garfield to leave the play should he receive a bona fide motion picture offer.

That demand caused the deal to fall through, and left all concerned facing a large vacuum. Who could fill the role of Stanley?

It was Liebling who first thought of Brando.

He had heretofore appeared on Broadway in several plays. He'd made his debut in 1944, in *I Remember Mama*, then he'd appeared in a drama called *Truckline Cafe*, he'd supported Paul

Muni in *A Flag Is Born,* by Ben Hecht, and played in Katharine
Cornell's revival of *Candida,* as the young Marchbanks. He was
talented, certainly, but as yet far from a star in the theater.

Liebling suggested Brando to Kazan, who at first was not especially enthusiastic, but eventually agreed to see the actor, and
to hear him read the part.

Now came another problem. Nobody knew where Brando
was.

Even then, he was a somewhat unpredictable character, given
to sudden disappearances, and when Liebling started looking for
him, Brando was not at any place where he could be reached.

Remember, in those days, any casting agent could represent
an actor for a part in a play, provided *he* reached that actor with
the offer first. So Liebling took steps to find Brando and to protect himself. He sent out word to the grapevine, among Brando's
friends and acquaintances, that he was anxious to speak to the
young actor. *Let him get in touch,* that was all.

Days passed. No sign of Brando.

Then, one day, out of the blue our receptionist announced
that there was a young man outside, looking to talk to Liebling,
name of Brando. In jeans, disheveled . . . definitely a Stanley
Kowalski.

"I hear you're looking for me," said Brando.

"That's absolutely true," said Liebling. He grabbed his hat
and escorted Brando out of the office, leaving word with the secretary to call Irene Selznick and inform her that he was on the
way over to the Henry Miller Theatre, where she had her offices.

As the two men walked across town, Liebling explained to
Brando what the meeting was about, described the part of
Stanley Kowalski, and suggested that he prepare himself for an
audition.

As they headed west, Liebling, as he often did, began to hum.

"Say," said Brando, "do you sing?"

Liebling allowed as how he had done some singing in his
time.

"I like to sing," said Brando. "Let's harmonize."

Adjusting their voices to the proper keys, the pair began to
harmonize, walking down the busy street, singing at the top of

their lungs a song which Liebling had once featured as part of his vaudeville act: "Dear Old Girl, the Robin Sings Above You."

The singing pair arrived at the Henry Miller Theatre. Upstairs, Brando was provided with the script of Williams' new play. Eventually he gave a reading as Stanley Kowalski for Mrs. Selznick and Mr. Kazan. Liebling's faith was once again justified; the producer and director were so impressed with Brando that they immediately decided he must repeat his reading for Tennessee Williams.

Williams had gone up to Cape Cod and rented a beachfront cottage, where he and some friends were vacationing. According to Williams' own memoirs, recently published, Kazan wired Williams that he was sending an extremely gifted actor up to the Cape for an audition, and for Williams' approval.

Liebling advanced Brando the fare. Brando thereupon vanished.

He did not reappear until three days later, when he finally arrived at Williams' cottage, accompanied by a lady friend. It was not a propitious time; the cottage was in a state of crisis. The electric power and the plumbing had simultaneously failed.

The resourceful Brando promptly went to work. He restored the electricity. He then proceeded to work on the antiquated plumbing until he had that functioning again. Then he picked up a copy of *Streetcar,* sat down in a corner, and with Williams cuing him, he proceeded to read the part of Stanley for the playwright and his good friend Margo Jones, the Texas-based director-producer.

According to Williams, not more than ten minutes of Brando's reading had passed before Miss Jones jumped up excitedly and shouted, "Get Kazan on the phone right away! This is the greatest reading I've ever heard—in or out of Texas!"

Next day, Brando and his friend departed the Cape. Soon the part was his. In New York, Liebling proceeded to negotiate a contract for his client. The terms were agreed upon, and the papers drawn; an old familiar problem arose. Once again, Brando had disappeared. No one in New York knew where he was.

Once again, Liebling sent out the word through the grapevine that he was looking for Brando.

Silence.

Then, several days later, disheveled, unshaven, in nondescript clothing, the Stanley Kowalski-to-be reappeared in the Liebling-Wood waiting room, casually asking for his friend Mr. L. Liebling hurried out, pointed a finger at Brando, and promptly launched into "Dear Old Girl"!

When their close harmony had ended, Liebling took Brando by the arm. "Get in here," he said. "I've got a contract for you to sign."

The salary he had negotiated for Brando was an excellent one —$550 per week—fifty dollars more than the young actor had ever received—and in those preinflation days, a fat fee.

The play opened in New Haven, at the Shubert Theatre, in early November 1947. The cast and its performance were well received. As for the play, it was not until it arrived in Boston that rave reviews began to appear. Audiences were moved and impressed by Miss Tandy as Blanche DuBois, and by Kim Hunter as Stanley Kowalski's wife. But when it came to Brando, the excitement was electric. Here, indeed, was a new star.

On the occasion of Brando's triumph, Liebling came up to Boston on the second night to take Brando out for a celebratory dinner. On this night, nothing but the dining room of the Ritz-Carlton would do. But knowing his client by now, Liebling instructed Brando that jeans and a sweat shirt would not be acceptable. He must dress properly for the Ritz. Brando protested. "A shirt, *and* a tie," insisted Liebling.

Brando conceded. He wore one of the shirts from his stage wardrobe and found a tie to go with it.

During their dinner, Brando casually remarked, "Say, Bill, I've got a chance to go to Hollywood and do a movie. They'll let me out of this play, won't they?"

"Of course they won't!" said Liebling, astonished. "You're a star—you're terrific—the play's sensational—and you signed a run-of-the-play contract!"

"I did?" asked Brando.

"Didn't you realize what you were signing?" demanded Liebling.

"Je-sus!" moaned Brando, furious. "Does that mean I have to stay with this play until it closes?"

That it certainly did.

Streetcar then came to New York, and was a tremendous hit. Its future as a long-running success was assured. Brando had achieved stardom, but he was a bit rueful about it.

During the next two years, Liebling and I would drop by the theater to check on how things were going with the play and the cast. Every so often, one of the lady ushers would report "Mr. Brando isn't feeling so well tonight."

"Why not?" Liebling would ask.

"Well, you see," she'd tell him, "the play just won another prize."

No matter how Brando felt then about his long-run captivity, the audiences admired and respected him. And it was due to that same prolonged run that he became inseparably identified with the part of Stanley Kowalski. For years, nightclub comics and mimics could draw instant applause by doing Brando, in his torn shirt, yelling "Stella . . . Stella baby!" His film stardom had to wait. But when the film producer Charles Feldman bought the screen rights to *Streetcar*, and hired Miss Vivien Leigh to play Blanche, there would be absolutely no hesitation over the choice of an actor for Stanley.

From then on, Brando was a major film star, and he has been one of the greats ever since.

His career on the screen has provided us with many classic performances—*On the Waterfront, Viva Zapata, The Godfather*, to name but a few.

But for Liebling, Marlon was not only a talented actor but a good tenor. I like to think that in other circumstances, years ago, he could have done a double act with Willie the Bass.

7

Mr. and Mrs. William Liebling

Last year, an invitation arrived on my desk. I was asked to come to City Hall, to be a guest at a reception given by the mayor honoring the ninetieth birthday of that venerable playwright Marc Connelly, who has since, alas, passed away.

Governor Carey, Mayor Koch, and a large group of theater people were to be served an early-morning breakfast, and the City would present Mr. Connelly with a commemorative scroll.

When the invitation arrived, I happened to be having a conference in my office with Paul Green, who was the author of many classic American plays. He had been writing for the theater since 1926, and is the author of *The Lost Colony, Native Son, Johnny Johnson* and *The House of Connelly*.

I promptly called downtown to ask if Paul Green could be invited.

He was an old friend of Marc's, and when the two men met over the municipal danish pastries and coffee, Marc said, "It was most appropriate that Paul come here. After all, *I* wrote a play called *The Green Pastures,* and Paul wrote *The House of Connelly!*"

That morning was the first time I'd been in City Hall since the day, many years back, when Liebling and I went down there to get our marriage license.

Like all love stories, ours had its complications. If the path of true love never did run smooth, let the record show that ours had more than its share of potholes.

To begin with, while I was certainly aware of Liebling's growing attachment for me, and mine for him, ours was, I thought, merely a commercial partnership. We shared our offices daily, we had meals together, went to the theater nightly and saw a good deal of each other.

How could I contemplate anything else? I was living on West Fifty-first Street with my mother, as a proper young unmarried female should. Each week I dutifully brought home a paycheck which supported us. You must remember—if you can—these were earlier, far less permissive times. Even though I'd grown up in show business, I'd somehow been shielded from those bright lights of Broadway, and the broken hearts which awaited innocent young lasses there.

And now, here I was, in partnership with this dapper, worldly Broadway-based gent, who lived alone (or perhaps did not; I never dared ask) at the Piccadilly Hotel on West Forty-fifth Street.

Strictly a business partnership, right?

Wrong. One morning—he'd evidently been building up to the moment for some time—Liebling, dapper as ever, arrived at our office, walked into my office, pounded his fist on my desk and shouted, "Audrey, are you or are you not going to marry me?"

I was astonished. Totally speechless, I looked off into space and did not reply.

Nor did I for some time.

I was not exactly without beaux. I'd been seeing a biochemist who was teaching at Princeton. I hadn't been thinking about marriage, nor had I considered Liebling, except as my partner in Liebling-Wood. Also there was my mother and the Lutheran church.

I gave him no affirmation. I needed time to think. I was confused. Not he. He'd flung the gauntlet; he continued to do so. Each morning after that first outburst, he'd arrive from the Piccadilly Hotel and continue to go into his desk-pounding inquisition. Which remained a soliloquy.

I continued to withhold any reply. If these were negotiations, they were strictly one-sided. Liebling then took to ending his harangue with an implied threat. "All right," he'd say. "I'm never going to talk to you again about this until you talk to *me*."

He'd leave my office and go into his own and slam the door!

But he'd be back, the next morning, to plead his case, always brilliantly.

It began to get through to me that William Liebling was absolutely determined to marry me, and by now I'd discovered I wasn't precisely opposed to the suggestion.

Then I discovered what a really fine agent he could be—not only for his clients, but for himself.

He talked me into it. "If you'll marry me," he suggested, one day, "you don't have to live with me until you work out all your problems with your mother and your home life. How about that?"

We closed the deal on those terms.

Now other problems surfaced. How and where to get married? Here was William Liebling, ten years older than I, of a different religious persuasion, as faithful to his Jewish upbringing as I was to my own Lutheran one.

We operated on the excellent theory, Marry first, explain later.

So we chose the time-honored dramatic ploy, beloved of all playwrights since Shakespeare, one which solves many plot problems—the clandestine elopement.

Some kind friends made all the necessary arrangements, and on the twelfth of February, in 1938, we went off in a car to Armonk, New York, and had a secret wedding before a justice of the peace. Afterward, we had a lovely wedding lunch, and then we returned to New York, man and wife, yes, but still living apart, he at the Piccadilly, I on Fifty-first Street.

In order to keep everything strictly under cover, my new husband took the license and my ring back to his hotel room at the Piccadilly, where they remained.

My mother, being a woman of some sensitivity—after all, she'd been around show business all her life—had begun to realize my relationship with William Liebling was a bit stronger and more involved than any simple business partnership.

Later that month, in February, she suggested I might like to join her on a vacation trip to Bermuda. Her ploy was very much part of the old-fashioned pattern of maternal behavior in earlier times: if your daughter was seeing someone of whom you did not approve, you packed her off on a trip, preferably by sea, thus rendering her unavailable to opportunity.

Dear Ida Wood, she didn't yet know the barn door she was locking—or trying to—was *ex post facto*.

But I agreed to go.

There we were, down at the ship, before sailing time, having a farewell party, and my secret husband, natty as ever, came down to see us off. He took charge of mixing all the drinks; not knowing anything at all about liquor, he managed to get most of the guests pie-eyed drunk. But before the ship sailed, he went over to my mother and took her aside. "Mrs. Wood," he said, gently, "I want to marry your daughter."

He understood she was an old-fashioned mother, one who firmly expected any suitor to make a proper request for my hand.

When she heard this, two or three tears dropped from my mother's eyes. But she made no comment.

The boat sailed. My new husband's instructions to me were clear. While I was in Bermuda, I was to inform my mother we were already married.

Somehow or other, I couldn't respond to my cue. Each day, I postponed the announcement. Mother was so happy to be with me I simply couldn't drop the bombshell.

We returned to New York, and Liebling met the boat. "Well?" he asked.

I shook my head and said, "Sorry—I haven't been able to tell her."

Even then he didn't have the courage to do so, either.

We'd been married three weeks, but we weren't man and wife.

Even though *Abie's Irish Rose* had been a Broadway hit for years, pleasing audiences with its story of an interfaith marriage, our own case was not quite as simple as playwright Anne Nichols' three-act plot made it out to be.

Something had to be done. I knew that, even if she agreed to the match, my mother would then expect a church wedding for her darling daughter.

But where? I went to my own church, the Lutheran church on Central Park West at Sixty-fifth Street, and asked the minister, a wonderful gentleman named Paul Scherer who was also a friend, whether or not he would marry me, in a religious ceremony, to a gentleman of another faith. He had no objection to such a wedding; however, there was a rule in the Lutheran doctrine which forbade a religious ceremony after a civil one had taken place.

Finally, I thought of a man I'd met, Dr. Randolph Ray, who presided at the Little Church Around the Corner, on Twenty-ninth Street near lower Park Avenue, and who had many theatrical people in his flock. Surely he could help us.

Dr. Ray's first question after I'd explained our plight was, "Would Mr. Liebling agree to be baptized?"

I did not even choose to put such a question to my husband. I knew he was a pious Jew who attended services at his synagogue and kept the ancient rituals of his faith. Since I respected his religious beliefs as much as he did mine, how could I expect him to change them?

Finally, as a special concession, Dr. Ray agreed to marry us, not in front of the altar of the church, but in his own parsonage.

We had the place. Now it was up to me to break the news to mother.

It was a situation to challenge the sharpest playwright. I had to explain I was going to marry Liebling, and we were going, not to the Lutheran church, but downtown to the Little Church Around the Corner, and not midday but late in the afternoon, in the parsonage, in front of the fireplace shortly after Dr. Ray's daughter finished her piano lesson!

I don't remember my dialogue. I talked fast and kept talking. My dialogue must have sufficed.

Because on the twenty-fourth of March, 1938, at 5 P.M., our second marriage took place.

Liebling's mother did not attend, nor did she know about it. I'd told my mother, but somehow he couldn't tell his. He'd gone up to see her on one of his many visits uptown—he was a fine upstanding son who took care of her until she died—and he asked Mrs. Liebling, an Orthodox Jew, "Mom, what would you say if I married a *shiksa?*"

Mrs. Liebling nodded and promptly replied, "You're a good son, you've always taken care of me. If that is what you want to do, you must do it. As for me, I'll just kill myself."

After we were married, my mother somehow found out Mrs. Liebling was unaware of her son's new wife, and we were planning to keep it that way. She said, "Where is this woman? I must talk to her! Why should I go through this *alone?*"

Liebling's mother and my mother never did meet. But I did meet her. On such occasions, I was introduced as his secretary. One night I attended a family dinner given by Liebling's brother, and I sat beside her at the table. She told me about Liebling, and proudly related how hard he worked at his job, what a success he was in show business, and continued to praise him. I merely listened and nodded. After all, I was long since convinced.

We left the Little Church Around the Corner, went to a small dinner afterward, and then we went to Atlantic City—properly Mr. and Mrs. William Liebling at last—for our long-delayed honeymoon. A weekend only; the office had to open Monday morning.

In those days, Atlantic City had for many years been a traditional theatrical tryout town.

Let the record show that our marriage was a hit and enjoyed a thirty-two-year run.

My mother was quite valiant about it all. For the first few years, she was willing to accept the fact of our marriage, even though she would not give way emotionally to her new son-in-law. Liebling came to adore her, but for a long time she withstood his tenderness. She persisted in holding him off; she was determined not to fall for this dapper interloper who had snatched away her only child. Finally, it happened. Five or six years later, she simply collapsed and responded to his affection.

From that point on, their adoration was mutual. It even surmounted the time in 1940, when Mother was packing certain papers to send off to California, where we'd opened an office, and accidentally discovered our original Armonk marriage certificate. "A *sneakaway* marriage?" she exclaimed, shocked. She refused to give up that certificate. By her rigid standards, our trip to Armonk had been a clandestine affair, unworthy of recognition. From that point on, it was always referred to as "the sneakaway marriage."

But she and Liebling had a unique relationship. He would put his arm about her, embrace her fervently, and she would shrug and explain to onlookers, "You know, he does this to me all the time." He would take her to Sardi's for dinner, and Mother would get into the taxicab; Liebling would begin embracing her in the back seat. Delightedly, Mother would complain, "Oh, Liebling, please don't!" Should the cabdriver turn to stare at such goings-on, Liebling would say, "Don't worry, it's only my mother-in-law." Should he continue his fondling, she would beam and say, "Sex, sex, sex! That's all you think about!"

When mother died, years later, Liebling's affection for her had grown to a point where he insisted on an obituary notice in the New York *Times* which included "loving mother-in-law of William Liebling."

We were never certain whether Mrs. Liebling suspected the truth about us. However, we were told by other relatives she'd had a dream one night in which, as she related it, she had seen a small, auburn-haired woman who'd become part of her son's life. It was never precisely explained by her to anybody exactly who this small woman was—but we surmised she had found out.

Until she passed away, however, I was never her daughter-in-law.

Merely her wonderful son's faithful secretary.

When we first were married, Liebling, who lived at the Piccadilly, decided that the nature of our business would be better served if we were not based in an apartment, with all the housekeeping chores. A furnished apartment would still entail laundry, cleaning and cooking, none of which either of us was prepared to take on. A friend of his, Eddie Diamond, a theatrical stage manager, suggested the Royalton on West Forty-fourth Street, and it's been home ever since.

The Royalton is a unique place: it's always been host to all sorts of theater and literary people. George Jean Nathan, the eminent critic, lived there, as did Robert Benchley. Carl Sandburg always stayed at the Royalton; Studs Terkel still does. Julie Haydon, Jed Harris—all sorts of interesting people.

Have you ever heard the wonderful story about Benchley and Frank Case, the owner of the prestigious Algonquin, which is just across the street? Benchley always frequented the Algonquin, but lived in the Royalton. One night he invited Frank Case to dinner, in his Royalton suite. When Case sat down to the table, at the Royalton, he discovered that everything in Benchley's suite—the tablecloth, the silverware, the dishes, etc.—was *all* from the Algonquin. Benchley had been preparing this elaborate practical joke for weeks!

My mother eventually gave up her apartment and came to live in the Royalton, in her own sixth-floor suite, so the hotel was truly home. The staff—some of whom are still there, after all these years—came to treat her as part of a large family.

One evening, my mother said to me, "Do you know who Thomas Wolfe is?" I told her he was a great American author. "Well," said my mother, "Mrs. Wolfe, who is his mother, is sitting right over there in the lobby, writing a letter." I spied the lady at a writing desk, a tall, imposing woman. "Would you like to meet her?" asked my mother. "She and I are friends." I allowed as how I certainly would, and mother brought me over to meet the lady, the model for Eliza Gant in the novel *Look*

Homeward, Angel. When we shook hands, I was impressed by
the strength of Mrs. Wolfe's grasp. So strong, such a titan of a
lady.

Mother also had small scenes with George Jean Nathan. He
was a flamboyant character, given to wearing fur-collared overcoats and broad-brimmed hats. One day he came to take the elevator up, and my mother stood outside the elevator. "Take Mr.
Nathan up," she announced to the elevator operator. "*I* will wait
for the *next* car." It seemed that Mr. Nathan never removed his
broad-brimmed hat in the elevator and Mother, an old-fashioned
lady, took that as a rebuff!

One day she reported to us that Julie Haydon, Mr. Nathan's
lady friend—who lived in a separate apartment, and who had a
small dog—had left the lobby and gone out to the street. "She
was kneeling on the curb, with the dog on its hind legs," reported my mother, "and she took the dog's paw and waved it to
Mr. Nathan, across the street. And do you know, Mr. Nathan
waved back!"

Nathan never acknowledged my presence, all through those
years. There was a tiny coffee shop in the Royalton, and we'd sit
and eat breakfast, never speaking. But I will always remember,
one morning, the counterman calling out: "Burn Mr. Nathan's
muffin!"

It seems like such a short time ago that there was such preju-
dice in the world we lived in. In the days when Ethel Waters
starred in *Mamba's Daughters* on Broadway, we invited her to
dinner in our Royalton suite. That was in the thirties, and
Liebling made very certain there would be no argument downstairs when she came into the lobby. He spoke to the manager
before she arrived and insisted that this great lady, who was our
guest, not be directed to the service elevator. Can you imagine
such a situation today? (Lest you think I am overdramatizing
the case, I can tell you what DuBose Heyward reported to me,
back in the days when *Porgy and Bess* was rehearsing. All the
members of the cast of that show were required, in whatever
hotel they were rehearsing, to use the service elevator.)

We have come a long way in race relations since then.

8

Some Early
Entrances and Exits

Play Agents in New York City . . .
Audrey Wood, 551 Fifth Avenue. Sells a lot of plays. Will
spend four years, sometimes, selling a play she has faith in.
Very hard worker, very devoted to playwrights.

Writer's Digest, June 1942

Our first hit, *Room Service,* was doing standing-room-only business at the Cort Theatre, and the new firm of Liebling-Wood,
Inc., was thriving. We represented one of the biggest smash hits
on Broadway, and since show business is where the old adage
"Nothing succeeds like success" was invented, we'd become
"hot." In the space of two short months, we'd accomplished—
with the considerable assistance of Messrs. Abbott, Murray and
Boretz—what most theatrical agencies take many years to
achieve.

My office phone rang constantly. Authors were seeking appointments. Producers wanted new plays. Through the doors
surged actors and actresses, in eager pursuit of Liebling. When
my secretary announced to the party on the other end of the call

that Miss Audrey Wood was anxious to speak, there was a subtle difference to the response. No one placed my call on hold.

And each morning, the mailman arrived loaded with mailbags full of manila envelopes, bundles of unsolicited manuscripts from hopeful playwrights who'd invested time, energy, typing paper and postage in their own talent.

Forty-odd years later, the envelopes still arrive. I try faithfully to read as many of them as I can, but out of respect for my eyes, I now have assistants to screen out the obvious impossibles. But back in those days, I dutifully stayed up nights reading them all.

I've never been able to explain how I know when I'm reading a good play. Talent—real talent—is amorphous, but one thing I've become certain of, after plowing through thousands of Act One, Scene Ones, I can read two or three pages of a script and know the author can write. Talent comes right off the pages, it knocks you out. Bowls you over, starts commanding your interest. Don't ask how I know; it's no trick. Some sort of signal light goes on in my head, and I know.

Which is not to say that once I'm sure I've discovered a good play, its eventual success is automatically guaranteed on the stage. The play may be the thing, but so many other elements must come into focus in the casting, the direction and the production to make it work in front of an audience. Getting a play into a producer's hand and arranging a contract giving him an option on its eventual production is very much like entering the Boston Marathon. Whether or not the play, and its author, will ever go the distance to the finish line is, in every instance, a long shot.

In the years which followed, I found quite a few good plays, and managed to get them produced. But the eventual results were not always gratifying, either for my playwright clients or for Liebling-Wood, Inc.

One of the first which comes to mind was an interesting historical drama called *Missouri Legend*, by a woman named Elizabeth B. Ginty. At that time middle-aged, Miss Ginty had spent years working as private secretary to the late great theatrical producer-writer David Belasco. Her play was pure Americana: she had dramatized the story of the two outlaw brothers Frank and Jesse James.

The play was produced by Guthrie McClintic and Max Gordon. Guthrie, who was Katharine Cornell's husband and a brilliant man of the theater, directed. He was the sort of craftsman who threw himself enthusiastically into the background of whatever play he was working on, and with *Missouri Legend* he went all the way. I can still remember this dapper, elegant gentleman arriving for rehearsals, appropriately dressed in jeans, a Western sombrero and a pair of high leather boots.

He did a fine job. Miss Ginty's play was well received by the critics when it opened at the Empire Theatre in the winter of 1938. But who could foresee that there would be a blizzard that week which would effectively tie up New York? Sufficient audiences never made it to the theater. Messrs. McClintic and Gordon had to post the closing notice. Unfortunately, Miss Ginty did not write another play. She died soon afterward, which was the theater's loss.

There was one redeeming event. A young actor named Dean Jagger, whom Liebling had cast as Jesse James, was spotted by a talent scout for a movie company. He sent Jagger out to Hollywood, where he had a long and prosperous career in front of the camera.

Some years before, when I was working at the Century Play Company, I had as clients DuBose and Dorothy Heyward. DuBose had written a novel called *Porgy*, which dealt with the black residents of Catfish Row, in South Carolina. The Heywards had adapted the book into a play. It had been produced in 1927. It was a sensitive and honest portrayal of people who had heretofore been treated by playwrights as caricature figures of fun. *Porgy* was a great success as a play. Produced by the Theatre Guild, it had been directed with enormous taste and imagination by Rouben Mamoulian. With a fine cast of talented black performers, *Porgy* had a successful run of 367 performances.

George Gershwin had read *Porgy* as a book, and was so excited by it that he suggested he make an opera of it. But the

Heywards had already begun to write their dramatization, and felt he should postpone his plans until after *Porgy* was produced as a play.

For several years after *Porgy* was produced as a play, Gershwin nursed his plan for an opera, but constant other commitments kept taking up his time. Meanwhile, the Theatre Guild approached other musical talents to adapt the story of Catfish Row and its people into a musical. At one point, the Guild proposed hiring Jerome Kern and Oscar Hammerstein II to create a musical comedy based on *Porgy* as a starring vehicle for the great Al Jolson.

Jolson embraced the plan enthusiastically. But in typical Jolson fashion, he wanted a traditional Broadway musical, not an opera, a show in which he could dominate the material.

DuBose, a lovely, soft-spoken Southern gentleman, was the kind of client who makes being an agent a pleasure. He insisted on discussing everything with me. I was young and relatively new at the business, but that didn't matter to him. I was also somewhat in awe of him. In fact, for years, I always called him "Mr. Heyward." DuBose would say, "For God's sake, Audrey, can't you say DuBose? Must you always say '*Mistuh* Heyward'?"

Somehow I continued with the formal form of address.

We had many discussions about the Guild's proposal to do the show with Jolson, but I was against it. I held out for Gershwin. I felt his interest was of important substance, and because of his great ability, I thought *Porgy* should be done as an opera, not as a routine musical comedy starring Jolson, no matter how dynamic a performer he might be. Young as I was, I spoke my mind to Mr. Heyward. *DuBose.*

He agreed with me and insisted that the Theatre Guild should wait for Gershwin's availability, no matter how long it took for the composer to get around to the project. The Guild wasn't happy about it, but they had to abide by his decision. Jolson went off to make *The Jazz Singer* as a film. We waited for Gershwin.

When Gershwin finally got around to the opera, he attacked the project with all his considerable talent. We were all excited at the prospect. I can still remember the day I took the contracts to Gershwin—the collaboration agreements between all parties concerned. I arrived at Gershwin's apartment in the seventies, and I waited. I'd never met him before; meanwhile, there were many of his paintings in the foyer which I looked at and admired. Finally Gershwin appeared, young and charming and enormously gracious. He went about the business of signing. He was effusive about DuBose and said what a great joy it was to work with him. He'd previously gone down to Charleston and spent a month there with the Heywards, where they'd done an outline and he'd begun work on the score. Some of the lyrics were being written by DuBose, others would be done by Ira Gershwin. That day Gershwin was bursting with excitement for the forthcoming project. He planned to return to Folly Beach and to spend months there, steeping himself in the rhythms, the speech patterns and the life patterns of the Gullah Negroes.

As I left, I mentioned I particularly admired one of his paintings in the hallway. It was of a bearded patriarch, beautifully done. Gershwin beamed. "I'm so glad you like that painting, Miss Wood," he said. "That's my grandfather."

Then I went across the street to bring the contracts to Ira for his signature. I remember how bright and cheerful he was that day. Proudly he proceeded to show me *his* artwork. Ira painted in a totally different style from George. His work, like his lyrics, had a wonderful innate sense of humor. One of his paintings was a self-portrait, standing, in his shorts, before the easel, peering at himself critically.

Eleven months passed, during which Gershwin completed the score of *Porgy and Bess*. When he had finished, it ran to some seven hundred pages of music. Uncut, it would have taken four and a half hours to perform. It was certainly his masterwork, and well worth waiting for. In 1935, the Theatre Guild produced *Porgy and Bess* at the Alvin Theatre. It was well received and had a respectable run, but it was not until years later, after Gershwin's tragic and untimely death, that his opera would be revived, to become a classic, one constantly seen and heard in opera houses all over the world.

After I left the Century Play Company, I had continued to represent the Heywards, and in 1939, they sent me a play called

Mamba's Daughters, based on a novel by DuBose. It was a strong and moving drama about a black matriarch and her struggles to raise her family. Guthrie McClintic optioned it and went to work to cast the major role.

That's when Ethel Waters came into my life.

Guthrie decided to cast her as Mamba. It was a bold idea. Heretofore, Miss Waters had been a headliner in nightclubs, vaudeville and musical revues. She was an exciting stage personality and a marvelous singer, she'd introduced such great songs as Irving Berlin's "Heat Wave" and "Supper Time" in his show *As Thousands Cheer,* she'd starred in *At Home Abroad,* but to cast her as a dramatic leading lady in a straight play was in those days a considerable risk. For audiences to accept Miss Waters as an entertainer was assured. But the Broadway theater did not offer blacks serious roles in those days. Who could be sure ticket buyers would support such a play?

Months before, I had sold *Mamba's Daughters* to another producer, and he'd tried to launch the play with Waters as a lead. After searching for backing, he had come up with none. He dropped his option. DuBose and I had been told the bad news before Ethel, and went to visit her, to break it to her, as tactfully as we could.

Ethel looked at us quite serenely, and then, very simply, said, "Well, I've known this was going to happen for a long time."

Then she smiled beatifically. "It's no problem," she continued. "Another producer will come along, and the play *will* be produced, and I will play Mamba."

She was right, of course, but I remember wondering, afterward, how could she have known?

The answer proved to be somewhat surprising.

Ethel told me later she had a good friend in Cleveland, a lady who foretold everything that was going to happen to her, professionally and privately, and everything pertaining to *Mamba's Daughters* so far had been previously predicted by her seeress friend.

For a while, I suspended judgment on this remarkable so-called medium, fortune-teller, mind-reader—whatever; I was quietly skeptical. But after the play had opened at the Empire Theatre, I went back one night to Ethel's dressing room, and there she introduced me to her "friend," a serene quiet woman.

After we'd been introduced, this lady, who had never seen me before, proceeded to tell me a good deal about myself. Softly, she described the apartment on Fifty-first Street in which my family had lived, and where I'd been born, and then she went on to discuss a woman who'd played an important role in my life. "She's black, and from the South," she said, "and she's very close to you even now, isn't that so?"

Laura Plummer was a woman who'd worked for my mother. She was from the South, she'd raised me and cared for me, and in later years she went into business for herself, working as a manicurist and hairdresser. We'd never lost touch. Laura came in to see my mother each week and to do her hair. She remained a dear friend of our family until she died.

How did Ethel's friend know all that?

I can't explain, but ever since then, I've never been skeptical about that particular lady's powers.

Perhaps we should have consulted Ethel's friend about the eventual fate of *Mamba's Daughters,* and she might have told us about the future. Ethel, who was the first black ever to star on the stage of the Empire, gave a magnificent performance. But the next morning, the all-important review from Brooks Atkinson, of the New York *Times,* was somewhat less than enthusiastic.

For the next week, business at the Empire box office was not very good. A group of theatrical people, friends of Ethel's and other prominent professionals, were so incensed by Atkinson's review that they spontaneously met, raised some money and took an ad in the *Times,* to rave about Ethel Waters' performance in *Mamba's Daughters,* and to plead with the New York audience to support this fine actress in DuBose and Dorothy's play.

The following Sunday, remarkably, Mr. Atkinson printed another appraisal of the play, one in which he heaped praise on Ethel (it was titled "Mamba's Waters") and apologized to his readers for having slighted *Mamba's Daughters* in his original review. He mentioned he had been suffering on opening night from a bad cold, and it had obviously affected his judgment.

Even after that, business didn't pick up too much. Eventually, *Mamba's Daughters* closed, a financial failure but a great personal success for Ethel. "And what an expensive cold for *us*," remarked DuBose, sadly.

Luckily, I would have more to do with Ethel.

Two years later, she was to play the lead in the first musical comedy hit our office represented. It was a delightful show called *Cabin in the Sky*, with a book by Lynn Root and a lovely score by Vernon Duke and John LaTouche.

The producer was Albert Lewis, a dear man who, like Liebling, came from the Lower East Side and had begun his career as a vaudeville performer. He was diminutive in stature, but possessed of enormous energy. He was also extremely shrewd in matters theatrical. He had been Max Gordon's partner in the successful production of vaudeville acts, and then gone on to be involved in such Broadway hits as *Rain* and *The Jazz Singer*. He'd spent many years in California as a successful film producer, but he'd found *Cabin in the Sky* and decided to come back to his first love, the legitimate theater, as its producer.

The show was a joyful, imaginative treatment of a fantasy plot, in which the forces of good and evil do battle for the soul of Little Joe, a gambling man. Little Joe was played by Dooley Wilson. (He will forever be immortal, however, for his performance on film as Sam, who played and sang "As Time Goes By" for his boss, Humphrey Bogart, in *Casablanca*.)

Ethel was cast as Sam's faithful wife, who does battle on his behalf with the Devil himself, and she was truly marvelous. Night after night, she would step out in front of the curtain and stop the show cold with one particular song, the classic "Taking a Chance on Love," a charming Duke melody to which John LaTouche and Ted Fetter wrote chorus after chorus of lovely lyrics.

There was another talented lady in *Cabin in the Sky*. Katherine Dunham, the dancer, had brought her troupe of dancers into the show and choreographed several of the major numbers.

Between Miss Dunham and Ethel there developed a certain amount of friction. Such backstage tensions are far from rare in the theater. Both were strong personalities and each refused to give way to the other.

I went backstage one night to visit Ethel, and she welcomed me, and proceeded to sit me down and tell me of all the difficulties she'd been going through during rehearsals and preparations. Miss Dunham's dressing room was upstairs, and I can still remember Ethel, pointing her finger up at the ceiling and saying, "That woman up there has done all she could to destroy me, *but*"—and she smiled, that great placid smile—"I have just kept on praying. God has stood by me, and I have come through!"

They were both troupers. The show became a big hit, and I am certain none of the paying customers were ever aware of the personal differences between those two ladies.

Ethel went off to Hollywood to repeat her great performance in the film version of *Cabin in the Sky* at MGM. At the studio, producer Arthur Freed assigned Yip Harburg and Harold Arlen to write more songs for the picture, one of which became certainly the most superb melding of singer and song that I have ever heard, or hope to hear: Ethel singing "Happiness Is Just a Thing Called Joe."

Fortunately for us, and for future generations, her performance of that song is preserved on film, as is the last play Ethel starred in, *The Member of the Wedding*.

Which brings me to my client Carson McCullers.

That extremely talented writer came into my life through the efforts of Tennessee Williams. Carson was a close friend of his, and someone whose talents he greatly admired. How *The Member of the Wedding* came to be a Broadway success is a remarkable story.

It had originally been written by Carson as a novel, which when published achieved great critical success. Before I became involved with Carson, another agent had brought her together with a playwright, and a deal was made by which her book would be dramatized for Broadway. I never read this version, but when Carson finally read the dramatization she was so emotionally disturbed that her dismay caused a physical reaction. She became quite ill; it may even have been the beginning of the stroke which eventually felled her.

There ensued an arbitration, at which Carson demanded the return of her dramatic rights. Tennessee was her chief witness and, as always, was most eloquent. Eventually it was decided she was entitled to the return of her rights. Carson then decided to do her own dramatization.

In the summer of 1946, she and Tennessee went up to Nantucket and shared a rented cottage. There, at opposite ends of a long table, the two worked each day, Tennessee on his play *Summer and Smoke* and Carson at her theater adaptation of her novel.

I have no idea how much help Tennessee actually gave her on the play. But one thing is clear: he gave her the most necessary assistance. Each day, through all that time, he sat with her, impelling her forward. If he hadn't, it's safe to say there might never have been a finished play.

Tennessee persuaded Carson to bring it to me. When I'd read it, I realized it was unique: a sensitive story of the coming of age of Frankie Adams, the Southern adolescent girl. But the play presented enormous problems. Whoever produced *The Member of the Wedding* would need brilliant actors to fill its three major roles—Frankie, the teenager, her seven-year-old cousin, and the loving black lady who was the family cook. Hardly what one considered a "star" Broadway cast. Nor was Carson's subject matter, in any sense of the word, so-called commercial theater.

Then, when I met Carson and we talked about her play, I realized this talented lady had absolutely no concept of how much time and work, how complex the preparations involved, how difficult the production process of a play can be. Carson was, to put it mildly, naïve and charmingly innocent about the theater. She believed it would all happen, and that was that.

I realized she would need a very special sort of producer—someone who was knowledgeable in the theater, who had great taste, who had the necessary boldness to put on this play—and, most importantly, someone who would be sympathetic to this extraordinarily gifted woman on her first venture into playwriting.

After I'd thought hard about who that producer might be, I finally decided on Robert Whitehead. I was delighted when he read Carson's script and agreed to bring it to Broadway. His coproducers were Oliver Rea and Stanley Martineau.

Carson lived at that time with her husband, Reeves, up in Nyack, on the Hudson, and I well remember the day we all went up to discuss the future production. By that time, Whitehead had hired the late Harold Clurman, a veteran of the Group Theatre and a thorough theater man, to direct. He'd never met Carson before, and we spent several hours that day at her house. Dear Carson, lanky, her hair cropped short, smiling, almost childish in her enthusiastic responses to the professional discussion which dealt with casting, scenery and costumes. She approached it all with the anticipatory glee youngsters have when putting on a play in the attic. It was her first venture into the theater; how could she imagine all the problems that awaited us?

When we left and headed back to New York, Clurman, who'd been listening all afternoon to Carson's wide-eyed comments, turned to me and shook his head. "Audrey," he asked softly, "what do we do if we get into trouble in Philadelphia?"

I understood what he meant. His playwright had no previous theatrical background; to whom could he turn for the inevitable rewrites?

I had no idea. "Harold," I said, "let's wait till we get to Philadelphia."

Which was the best I could do for him. Besides pray.

When Whitehead and Clurman finally cast the play, our three leads were Ethel Waters, who played Berenice Sadie Brown, the cook; young Julie Harris as Frankie Adams, a gangly girl of fourteen; and in his stage debut, a lovely little blond boy, Brandon de Wilde, aged seven, as Frankie's small cousin. The time was 1945, the place a small Southern town.

Then we went to Philadelphia. The rehearsals had gone well; there hadn't been any problems yet. Then, on the Sunday night before the opening, we had a dress rehearsal. In the theater that night were only a few people, members of the staff, a few friends and relatives. Carson and her husband, Reeves, sat nearby.

The dress rehearsal was a total disaster. There were infinite problems with the scenery and lighting, the performances were shaky—all in all, when the curtain finally, mercifully fell, we all knew we'd witnessed one of the worst theatrical evenings I've ever suffered through.

Carson, a tall wavering figure in the gloom, stood up. She said cheerfully, in her Southern drawl, "It was just lovely. I enjoyed every minute of it. Now if you all will excuse me, I'm going back to my hotel and get a night's sleep."

We burst out laughing.

Carson looked at us as if we'd all gone mad. She truly did not have the slightest idea of how dreadful this night had been.

We opened the following night. And that was also a strange experience. Little Brandon de Wilde, playing his first part in a play; nobody had bothered to tell him there would be people sitting in those chairs out front.

All of us professionals had merely assumed he'd *know* they'd be out there.

When *The Member of the Wedding* begins, the little boy is onstage. So that night, when Brandon got ready to play his first scene, on the stage, before the curtain went up, from out front he heard the rising sound of voices. He looked through the peephole in the curtain, saw a crowd in the seats—and promptly went into hysterics. Terrified and upset, he began to cry.

Harold, that sensitive man, took Brandon aside, calmed him down, and spent a few minutes talking very quietly to the boy. To this day I do not know what Harold said, but his words were magical. Brandon quieted down and returned to his place onstage. The house lights went down, the curtain went up, Brandon spoke his first lines and began his career.

During that Philadelphia tryout, Clurman's fears were to prove unnecessary. The play was gentle, yet unmistakably moving to audiences. Later, Brooks Atkinson would write, ". . . although the structure of the play was inept, it filled the theatre with charm and understanding because Harold Clurman staged it like a ballad, full of tenderness, childish audacity, and humor. It was endowed with inner life by the spontaneity of the acting. . . ."

Out of town, there were no crises. One brief scene, in which Frankie went into a small downtown bar, seemed completely superfluous to the action of the play. After a conference, it was decided to remove it. Carson agreed, and it was excised from the play as deftly as if it had been removed by a surgeon. So when we arrived in New York, to open on Broadway, Carson had not been required to do a single rewrite!

Opening night, Ethel Waters was once again a star, and, appropriately enough, in the Empire Theatre, where she'd played *Mamba's Daughters* by Dorothy and DuBose Heyward.

The performance went well, but I clearly remember the faces of some of our various friends coming up the aisle as the play ended—some of the so-called wise-money types, Broadway and Hollywood critics, smiling compassionately at Clurman, Whitehead, Liebling and me. Obviously, they were thinking, "Poor dears, they undoubtedly think this is a beautiful play, but it's a fragile thing which hasn't a chance in the world of ever making it here on Broadway . . ."

They were wrong. The next day's reviews were ecstatic. *The Member of the Wedding* was a smash hit. It was subsequently purchased by Stanley Kramer, who made it into a film in 1953, starring Ethel, Julie and Brandon, all repeating their marvelous performances under Fred Zinnemann's direction.

As for Carson, it was a lovely experience for the lady. Having been so well served on Broadway, so successfully, in such a remarkably uneventful fashion, with all those lush royalty checks in her mailbox up at Nyack, I'm certain she must have told herself, "This is for sure a simple way to earn a living!"

And who could blame her?

Three years later, she wrote another play. By that time, she'd become involved with Saint Subber. Saint was a very successful producer who'd been responsible for *Kiss Me Kate*, and had done such early Neil Simon hits as *The Odd Couple* and *Barefoot in the Park*.

Carson had come up with an idea for a play she called *The Square Root of Wonderful*. Saint was very patient. He made many trips to Nyack to try to help Carson push her play to its completion. It took a long time and a good deal of patience on his part to get to the point where Carson was able to finish the script. Her health was deteriorating, but she worked bravely on. Finally, in 1957, he began to produce her new play.

As director, Saint hired José Quintero. When he brought José up to Nyack to meet Carson, it was love at first sight for her. She was fascinated by the darkly handsome José; she became so enthralled by him that when José admired a rug she had—a lovely Persian in one of the rooms—Carson promptly decided to present it to him.

Then the play went into rehearsal.

Every day or so, I would hear from Carson. She'd call from home, or wherever she might be, and we would have long drawn-out conversations in which she'd talk about everything under the sun, chatting away in a neighborly fashion. It was only after a long while that she would get to the point of any call.

One day it went like this. She said, "Audrey, I had the most wonderful dream last night."

I said, "Carson, what did you dream?"

"Well," she drawled, "you know that rug I gave José?"

"Yes, Carson," I said, "I certainly do."

"Well," said Carson, "I dreamed José gave it back to me. Wasn't that a *wonderful* dream, Audrey?"

Later that day, I reported this dream to José, and he said, "Oh no! She should just try and get it back!"

Saint Subber took *The Square Root of Wonderful* down to Princeton, New Jersey, with Anne Baxter playing the lead, for its pre-Broadway tryout. After the curtain came down on the opening performance, José asked me if I would take a walk with him. I was with MCA then, and since he was a client of our office, he wished to consult with me. As we walked through the quiet Princeton streets, he abruptly announced he couldn't go any further with this play. He was at the end of his rope; he wished to withdraw. "There's really nothing more for me to contribute," he said, and as hard as I tried to change his mind—I assumed this was merely temporary depression—José was adamant. There were no hard feelings between him and Carson. He merely felt he was finished.

Saint brought in Joseph Mankiewicz, the film director, whose firm Figaro was a coproducer, and Mankiewicz did a valiant job of trying to redirect, but the play was a lost cause. George Keathley was brought in finally before the play opened in New York. Poor Carson was by now physically incapable of doing whatever work was needed; the stroke she had suffered had paralyzed her to a point where she could barely use one hand. *The Square Root of Wonderful*—such an ironic title. The play ran forty-five performances in New York.

But Carson's *The Member of the Wedding* remains alive today, a classic American play, a fitting memorial to a gallant lady.

As I think back on it now, what a marvelous experience the production must have been for Carson—even though she couldn't realize it was unique. No work to be done in Philadelphia, no tortured late-night conferences, none of that endless stress and anguish which has been the lot of so many of my other clients. She'd been blessed with a wonderful cast, a fine sensitive director and producers who believed in the play from the very beginning. How good to remember Carson, sitting in the audience, having herself a wonderful evening watching all her characters up there on the stage, playing out their stories, just as she'd imagined it all!

That was three decades ago, but I can still vividly call back the sound of Ethel Waters' rich, vibrant voice, as she held young Julie Harris in her lap, cuddled Brandon de Wilde close to her and sang the great spiritual "His Eye Is on the Sparrow, and I Know He Watches Me."

Such moments in the theater are what have kept me permanently stagestruck.

It isn't always so rewarding. Far from it. A great deal of the time there are tensions, arguments and passionate disagreements, which explode at all hours of the day or night. I found out early on that an agent's job calls for diplomacy, legal skills, tact and endless amounts of patience.

I remember once, when I was much younger, I represented Dorothy Heyward, the great legendary producer-director Jed Harris wanted to buy a play she'd written. An entire chapter could be written about the demoniac Mr. Harris but I think I can typify him by recalling what happened between us. We had considerable difficulty in getting him to sign a production contract; I drew up contracts and finally got an appointment with him at his hotel, the St. Moritz.

When I arrived at his suite, he opened the door. I knew he would do anything to put me at a disadvantage. He looked at me and said, "You've gained weight." I was so well prepared for this that I said, "Isn't it wonderful—ten pounds!"

This threw him off. We sat down and discussed terms. I kept my voice low, and that made him sit close. I said, "Jed, I must ask you to be at your very best with this woman. I've known her for many years, her husband DuBose and I were great friends, and she is alone. I don't want any of your shenanigans; I don't want you to do unpleasant things to this woman." Whereupon, looking me in the eye—we were almost nose to nose—he said, "If you were a man, I would punch you in the nose."

Whereupon I said, "Jed, I'm sorry I'm *not* a man." And that's how we reached our understanding.

Later on, there were problems, considerable problems. Jed would disappear, and poor Dorothy had no idea what was happening with her play. She lost her patience and so did I: the contract hadn't been signed and there was no advance paid (typical Jed Harris behavior—no money, no signature). Finally Dorothy wrote him a note saying let's forget it. Whereupon Jed sent her a wire saying, "AUDREY WOOD HAS PURSUED ME WITH TALMUDIC FURY." Ever since, "Talmudic fury" has been my pet phrase about my own conduct.

Many years later, I ran into Jed in the lobby of my hotel, the Royalton, where he was staying; it was a few months before he died. Jed asked me to have coffee with him, and even though he was genial and friendly, I simply could not start in with him again. So I made an excuse and hurried off to my office.

Later, Charlie Abramson, an agent who also lives in the hotel, reported to me that Jed had come to him and said, very seriously, "You know, I don't think Audrey likes me. . . ."

I once handled a play by Rube Goldberg, the great cartoonist. It was his first play, called *The Day of Rest*. This entire play was about a man trying to relax on a Sunday and what happens to interfere with his day of rest. When I read it, I got this very odd notion that Robert Benchley would be the perfect actor to play this leading role. He lived at the Royalton, too, and, being adventurous, one day I left the script with a letter suggesting to Mr. Benchley that he read it and consider becoming an actor in the Broadway theater. At this period, the early thirties, Benchley had done a few short films and he had also appeared, years before, in one of the famous *Music Box Revues* (produced by Sam Harris and Irving Berlin), doing his hilarious monologue "The Treasurer's Report." So I was very hopeful about all this.

Well, many days passed and there was no word from Mr. B., and I was trying to be very discreet and diplomatic, so now and again I would leave a little note, which I tried to keep on the light side, but always asking if he'd read the play yet. I didn't hear anything, and then, one day, in my mailbox, there was a note from him. In the envelope he enclosed one thing—his Actor's Equity card—*canceled*.

Never have I had an actor go to such lengths to prove to me he couldn't act anymore. He'd gone and had it canceled! So typical of Benchley.

I remember another play called *Mr. Sycamore*, adapted by the late Ketti Frings from a novella by my client Robert Ayres. It was a gentle fantasy about a postman who decides he'd rather be a tree. How he manages the feat and the reaction of his family made a rather fragile play. It was produced by the Theatre Guild in 1942 with Stuart Erwin as the man-tree, and Lillian Gish as his perturbed wife.

I went to New Haven for the tryout opening. By that time, I was accustomed to bad out-of-town premieres, but so many things were wrong with *Mr. Sycamore* I was truly dismayed. In the postmortem which took place after the last curtain—a theatrical ritual where they separate the men from the boys—I proceeded to tell Lawrence Langner and Theresa Helburn what I thought needed to be done. I gave them a long itemization of the errors that needed to be rectified, not only in the dramaturgy, but in the performance and the staging.

When I'd finished, Lawrence smiled weakly and said, "You know, Audrey, you always make me feel as if I'm the agent, and *you're* the producer."

(I believe he meant that as a compliment.)

We all agreed a great deal of work needed to be done by Miss Frings. At a later period in her career she was to write a successful adaptation for the stage of Thomas Wolfe's *Look Homeward, Angel*. At that time she was a Christian Scientist.

After Ketti listened to all the objections, the suggestions and requests for rewrites, she smiled cheerfully at me and said, "Audrey, it will all be better when we get to Boston."

Faith may move mountains, but it did not rescue *Mr. Sycamore*. It wasn't better in Boston, and it wasn't better in New York. The New York critics did a rapid job of felling Miss Frings' tree, and shortly afterward, the play became one more statistic in theatrical history.

Somehow we had much better luck with musicals. Not only did Liebling-Wood represent *By Jupiter,* but in 1944 Yip Harburg returned from Hollywood with a new project. He and Fred Saidy and Sig Herzig had written the book, and the score was by Harold Arlen, with Harburg's lyrics.

Harburg, who had always been an amalgam of shrewd showman and political activist, anticipated Betty Friedan and Gloria Steinem by three decades. His new show was based on the story of Amelia Bloomer, the eighteen-sixties feminist who crusaded for temperance, women's rights and the abolitionist cause, and for whom the bloomer, which she invented, had been named.

Bloomer Girl was produced on Broadway by John C. Wilson,

a very elegant and social gent who'd heretofore spent most of his career involved with the works of Noël Coward. Nat C. Goldstone, a Hollywood agent, was the coproducer. They were an odd theatrical couple indeed, but the partnership worked. They assembled a fine cast including Celeste Holm and Joan McCracken, both of whom had made a success the year before in *Oklahoma!*, and once again Dooley Wilson was part of the company.

Arlen and Harburg provided a splendid score, one that had a delicate balance of lovely ballads such as "Evalina," and "Right As the Rain," rousing marches ("It Was Good Enough for Grandma") and a song of great social significance, "The Eagle and Me."

Bloomer Girl ran for 654 performances and made stars out of Celeste and Joan. There was a good deal of discussion about turning it into a film, and over the years since then, a number of Hollywood producers have tackled the project. Somehow or other, it's never happened. I'm convinced *Bloomer Girl* would make a splendid revival for today. One day, I'm certain, theatergoers will once again enjoy *Bloomer Girl*.

Two years later, in 1946, Yip was back with another book he'd written with Fred Saidy, and a score for it he'd done, this time with Burton Lane. These talented men had combined two totally disparate themes, the story of a whimsical Irishman searching for a pot of leprechaun gold and the race struggle between whites and blacks down South, into a rollicking musical—*Finian's Rainbow*. Once again, Harburg was anticipating one of the great movements of the postwar society. In 1946, the show was truly avant-garde. What Broadway producer of that era would have contemplated a plot in which a Southern senator named Billboard Rawkins, an implacable segregationist, falls asleep and is transformed by Finian, with one magic wish, into a black evangelist?

In the script was a part that was not easy to cast. Og was an ageless leprechaun, the guardian of the fairy pot of gold, an elfin creature who would fall in love and then sing a delightful song, "When I'm Not Near the Girl I Love, I Love the Girl I'm Near."

Once again, Liebling demonstrated his tenacity. He had decided a young actor named David Wayne was absolutely the right choice for Og. Wayne had previously been in several plays, but this part was a big departure from his earlier roles. And Og was absolutely pivotal to the plot. Liebling brought him in to audition and, after much discussion, Wayne was engaged.

The out-of-town tryout of a musical show is a hectic, intense torture chamber, with the creative personalities involved all grappling with each other over necessary cuts and changes. Uncertainties constantly surface and become the seeds of all-night debates. *Finian's Rainbow* was no exception. Even though audiences in Philadelphia enjoyed it, there was a high quotient of backstage tension.

Three or four days before the show was due to open in Philadelphia and head for its New York premiere, Burton Lane came to Liebling and took him aside. "Bill," he said, "David Wayne won't make it. He has to be replaced."

Liebling stood firm. "Just let him open," he said, and walked away. No amount of discussion could change Liebling's stand. Somehow he prevailed.

Wayne did open, and he was superb. He more than justified Liebling's faith. From that day until this, there have been no further doubts about David Wayne's abilities, either onstage or in films or on TV.

The late Ella Logan was the female lead in *Finian's Rainbow*, and she was marvelous, especially when she sang such lovely songs as "Look to the Rainbow," and the classic "How Are Things in Glocca Morra?"

But I remember a rather sad episode involving Miss Logan. There had been an early stipulation made by the producers that none of the cast of the show would receive star billing. No performer's name would be billed above the title.

However, when the cast and crew arrived in Philadelphia for the tryout, it was discovered that one of the house electricians there, assigned to set up the electric sign on the marquee, had inadvertently placed Miss Logan's name up in lights, above the title.

Somehow or other, Miss Logan decided that, mistake or no, the presence of the sign and her name on it was sufficient to guarantee her further star billing, and for the next few weeks she insisted on it. Even though her contract clearly stated that there would be no such billing, she instructed Liebling to do battle for her.

Finian's Rainbow opened in New York, and was a smash. There were lines at the box office each day, but on the Forty-sixth Street Theatre marquee, Miss Logan's name did not appear. Although she had scored a great personal success, she became obsessed by the omission. Nothing could deter her from fighting for what a hapless electrician in Philadelphia had given her by mistake.

Liebling tried to explain her case, although he was personally dubious as to its merits. Every day, she brought up her complaint. It was argued down by the producers, who pointed to her contract and insisted they were abiding by its terms.

Eventually, Miss Logan hired the legendary Irving "Swifty" Lazar to bring her case to a satisfactory resolution. Even he was unable to sway the producers. Miss Logan continued to insist. Eventually, dissatisfied, she left the show.

Finian's Rainbow was the high spot of her career. Certainly the part she played was the best she'd ever had, as were those lovely songs she introduced. It has always seemed so ironic and sad that such a talented performer would permit anything so temporal to anger her to the point where she could become self-destructive.

But it doesn't surprise me. She was not the first nor would she be the last client I've done business for who placed such emphasis on the size and placement of her name in advertising and publicity. In the years I've been an agent, I've often been involved in bloody contractual wrestling matches where the fine points of billing became as vital as the lines drawn on a postwar peace treaty.

When Shakespeare wrote "What's in a name?" he certainly wasn't referring to show business.

Personally, I've been lucky. Even though I've done battle for my clients, I've never had much of an ego problem about my own billing.

But then, Wood is a hard name to misspell.

One day in 1946, when *Finian's Rainbow* was selling standing-room, I received a call, completely out of the blue, from California. On the other end was an actor whom I'd never met, Mr. Charles Laughton.

"I have written an adaptation of a play called *Galileo* with Bertolt Brecht," he announced crisply. "I am coming to New York and we both wish you to represent this project. Therefore, Miss Wood, I would like to arrange a meeting at which time I can read the play to you."

I was enormously flattered. Brecht was an outstanding playwright and Laughton a superb actor. Certainly I wished to represent them, but I told Laughton he would be better served if he sent the play along and allowed me to read it for myself. I tried to explain to him I always preferred to operate that way. "I trust my eye, and not my ear, Mr. Laughton," I said.

I was well aware of what a superb reader he was. It was legendary in the business that Laughton could pick up the telephone book, read from it and hold an audience spellbound.

"I see," said Mr. Laughton. "Then I shall call you when I arrive in New York."

Shortly afterward, I received another call, this time from Orson Welles, another performer well known for his ability to mesmerize audiences. He explained to me that he was considering directing *Galileo,* with Laughton as the star, and he had heard from Charles that I did not wish him to read the play aloud to me. "Who the hell do you think you are, not to permit him to read it?" he demanded. "This is easily the most insulting thing that has ever happened to an actor of his stature!"

Faced with this onslaught, I conceded I would break my rule. I made a date to meet with Laughton at his hotel the following week.

Laughton was in New York living at the Gotham. He suggested that Liebling and I come to his suite at 11 P.M. It seemed his wife, Elsa Lanchester, had a social engagement that

urrounded by friends and clients, Tennessee Williams, William Inge, Maurice Valency
nd Carson McCullers. (PHOTOGRAPHED BY RICHARD AVEDON)

Mr. Williams' inscription says it all: "'F
Audrey — Whether the cup with sweet
bitter run.' — Tennessee"

Arthur Kopit, who wrote on the back of
this photo:

> To Audrey . . .
> Short in height
> Great in power,
> Infinite in spirit, with love,
>
> Arthur
> (The Tall One guarding Miss Wood)

Preston Jones and me, at the opening of *A Texas Trilogy*.

...bert Anderson, my longest-running ...nt.

DuBose and Dorothy Heyward and daughter, Jennifer, at home in Charleston, South Carolina.

Brian Friel, of the Abbey in Dublin, London's West End and Broadway.

James Costigan, who waited patiently for almost a decade before his *Love Among the Ruins* found its cast, director and audience on TV.

evening, and Liebling and I could come and listen to *Galileo,* sans any interruption. Welles would also be there.

To me Liebling demured. He protested that after a hard day at the office, attending to all the business chores of his job, he could better use a night's rest. Should he attend he might well fall asleep.

Therefore, I went alone.

I knocked on the hotel suite door. Laughton opened it. He was wearing an open shirt, as I remember, and was barefoot. He welcomed me. We were alone. Mr. Welles had not yet arrived.

"We shall wait a few minutes for him, and then I think we should proceed, don't you agree?" he asked.

"I certainly do," I said.

He led me over to a small card table, pulled over two chairs. We sat down, face to face, and waited.

Then he glanced at his watch. "Let's begin," he said.

He opened the script and began to read *Galileo* aloud, to an audience of one.

Laughton was a consummate actor. He read directly to me, fastening his sharp eyes on mine. It was probably the most marvelous reading of a play I've ever heard, before or since.

But it was late, and I'd already had a long, hard day. The play went on and on, and despite Laughton's brilliance, there were times when I fought off drowsiness. Whenever his eyes darted down to the printed page, I surreptitiously pushed my eyelids upward, so as to remain alert. I dared not insult this man by showing the slightest sign of inattention.

It was well after 1 A.M. when he finished.

Then there was a knock on the door. There stood Mr. Welles. He had just had himself a long nap, awakened and hurried over to the Gotham, fresh and alert, and was now ready to discuss the production of *Galileo*.

It seemed both men were ready to spend the rest of the night, if need be.

Then, mercifully, the telephone rang. "For you," announced Laughton, who looked surprised at this late call.

It was Liebling. "Listen," he said, urgently, "I'm downstairs, with a cab waiting. Get the hell out of there and come home!"

He'd felt so guilty at having left me to go it alone he'd awakened, gotten dressed and come over. But I could not explain to Laughton that it was my husband downstairs; I'd already lied in his behalf and told him Liebling was out of town! So I made some excuse to my two hosts, suggested we must discuss the play further the following day, and said good night.

Laughton graciously offered to escort me out. Barefoot, in his careless dress, he padded down the hall with me through the quiet hotel, to the elevator. I remember praying he wouldn't escort me to the lobby, not only because of his attire, but also because there he'd meet Liebling, and how would I possibly be able to explain his presence?

Strangely enough, I had another play in my office at the time called *Lamp at Midnight* by Barrie Stavis, and it, too, dealt with Galileo and his struggles. It seemed impossible for me to handle two plays on the same subject, and I had to be fair to Mr. Stavis. I explained the situation to him, and I suggested another play agent whom I'd spoken to, who was willing to represent him. The problem was thus resolved. *Lamp at Midnight* was eventually produced with an excellent cast at a new theater downtown called New Stages, and I was free to cope with the problems of Laughton and Brecht.

During the next few days, I went looking for a producer for *Galileo*. The Theatre Guild was definitely interested, and we began discussions about a future production.

Laughton called to announce he was going out to spend the weekend at Westhampton, Long Island, and he planned to take a copy of the play along, to read to a group of friends and acquaintances, most of whom were involved in the theater.

"No, no!" I said. "You must not do that!"

"Why not?" he demanded.

I explained to him that each one of the members of his weekend audience was a possible source of future theatrical interest. The theater being a small, inbred world, certainly the morning after his reading each one of his listeners would be on the phone, discussing a play which I had in submission to the Guild. "By Monday morning, it will be all over the town," I said. "It's a very bad thing to do, believe me."

"Do you really think so?" he said, like some small boy who'd been chastized.

"It may very well hurt the sale," I insisted. "Please—do *not* read the play."

"I'm not certain you're right, but I'll think about it," he promised, and hung up.

I wasn't at all sure he'd listen to me. Then, the following Monday, I received a call from Stanley Young, a playwright client of mine who had a home on Long Island. He wanted to tell me what had happened out there. It seemed he'd been invited to a reading of *Galileo* by Laughton, and naturally, he'd been looking forward to such a performance with keen anticipation. "Audrey," he said, "do you know what happened? When we got there, Laughton announced to us he would not be reading the play—and then, do you know what he did read for the next three hours? The *Bible!*"

It was one of the few times I've ever given direction to an actor—and the actor took it.

The deal with the Theatre Guild did not materialize. Welles went off to other projects. But I did eventually make a contract with T. Edward Hambleton and John Houseman to produce *Galileo,* not in New York, but at a small theater in Los Angeles called the Coronet.

Galileo, starring Laughton, opened there in July 1947. The reviews were respectful, but not wildly encouraging. One newspaper, the *Herald-Examiner,* took particular aim at the star, complaining that he portrayed the great legendary Galileo as "a porcine boor." But Hambleton and Houseman were determined to bring the production to New York.

It was a difficult time for that venture. For one thing, the House Un-American Activities Committee, embarked on a political witch-hunt, had during that summer begun calling in "unfriendly witnesses," in an attempt to probe the so-called Communistic conspiracy in the arts. Foremost on the list of the committee's earliest targets were Bertolt Brecht, as well as Hanns Eisler, the German composer who had written an original score for *Galileo.*

Houseman recently wrote: "When *Galileo* was presented to

New York that fall, its performance generated none of the cultural and social excitement that had marked its California premiere. For one thing, the climate had changed; for another, Brecht himself was not present. Summoned to Washington as the 19th member of the 'Hollywood 18,' he appeared before the House Un-American Activities Committee. Wreathed in cigar smoke, his answer to the incriminating question as to whether or not he had ever been a member of the Communist party was 'No, no, no, no, never!' . . . Arrangements for his departure had already been made. Within hours of his interrogation, he left by plane for Europe and never returned. . . ."

It was within such an ominous atmosphere that Hambleton and Houseman prepared the New York production.

Since I was agent for Laughton and the now-vanished Brecht, there were many times when I needed to consult with Laughton on matters concerning his position as coauthor. Brecht was inaccessible, somewhere in Europe. By now we were on an amicable basis—except for one afternoon when I came up to his hotel room for a conference.

When I knocked, Laughton called "Come in, the door's unlocked!"

He was lying on a couch, barefoot, his shirt wide open, its rumpled tails bagged wildly loose above an equally rumpled pair of trousers. On his capacious stomach was set a bowl of fruit, which he was fondling, one piece at a time.

This remarkably talented client, who for years had stirred audiences with his many performances, looked up at me, and said, sharply, "You have either misbuttoned your coat, my dear Miss Wood, or one button is missing."

That did it. I said, "Charles Laughton, I have taken a great deal from you, but I will have no criticism of the way *I* dress, thank you!"

He smiled, nodded meekly, and never again did he bring up the subject of clothing, either his or mine.

Galileo was received respectfully by the New York critics. All the electricity and excitement Laughton had communicated the memorable night in his hotel room was there, on the stage. Brecht and he had a stirring message to impart, one that affirmed the ability of a single man to struggle against repression, a theme that was singularly apt for those dark and stormy days.

Perhaps it was because of the clouds which hung above the production, those symbols of the departed Brecht and Eisler; it may also have been that audiences expected Laughton in less dramatic roles. Whatever the reason, *Galileo* did not run very long.

I remember one afternoon, during rehearsals, sitting in the rear of the darkened theater in New York, watching Laughton up onstage doing one of his highly emotional scenes. Behind me, the company manager, Theron Bamberger, was holding a discussion with one of his assistants in what Bamberger obviously considered to be a stage whisper. The Bamberger whisper was far louder than it might have been. Suddenly, onstage, Laughton stopped rehearsing and walked imperiously to the footlights. He glared out into the darkened house.

"Theron Bamberger," he announced, his tone sepulchral, his diction immaculate as always, "I can . . . *hear* . . . you!"

It's many years later, and Laughton is gone. *Galileo* has survived, and become a permanent part of the Brechtian repertory, revived all over the world. But I am grateful I can still hear, quite clearly, the echoes of Charles Laughton.

Molly Day Thatcher was another good friend. She was married to Elia Kazan, who was then an actor and a member of the legendary Group Theatre. It was back in 1939, when Molly worked at the Group as part of the staff and play reader, that the Group had decided to hold a contest to discover talented young playwrights. The prize was a hundred dollars—not much by today's standards, but back in those days a substantial sum.

One day Molly called to tell me she had read some one-act plays submitted by a young writer under the title *American Blues*, and the Group was awarding him the prize for his work. She was very excited by what she'd read, and suggested I might be interested in becoming his agent, and sent over his address, in California.

I wrote the young author and told him I was interested in

reading his work. For quite a while, nothing happened, and then I received a reply. He said he'd received my letter and he'd also received letters from other New York agents. The news of his award had been reported in theatrical columns, he was thinking the situation over and he would let me know what his decision was.

At the time, I thought all this rather amusing. After all, we were an established agency—even in California people knew who Liebling-Wood, Inc., was—and here was a struggling author with no credits whatsoever!

Some weeks passed, and I received another note saying he'd decided to come with our agency. He'd liked my letter, and he sent along a batch of work. In that manila envelope were his winning one-act plays, as well as other drafts of work he'd done since.

I read what he sent, and almost immediately I had that old reliable signal. His longer plays were far from ready for production, but those one-acters were special. He obviously had enormous talent.

He promised to come. I waited.

One day I came out into the outer office at 30 Rockefeller Plaza. Liebling was, as usual, dealing with hopeful actors. They came and went, but there was a young man seated on the bench, the same bench I'd sat on the first day I'd come up to meet Liebling.

Liebling, who obviously assumed the young man was an actor, walked over to him and said, "Sorry, nothing for you today."

The young man replied, "I don't want anything today, except to meet Miss Wood."

I went over and said, "Did you want to see me about something?"

He said, "If your name is Audrey Wood, I do. My name is Tennessee Williams."

9

The Dragon Lady
and the Gentleman Caller

He spoke with a soft Southern accent, he was young, he was enormously gifted.

He had hitchhiked to New York, and he was quite broke.

He was not only already capable of writing such excellent one-act plays as *American Blues,* but would later demonstrate a considerable talent for poetry and for fiction. Wherever he went, even then, as he has done all his life, he worked long and hard, totally dedicated to his craft.

But talent, even genius, is only part of the game. That obstacle course which lies between the act of writing *"The curtain falls"* on a manuscript page and the ultimate sound of audience applause in a theater (if it comes) is a fearful path. It is truly a marathon which only the hardiest can complete, and it is always there, with each new project. No wonder there are so many authors and playwrights who have only run it once.

To break down the doors that would lead him to his great success—Tennessee is unarguably the foremost American playwright of the postwar theater—would take a considerable time. Six years, in fact, from that first day he arrived in 1939, in our office waiting room, until his first great success, *The Glass Menagerie,* would open on Broadway.

It would be a long hard climb for both of us, the longest, in fact, I've ever experienced before I could induce something affirmative for one of my clients.

Liebling and I were faced with his financial problems. We tried to get him a job selling shoes at Macy's, but that was a stopgap. Finally we advanced him enough money so that he could go back to his family in St. Louis. Soon, I began to receive letters from there:

"I am still here in St. Louis by virtue of necessity—the smother of invention. All optimism has departed." He left St. Louis. In May 1939 he wrote me, "I have about thirty bucks and when that is gone I shall have to start to write desperate letters home, hocking my typewriter and guitar. That kind of living is pleasantly exciting but not conducive to 'emotion remembered in tranquillity,' from which the highest art is expected to spring."

In June I sent him an application for a fellowship to a fund that had been set up at the Dramatists Guild in New York by the Rockefeller Fund. I was also delighted to sell one of his short stories to *Story* magazine, run by Whit Burnett and Martha Foley. It was called "The Field of Blue Children," and for it we received twenty-five preinflation dollars.

"The twenty-five dollars looms quite large in my own perspective," he wrote. "On the strength of it I am having my typewriter repaired and planning a trip to San Francisco to see William Saroyan and the World's Fair." Once that money was gone, I received another note. "Do you market verse? I have a great mass of it—both modern and traditional, short and long, which I have only used so far as a lining for chiffonier drawers."

Then, astonishingly, Williams was awarded the Rockefeller fellowship, the then mammoth sum of one thousand dollars. I wired him, "SO PROUD YOU HAVE WON."

Back came his answer: "Needless to say, I now understand how Lazarus felt when he sat up and saw daylight again. My happiness has sort of numbed me. I am warm all through my very bones with gratitude."

I took charge of the money, and since he was traveling all over the country, I doled it out to him in installments of twenty-five dollars a week. But I received a stream of collect wires, always pleading for further advances; they came from everywhere, and as I recall, provided me with a tapestry of geographical America.

He lived almost penuriously, worked at any and all sorts of jobs, but always kept on writing. That original Rockefeller cash grant did not last very long, nor did the renewal of it which he later received, a check for five hundred dollars.

He came back to New York, and kept on writing. One of his plays, a one-acter, *The Long Goodbye* was produced downtown at the New School, prestigious but financially unrewarding.

His primary need was survival. It was an unending struggle to stay alive and fed until we could find a producer who would give his work a production. Tennessee needed every penny of the sustenance we could find him. Hume Cronyn volunteered to option Tennessee's one-act plays for production, and even though there was little possibility that he could ever find a place where they might be presented, he renewed the option, a small sum but a vital one, for several years. That was truly an act of faith on Hume's part; the money came out of his own pocket, not from backers.

(In an interview with Hobe Morrison many years later, Hume recalled, "I had taken an option on one of Tennessee's scripts, and after re-reading it and thinking about it for a good while, I sent it back to Audrey with a note saying that I was relinquishing my option, because I had finally become convinced that the play wasn't right and wouldn't succeed on the stage.

"When Audrey received my note, she phoned me and pleaded with me to renew my option. 'I respect your reasons for not producing the play,' she told me, 'I can't quarrel with your decision about that. But you simply must not turn down Tennessee. It's too important to him, and he's too important to the theatre.

"'Option money is the only income Tennessee has. He just barely keeps alive on it, and he must not be forced to go back to some kind of job that will take his time and energy away from writing. I wouldn't try to tell you that you should or even can produce this play—maybe no one will ever produce it.

" 'But if you renew the option on it, the money will enable Tennessee to write. Someday he's going to write great plays. I know it, and you must realize it too, from the beautiful writing in this script. I'm asking you to invest this much—the amount of another option royalty—on his future and the future of the theatre.' "

"How could I refuse such an appeal?" Cronyn recalled later. "I renewed my option and of course didn't even think further about producing the play. As a matter of fact, it never was produced. But I like to feel that I had something to do with all the plays Tennessee later wrote. It gives me satisfaction to think that I was a factor in the creation of plays like *The Glass Menagerie, A Streetcar Named Desire, Cat on a Hot Tin Roof,* and others.")

One very cold winter, I remember that Carly Wharton, a generous lady who was then married to the late theatrical lawyer John Wharton, insisted on giving Tennessee an overcoat as well as small sums of cash.

There were few, very few, affirmative signs. Here and there I was able to find him other small sales, the proceeds of which were helpful in sustaining him. Out of my files I find two letters that sharply underscore his situation.

DODD, MEAD & COMPANY
432 Fourth Ave.—New York
Publishers Since 1939

December 3, 1941

Miss Audrey Wood
551 Fifth Avenue
New York, N. Y.

Dear Miss Wood:

Miss Margaret Mayorga tells me that you made an urgent request on behalf of Tennessee Williams that we pay the fee for permission to include his play in THE BEST

ONE ACTS PLAYS now instead of when it is due, on publication day. We are glad to accommodate you in this respect
and accordingly I am enclosing a check for $20.

Sincerely yours,

E. H. Dodd Jr.

December 8th 1941

Dear Mr. Dodd:

I want to thank you sincerely for your great kindness in
sending the $20.00 check for permission to include Tennessee
Williams' one-act play *The Lady of Larkspur Lotion* in the
Best One Act Plays of 1941.

I have great faith in Williams and my biggest job is
devoted to keeping him alive and eating until he breaks.
Your special thoughtfulness in this instance is, therefore,
doubly appreciated.

Cordially,

Audrey Wood.

His first produced play was *Battle of Angels,* which was optioned by the Theatre Guild in April 1940. The Guild engaged
Margaret Webster, an English lady, to direct. It was a rather
odd choice: Williams had written a highly melodramatic play
about people in the South, and Miss Webster's prior work here
had been as director of Shakespearean productions starring
Maurice Evans.

In later years, Tennessee used to say, "The Theatre Guild sent
Peggy Webster down to the deep South, and having been there
two weeks, she absorbed the entire deep South, returned to New
York and proceeded to put the play into rehearsal."

Battle of Angels was a strong drama, far ahead of its time in
the author's use of explicit sexual scenes and in outspoken dialogue. Williams' plot dealt with a heroine who indulged in extremely free roaming sexual relationships. Very strong stuff for
1940.

The Theatre Guild's plan to open such a play in Boston seems, in retrospect, to have been a manifestation of a deep collective death wish. Philadelphia, Washington, New Haven—perhaps such towns might have appreciated the onslaught of Tennessee's bold first drama. But Boston? For years that city had been an ironbound bastion of purity in the arts and letters. "Banned in Boston" has long since become part of the language as a euphemism for censorship. In the case of *Battle of Angels*, that saying was quickly altered to "bombed in Boston."

Years afterward, in 1966, I wrote Tennessee a letter in which I set down my recollections of that disaster. "Your letter from Positano recalled our morning walk across the Boston Common in late 1940 and the many other walks this led us into. Memory is tricky. Some things vanish practically before they happen—other events grow brighter through the years. But like you—I remember the classic morning in Boston, the morning after *Battle of Angels* had roared into life, kicking and screaming all the way. I still tremble remembering the third act curtain falling as the smoke pots miscarried and spewed grey clouds over the auditorium. The older generation of Theatre Guild subscribers coughing and running for their lives up the aisles to escape. The organ music offstage rising to an impassioned height of intensity while Wesley Addy carried the limp or by now quite dead body of Miriam Hopkins up a flight of stairs to the theatrical heaven provided by Peggy Webster.

"And that 'morning after' conference the Guild summoned us to at the Ritz-Carlton. But before that, we met for breakfast sitting at a drug store stool close by the far less elegant Touraine Hotel. The morning papers were spread out over the counter. Each of us knew the Guild would shortly be joining the chorus of woe. So when we finished our coffee we sauntered across the Common. There was no need to hurry. Our shame was now public knowledge. And then there came that small boy with a cap pistol and a sudden pop which seemed to us the roar of a cannon. We clutched at each other and you cried out, 'It's the Guild. They're after me!' And we both rocked with laughter because we knew in a few minutes it was all about to begin and there wasn't time for anything other than laughter.

"Then there was that meeting at the Ritz. Pert, articulate Terry Helburn all business and no funny business, please. Lawrence Langner looking as though he might never lift up his head in public again. And Peggy Webster—the most understanding but with least power. Words flowed but there wasn't much said if anything that would prove helpful to a playwright that morning. Ultimately, true misery came from the depths of Lawrence when he hissed in rebuttal that the Guild was despite this tragedy truly an art institution. 'If we were not,' he continued, 'we would all be sunning ourselves in Florida on the profits of *Twelfth Night* (starring Helen Hayes), but since we continue to be art producers we are struggling in Boston with an unknown playwright.' After that there was no place to go. Who could top that?

"You looked at me and giggled before Lawrence caught you at it. As I remember it was followed by a wise wink. At that moment I realized whatever would befall you in the future you would hold your own and 'whether the cup with sweet or bitter run' you would stand up and take it. And by God, you have—and do and will—continue. All writers in the theatre should come from Indian fighting Tennessee pioneer stock. They'd last longer and so would the American theatre."

Tennessee packed his bag and left Boston. The best I could secure for him was an advance payment of one hundred dollars from the Theatre Guild, said sum being their endowment for him to go away and rewrite the script for a production in some hazy unscheduled time in the future. He went off to Key West, Florida, to begin his rewrite.

Terry Helburn and Lawrence Langner sent out a somewhat prophetic letter to their Boston subscribers:

> We chose to produce *The Battle of Angels* because we felt the young author has genuine poetic gifts and an interesting insight into a particular American scene. The treatment of the religious obsession of one of the characters, which sprang from frustration, did not justify, in our opinion, the censor's actions. It was, we felt, a sincere and honest attempt to present a true psychological picture.
>
> . . . *The Battle of Angels* turned out badly but who knows

whether the next one by the same author may not prove a success?

For years after that Boston debacle, in which the critics, the censors and the audience had driven Tennessee out of town, whenever I met Lawrence Langner on the train coming up to our home in Westport, he would remind me that he still had the scenery for *Battle of Angels* carefully stored away in the storage area of his Westport Country Playhouse. But when the play finally did reappear—Williams continued working on it over the years—it was retitled *Orpheus Descending*, and directed by Harold Clurman. Starring Maureen Stapleton and Cliff Robertson, it was presented on Broadway in 1956 by the Producers' Theatre. Later, it would be filmed by Sidney Lumet, with Marlon Brando and Anna Magnani as the leads, retitled *The Fugitive Kind*.

But all those events lay far in the future. After that Boston debacle, my young client went back to work. First he did the rewrite for the Guild, then he wrote poetry and short stories. In collaboration with another young writer, Donald Windham, he did an adaptation of a story by D. H. Lawrence called *You Touched Me!*

I did not know he was writing this. So naïve were the two young writers they were unaware that legally they had no rights in such a work; no one had told them that before one does an adaptation of another author's work, one must first clear the rights—in this case, with the Estate of D. H. Lawrence. I was quite surprised when they brought me the finished work, I read it and thought it was excellent. Luckily, I knew Alan Collins, at Curtis Brown, Ltd., who represented the Lawrence interests. When I got in touch with him, I found that by some miracle the dramatic rights to *You Touched Me!* were available. That was truly fortuitous; with such a major literary figure as D. H. Lawrence, the rights could well have been committed elsewhere. I made an arrangement on behalf of Williams and Windham, and set out to find a producer for this play.

But in the meantime, there was the battle to keep Tennessee solvent. To say that he struggled is an understatement. But no matter how tough things were, never did he stop working. He took various jobs, as an elevator operator, as a waiter; down in Florida he spent several months as a teletype operator with the U. S. Army Corps of Engineers. At one point, he actually made it to Broadway—but not quite in the exalted professional status he would later achieve there. He wore a uniform provided by Warner Bros. and served as an usher at their Forty-seventh Street film palace, the Strand. (Years later, that same firm, Warner Bros., would cheerfully pay him huge sums for the screen rights to several of his hit plays.)

Then, quite fortunately, came a sort of break. We at Liebling-Wood were able to secure him a six-month contract, with options, as a screenwriter for MGM, out in Hollywood. He was to go out to the Coast to work at Culver City for $250 a week, truly a remarkable sum of money for this young man who'd literally been scratching to stay alive. In fact, when I told him of the deal, he asked, "$250 a month?"

I replied "No—a *week.*"

Astonished, he answered, "That's—*dishonest!*"

He moved out to a small beach accommodation in Santa Monica in the summer of 1943, and commuted each day to Culver City. At a time when other studio employees were casually flaunting limousines and flashy convertibles, Tennessee used a secondhand motor scooter. Thrifty to the point of penury, he lived on a mere twenty-five dollars each week. I carefully banked the rest of his salary for him so eventually he would be able to utilize the savings to underwrite his future playwriting.

Hollywood, and especially affluent MGM, was definitely not Tennessee's métier. With their typical profligacy, the "story brains" at the studio promised him work writing an adaptation of a novel, *The Sun Is My Undoing*, as a possible vehicle for Lana Turner. Said promise did not materialize. Pandro Berman, a major producer (he was later to produce two films based on Williams' plays), suggested he try working on an original screenplay by Leonore Coffee, advising him it would be better for him to start on something simpler. Thereafter, he was transferred to a project designed to star MGM's leading child actress, Margaret

O'Brien. He sent me a note saying "*The Sun Is My Undoing* has not risen yet."

When the O'Brien project came to nothing, he set to work to write a screenplay of his own. In its original form, it emerged from his typewriter as a work he titled *The Gentleman Caller*. He finished it, and submitted it to the MGM story department.

Days passed. Then the manuscript mysteriously reappeared on his desk, sans any comment. No one from the MGM story department ever mentioned even having read it, so it is a fair assumption that if anyone at MGM actually read the work, he or she thought little of its merit as a possible film.

MGM subsequently did not choose to renew his employment contract.

My young client returned East, solvent enough to go up to Provincetown, on the Cape, and to go to work on that screenplay, with the intention of turning it into a play. When he finished work, he promptly sent it down to my office by mail. The only copy he had—*no* carbon, if you please—he entrusted to the U.S. mails.

I still shiver in fright at the risk he was taking with that lone typewritten script of the play, now retitled *The Glass Menagerie*.

Later on, when that play began to look as if it would be the great success it was, I heard from MGM. Lily Messenger, one of the executives who'd originally been responsible for bringing Tennessee out to the studio, was very angry. Apparently Tennessee had given an interview to some paper in which he'd made some remarks about the way he'd been treated at the studio. His comments were not scathing, merely the truth as he'd remembered it. According to Tennessee, he'd been dropped "in retaliation for my unwillingness to undertake another stupid assignment."

L. B. Mayer, the titan, himself got into the controversy, and for a while there I was embroiled in an argument. The MGM people claimed they had rights to *The Glass Menagerie* since he'd ostensibly written it on studio time, when he was being paid by them. Lily Messenger wrote to say that this was a classic case of a man biting the hand that had fed him.

I wrote back. "This is America, this is Williams' play," I said, "and MGM has no claim whatsoever to it. He wrote it when he was no longer in your employ."

Surprisingly enough, that seemed to end the discussion, once and for all.

The Glass Menagerie was a beautiful piece of playwriting, and I set about to find a producer for it. My choice was an actor-producer-director named Eddie Dowling.

I have always proceeded on the theory that as an agent I must cast the producer for a play as carefully as one would eventually cast the director, and the performers. Dowling seemed to be the right talent for this sensitive and lovely work by my young client. In previous seasons he had produced such imaginative plays as Paul Vincent Carroll's *The White Steed,* Philip Barry's allegorical *Here Come the Clowns* and young William Saroyan's *Love's Old Sweet Song,* and *Hello, Out There.*

Later on, Eddie used to give interviews in which he would tell writers this play was a poor, wilted manuscript I had submitted all over New York, and finally he'd seen it and had this great vision of its possibilities, and he'd bought it to rescue it from dark oblivion. Not true at all. He was the first theatrical producer to read it, and he optioned it right away. He had another script he was planning to produce out in Chicago, but he decided to put on *The Glass Menagerie* first, in partnership with his financial backer, a man named Louis Singer.

Singer had never been in the theater. He had made money by owning and operating a string of hotels. Dowling promised him *The Glass Menagerie* would be a hit. Singer permitted himself to be persuaded, and production began.

The major role in the play was Amanda Wingfield, the Mother. To find an actress capable of portraying the somewhat faded Southern gentlewoman was far from easy. George Jean Nathan, the eminent theater critic, suggested Laurette Taylor. His suggestion was brilliant, but it posed great difficulties. At this period, Miss Taylor, who had once been the toast of New York for her many memorable performances, was far from an employable actress. She hadn't been on Broadway much lately, due to her drinking problem. But thank heaven, she finally was given the part. Young Julie Haydon, an actress who was a friend of Mr. Nathan's, played the Daughter, Tony Ross played the Gentleman Caller and Dowling himself staged the play and took the part of the Son.

It was the first time I'd ever had a play by one of my clients produced in Chicago. We were booked to go into a small theater that was part of the Civic Opera House, far away from the regular theater district in the Loop, there was a war on and it was the dead of a brutal Chicago winter. These were far from helpful circumstances for a sensitive play by a hitherto new playwright.

During rehearsals, Miss Taylor seemed to be having trouble remembering her lines. But she was undeniably what is known in the theater as a "money performer." When the curtain went up in Chicago, she came onstage and gave a letter-perfect, magnificent performance. As did the rest of the cast.

The opening-night audience was respectful but hardly ecstatic. The reviews were good, especially that of Claudia Cassidy, the drama critic of the Chicago *Tribune*. She and Ashton Stevens, another respected critic, took it upon themselves to campaign for the survival of *The Glass Menagerie*. Each week they wrote pieces urging Chicago to respond to this play. Miss Cassidy told her readers Laurette Taylor ranked with Duse. The play kept on running, and business improved.

I remember the last rehearsal of *The Glass Menagerie*, the afternoon before the New York opening, at the Playhouse, in March 1945. It was a warm spring day, a Saturday.

The play had been running in Chicago since December. Now here it was preparing for the most important moment in the life of any playwright, the New York opening. For Tennessee, it was his first. For Laurette Taylor, it was a return after many years away from Broadway.

I don't remember where the author was that last afternoon, but I shan't ever forget sitting in an un-air-conditioned Playhouse Theatre. There was a frenetic veiling over everything—and everybody. The actors paced nervously before the run-through began. The light technicians tinkered with never-ending light cues and most of them came out just a little bit wrong. Having played their roles for months in Chicago meant absolutely nothing. This was the day of the New York opening. This was it. I kept remembering Liebling's remark, "You're only as good as the night they catch you." My stomach began to ache. My blood pressure hit a new high.

Laurette Taylor, who up to now had been a tower of strength, began a scene, an opening one, and after a few words in recognizable anguish said, "I'm sorry, I have to leave the stage. I'm going to be sick." And sick she was offstage and then returned to try once more, a little whiter than when she had first exited. This illness continued all afternoon.

Paul Bowles' sensitive incidental score roared out when it should have sounded like circus music, away off in the distance of memory. Julie Haydon was trying to keep a stiff upper lip, but her concern for Miss Taylor was considerable. The two men, Eddie Dowling and Tony Ross, may also have been scared to death, but they made a brave attempt at pretending they didn't care a damn what day it was.

The coproducer, Louis Singer, felt his way over to my side of the otherwise dark, empty auditorium where I was crouched down in my seat. Peering at me through the darkness, he said, "Tell me—you are supposed to know a great deal about the theater—is this or is it not the worst dress rehearsal you've ever seen in your life?" I nodded a vigorous "Yes."

I was too frightened to try and open my mouth.

Saturday evening at the Playhouse Theatre at the appointed hour the curtain went up. Laurette Taylor made her entrance on cue and played with all the artistry she possessed. The rest of the cast worked expertly. The lights worked with nary a blunder. The music was played the way the composer had dreamed it would be. The setting truly became the world in St. Louis where the Wingfield family lived.

During the intermission, Robert Edmond Jones, a scenic designer of fully equivalent talent to that of Jo Mielziner, who had designed *The Glass Menagerie* and who was my escort for the evening, said to me rather crossly, "Now, Audrey, stop all this hand clasping and stop digging your elbow into my side. Everything is going splendidly. You have absolutely nothing to worry about—any longer."

Suddenly the play was over—and everything had gone splendidly for everyone. There were the actors bowing to waves of delighted applause. There was a roar for Laurette. There were cries of "Author—author!" There was Tennessee bowing deeply in the aisle to the actors, not to the audience—presenting a view of his posterior for all the world to view.

The world went backstage after the performance to give thanks to the entire company, but most of all to pay homage to Laurette Taylor. I waited until the line of worshipers had come and gone. When I entered she was sitting dressed still as Amanda Wingfield. Her eyes were shining with triumph. Her head was high. Her spirits were even higher. She looked like a queen who had returned to her throne after a long journey away from home. As always, she had the scene, and the proper line to go with it. The opening night was the night before Easter Sunday. Her head now rested against the back of her chair. With great happiness, she chortled, "Jesus Christ will rise tomorrow—but *I* shan't."

Is it any wonder I decided years ago, to stay near the theater for the rest of my life?

The critical notices were marvelous, remarkably so. Except for George Jean Nathan, who, somewhat perversely, wrote a notice that said that Tennessee's play hardly mattered except for the performance of Miss Taylor.

Tennessee has remembered on opening night, Nathan sent Miss Taylor, as an opening-night present, a bottle of whiskey.

Later, she sent Nathan a note in which she said, quite briefly, "Thanks for the vote of confidence."

The Glass Menagerie was to receive all sorts of accolades. It was given the Drama Critics Circle Award as Best Play, but not the Pulitzer Prize, which was awarded to the comedy *Harvey*, by Mary Chase.

Somehow, the success of the play did not satisfy Eddie Dowling. Perhaps he felt upstaged by the attention being given to Tennessee and Laurette Taylor. Whatever the reason, he did not behave well. He treated Laurette badly, and this did not sit well with Tennessee at all, as well as with the rest of the cast. He, along with everyone else, felt the lady was giving one of the greatest performances ever seen on a Broadway stage. How sad it is that there is no filmed record for future generations. Dowling's behavior, added to the interviews he gave, in which he somewhat whimsically announced he had discovered this new young playwright at the bottom of a rain barrel, did not sit well with my client, nor with Liebling and me.

I remember one night Liebling and I went back to Dowling's dressing room at the Playhouse to tell him that *Billboard,* the theatrical newspaper, was going to give *The Glass Menagerie* an award as the best play of the season. We thought he would be pleased to hear the news, but with no humor whatsoever, Eddie glowered at us. "Too many prizes," he remarked. "It's *un-dignified.*"

It's now well known the character of Amanda Wingfield in *The Glass Menagerie* is based on Tennessee's own mother, Mrs. Edwina Williams, known to all as Miss Edwina, a lovely lady who passed away only a couple of years ago.

According to Tennessee, when his mother first saw the play, in Chicago, back in 1944, she came backstage after the performance to pay her respects to Laurette Taylor.

Miss Taylor glanced at Miss Edwina, smiled and asked, "Well, Mrs. Williams, how did you like yourself?"

"Myself?" asked Miss Edwina, most innocently.

Later on, when the play had opened in New York, Miss Edwina came to town to see it again. By that time, I was friendly with her, and invited Laurette Taylor and Mrs. Williams to be my guests at lunch at Sardi's. Those were the days when we ladies wore tiny hats and gloves, and were, oh, so feminine. We sat there, all three of us, having our lunch, and then Laurette, with her wonderful fey Irish sense of humor, said to Miss Edwina, "You see these bangs I wear? I have to wear them playing this part, for I actually have a high, intellectual forehead."

"Is that so?" replied Miss Edwina, sweetly. She removed her tiny hat, and then she said, "I wish you would look at my forehead, Miss Taylor. I hope you will notice *I* have an intellectual brow, too."

Later that year, President and Mrs. Truman invited the original company of *The Glass Menagerie* to the White House for a reception on the occasion of a command performance of the play in Washington given as a benefit for the polio fund.

By that time, Tennessee had gone to live in New Orleans. Very rapidly, he had become solvent. The weekly royalties from his first success had provided him with a new and welcome affluence. I asked him to come up for this important occasion.

He seemed reluctant to do so. At that time he didn't fly, and it would mean a long train trip. I was quite annoyed. The idea of seeing Tennessee being honored in the White House must have appealed to my maternal soul. Finally, he agreed to come. He phoned me from New Orleans and said, "Please bring to Washington some ties and some socks."

A police escort was assigned to meet Tennessee at the train station and drive him to his hotel, a short while before he was expected for tea at the White House.

Liebling and I arrived at the White House, and we were greeted by the Trumans. We chatted with everyone on the receiving line, and all the assembled political dignitaries, but as time passed, there was no sign of the guest of honor. Liebling went in search of Tennessee, but nowhere was he to be found.

Finally Bess Truman herself came over to ask me where he might be. I knew Tennessee had a propensity for being late.

"Knowing Mr. Williams," I said, "I'm sure he will arrive this time tomorrow." I smiled my most cheerful smile.

"Well, if he does," Mrs. Truman told me, "he'll find three hundred congressmen's wives having tea."

I got the message. I may well have been the first guest at the White House to ask a First Lady, "Is there a phone in the place?"

Finally I located Tennessee. He had been fast asleep in his hotel room, having arrived after a grueling twenty-four-hour train trip. I was practically in tears. I told him, "By God, you've been very rude. You're a good Democrat, and you're going to apologize to Mrs. Truman."

That night, before the play was performed, in the Presidential Box at the theater, he did exactly that.

10

The Catastrophe of Success

For the next twenty years, Tennessee's writing career would be marked by a steadily mounting series of triumphs, both in the theater and in his published works including fiction and poetry. The films that were based on his works would be equally successful, for the producers and for him.

If there were difficult times for him along the way, and there were, the cause was no longer any economic stress. His health was often violently threatened, and he underwent serious bouts with various infections. But never once did this remarkably talented writer stop working for more than a brief time. Certainly, there would be dark periods in which he might give way to momentary depression, but invariably, wherever he might be, no matter what the cause of his problem, whether it be emotional involvements or whatever, the following morning would find Tennessee hard at work. No socializing, no telephone calls, nothing could intrude until he had done enough writing—or rewriting—he would never cease to find ways to improve his works—so that he could feel justified that day.

The theater adaptation he and Donald Windham had done of

the D. H. Lawrence story *You Touched Me!* was produced in New York in 1945.

I've always admired this play. It was produced and directed by Guthrie McClintic and it starred Edmund Gwenn, Catherine Willard and an exciting young actor new to Broadway named Montgomery Clift. It is the only play Tennessee ever collaborated on, and it's also one of the very few I was unable to sell as a film, even though I've always thought it would make a marvelous motion picture. *You Touched Me!* opened in September and had a very brief run. It closed in New York January 1946.

Windham was to write another play called *The Starless Air*, and years later he asked Tennessee to direct it in Houston. That was in 1953, and the play was received well enough so that the Theatre Guild made plans to do it in New York, with Tennessee directing. But the theater is a chancy business, built on "futures," projects that are announced and somehow never materialize. One of those was *The Starless Air*.

Ever since she'd worked as assistant director to Eddie Dowling on *The Glass Menagerie*, Margo Jones had become one of Tennessee's most devoted friends and boosters. Known to her friends as the Texas Tornado, Margo had gone out to direct a production of Tennessee's next play, *Stairs to the Roof*, at the Pasadena Playhouse. After the war, she'd gone back to Dallas and founded a most successful theater in the round, which she called Theatre 47.

Tennessee, having recovered from an abdominal operation in Taos, New Mexico, in 1946, spent the summer in a rented cottage on the island of Nantucket with Carson McCullers, who was adapting *Member of the Wedding* into a play. Tennessee was working on a play he would call *Summer and Smoke*.

Tennessee so admired Margo Jones's drive, her ambition, and he responded so to her admiration for him and his work, that he showed her the play and she immediately made plans to give it a premiere at Theatre 47, in Dallas. It opened there, directed by her, on July 11, 1947.

The night was truly remarkable. In those years, there wasn't much tributary theater in America, not even in affluent Dallas;

Margo was a pioneer. When I arrived at her theater, however, I found an audience composed of not only Texans but people who had gathered there from Los Angeles and New York. Broadway producers, show business people, even Brooks Atkinson, the drama critic of the New York *Times*. A very smart crowd indeed.

The performance was well received. After the curtain fell, we were taken in cars to a party in a fashionable suburb of Dallas. It was my first introduction to the Texas style of doing things. In the distance, on the horizon, lights began to appear, to glow and reflect, and then we arrived at a huge mansion. On the lawn had been set up a tent, there was an orchestra playing, servants moving everywhere, passing food and champagne to a crowd of guests. "Why, it's just a small Texas party," someone told me.

Somehow or other, there was an ironic contrast between the night's splendid gathering and the epigraph Tennessee had chosen as the key to *Summer and Smoke,* which came from the poet Rilke. It said, "Who, if I were to cry out, would hear me among the angelic orders?"

Back in 1945, I'd received an outline from Tennessee that dealt with a play which he had decided he would like to write for Katharine Cornell, then the most respected major star of the American stage. He had begun working on it, and according to his letter it had four different titles: *The Moth, The Poker Night, The Primary Colors,* and *Blanche's Chair in the Moon.*

"It is about two sisters," he went on, "the remains of a fallen Southern family. The younger, Stella, has accepted the situation, married beneath her socially and moved to a southern city with her coarsely attractive, plebeian mate. But Blanche [the Cornell part] has remained at Bellereve, the home place in ruins, and struggled for five years to maintain the old order. . . . The place is finally lost, Bellereve, and Blanche, destitute, gives up the struggle and takes refuge with Stella in the southern city. She arrives broken by the failing struggle (arrival first scene of the play) and is at the mercy of the tough young husband, Ralph. A strong sex situation develops, Ralph and Blanche being completely antipathetic types, he challenged and angered by her delicacy, she repelled and fascinated by his coarse strength. His friends are similar types who meet Saturday nights at the house for poker. . . ."

The outline went on, very detailed, and then at the end of the third page, he wrote, "There are at least three possible ends. One, Blanche simply leaves, with no destination. Two, goes mad. Three, throws herself in front of a train in the freight-yards, the roar of which has been an ominous undertone throughout the play.

"Treatment is everything in a play of this type," Tennessee added, "but some of the scenes already have a good deal of dramatic texture, so I think I will go on with it."

How fortunate it was for us, and for the American theater, he did so. I, however, did not submit the synopsis to Miss Cornell, a great actress but not right for the role of Blanche, in my opinion.

When the completed manuscript arrived at my office in 1947, it was called *The Poker Night*.

Some years later, writing in an article for *Esquire,* Tennessee said, ". . . it is a harrowing thing to submit a script to her. It makes me shiver and shake to deposit in a post-office slot the first draft of a new play addressed to Miss Audrey Wood, and till she gives a report on her reaction, which may be two or three weeks after I mailed it, the shakes and shivers continue and steadily increase. . . . You may wonder why she waits that long to respond, and sometimes I wonder, too. My guess is that if the wait is a long one, her silence is to let me know that the play is not up to scratch. But when you're so morbidly uncertain about the quality of your work as I am, you are likely to misinterpret expressed opinions of it, as well as the long, silent wait."

In the case of this new play, there was no such wait. The play was obviously a marvelous theater piece, and Tennessee had expanded on his original outline to such a point that Blanche du Bois's decline and final fall into madness became stunning drama. I did not wait at all; I hurried to tell him so.

I had only one objection, and that was his title. His manuscript was called *The Poker Night*. I told him it suggested a

Western action novel by some long since forgotten author, perhaps Rex Beach.

Looking away—very often in those days, Tennessee was sufficiently shy that he couldn't look one in the eye—he said, "Well, I have another title but I don't know if it's any good."

I asked him what it was. "*A Streetcar Called Desire*," he said.

"Wonderful!" I said. The one word was changed to *Named*, and that's where it stayed. He'd had the second title tucked away all the time.

Margo Jones wanted to bring *Summer and Smoke* into New York immediately, but having read *Streetcar*, I knew it was important to get it on first. But we drew up a contract giving Margo the rights to produce *Summer and Smoke* in New York with a production date that could only be decided upon after *Streetcar* had opened.

Now came the difficult problem of finding the right producer for this remarkable play. In doing my customary "casting" for that someone, I would make many enemies.

I would not consider Eddie Dowling, certainly not after the various public quotes he had delivered to the press about Tennessee in the past. The Theatre Guild seemed a dubious choice after the original Boston fiasco. Even though Hume Cronyn and Carly Wharton had helped Tennessee so considerably, they were not then actually producing. I truly felt that after what Williams had been through in the past, he had to have complete protection, artistically as well as financially. Whomever I ultimately chose, I knew I'd lose friends, but the move had to be accomplished.

Previously I had received letters from California from some of my friends there about a woman, Irene Selznick. She was Louis B. Mayer's daughter, and she wanted to come and be a theatrical producer in New York. I believe it was Rouben Mamoulian, who'd originally done *Porgy and Bess*, who wrote me and suggested that I look for scripts she might produce.

By now she'd come to New York and opened a production office. Liebling and I discussed the possibility of Irene Selznick doing *Streetcar*. Even though she was an unknown quantity, she had plus qualities. I wanted to find someone with money enough to keep a play out of town for as long as I thought it should be there, and also enough funds to cast the play perfectly, and to engage the right director for it. Certainly Irene Selznick could afford such expense.

She was then currently producing a play by Arthur Laurents called *Heartsong*, and Liebling and I decided to go to Philadelphia, where it was trying out, to see what sort of a job she could do as a producer. Later on, Irene was to give interviews to the press in which she said Audrey Wood and Bill Liebling had come to Philadelphia to "case the joint," and that was quite so. We were being fantastically careful about *Streetcar* and Tennessee.

Irene's project did not make it to New York, but by then we'd decided she was the perfect producer for Tennessee's play. Not only did she have an ample bankroll, but she was serious and had taste. So I sent her the script.

She read it overnight.

It must have been as remarkable an experience for her as it had been for us, because Tennessee's script was as close to the finished play which opened in New York as anything he's ever written, before or since. All the work he would later do during rehearsals was minor; truly, he'd already written a nearly complete masterpiece.

Irene called me the next day to ask, "Can I have two days to make a decision about my life?"

It seemed at the time there was a gentleman caller in *her* living room, and she had seriously been contemplating marriage.

Two days later she called and said "I've decided I want to produce this play."

Tennessee had never heard of Irene Selznick. He was then in New Orleans. I called him to tell him what I was doing and I remember getting back a wire which said: "THIS WOMAN HAD BETTER BE GOOD."

Since they'd never met, I decided they must do so before we signed production contracts. By this time word had gotten around Forty-fifth Street that Tennessee had finished a new play, and since he was the newest "hotshot" among the playwrights, there was a good deal of interest in who'd be the producer, who'd direct, who'd star, and all the other aspects of the future production.

In order to keep things quiet until they were actually settled, I decided to have Irene and Tennessee meet somewhere far away from voracious producers, Sardi's and Sam Zolotow, that eager, omniscient drama reporter whose job it was to smell out the news ahead of everyone for the New York *Times*.

Out of sheer nostalgia for my good friend and early client DuBose Heyward, I chose the lovely city of Charleston, South Carolina. I notified Tennessee that Irene and I would be coming down by train, and he should come up from New Orleans.

Irene and I arrived first, checked into our hotel and waited for him. His was the much longer train trip, and we had to wait until he arrived. Finally he was there. Feeling like a marriage broker, I met them downstairs in the lobby.

I said "Now, you two take a walk. Talk. I'll stay here."

I sat in the hotel lobby, reading and waiting until they returned.

When they finally returned an hour later, Tennessee came up to me and said, "Where are the contracts? I'll sign."

He signed, and the marriage was fact.

At that time, there was some sort of telephone strike going on. Irene wanted to notify her general manager, Irving Schneider, in New York, that the deal had been made. So she used the local Western Union office to send him a message, in a private code, so that nobody might get the news in advance: "BLANCHE HAS COME TO LIVE WITH US."

Irene agreed with Liebling and me that Elia Kazan would be an excellent choice for the director, so we promptly sent him a script. He read it and turned it down. I am not certain what caused him to do so, but I believe it was the first time he'd been presented with a play which had such a strong female character as Blanche. But we persisted. I spoke to Molly Day Thatcher, his wife, who had been so important to Tennessee's career in the early one-act days of *American Blues,* and she agreed to keep after Kazan and try to change his mind. We decided to try to talk him into it, and Molly persuaded Elia—known to all as "Gadge"—to come see us at our Royalton apartment. We had a meeting with him there, just the four of us, she and Gadge, Liebling and I. Liebling and I assured him he was the absolute perfect choice. Finally, Gadge gave in and agreed to do it. It was a lucky change of mind for all of us.

Liebling went to work to assemble the cast, and it proved to be one of his best jobs. As I've told earlier, he brought in Brando and cast Kim Hunter as Stanley's wife, Stella. Young Karl Malden was hired to play Stanley's good friend, and lovely Jessica Tandy, Hume Cronyn's wife, was cast in the vital role of Blanche du Bois.

Streetcar opened in New Haven in the fall of 1947, and got good but not great notices. By the time it reached Boston, it was giving off good vibrations. It was in the Boston theater that Gadge turned to Tennessee one night during a performance and whispered, "This smells like a hit." Future events proved Kazan had delivered the understatement of the decade.

The play opened in New York at the Ethel Barrymore Theatre November 1947 and became a mammoth hit.

"Tennessee Williams has brought us a superb drama," wrote Brooks Atkinson, of the New York *Times.* "And Jessica Tandy gives a superb performance as a rueful heroine whose misery Mr. Williams is tenderly recording. This must be one of the most perfect marriages of acting and playwriting. For the acting and playwriting are perfectly blended in a limpid performance, and it is impossible to tell where Miss Tandy begins to give form and warmth to the mood Mr. Williams has created."

The rest of the reviews were equally good. The play was a huge success for Tennessee, for Gadge, for that now legendary cast and for Irene Selznick.

For some time after the opening, remarkably, there was no motion-picture interest in *Streetcar. The Glass Menagerie* had earlier been sold to Charles Feldman, who was to film it for a Warner Bros. release, with Tennessee working on his own adaptation.

Sadly enough, there was no possibility of recording Laurette Taylor's performance as Amanda Wingfield. That great lady had since died. Most peculiarly, the film producers had decided on the late great English star Gertrude Lawrence, to play the Southern lady.

It became perplexing. After months of sellout business, during which *Streetcar* had won the Critics Circle Award, the Donaldson Award, and the Pulitzer Prize for best play of the year, we still had not received a single offer from any Hollywood studio.

Perhaps, back in those days of the forties, the producers were timid about depicting sexual relationships as blunt as the ones Tennessee had dramatized between Stanley, Blanche and Stella. Whatever it was, there we were, with the smash hit of the season and no picture sale.

One day Tennessee in California called me in Westport to tell me *The Glass Menagerie* was to begin filming, and to celebrate this event, Charles Feldman, a producer given to lavish gestures, was throwing a large Hollywood-style party. Those were the days of the fashionable bacchanales where the host engaged a large Sunset Strip restaurant, such as the Trocadero, or Ciro's, or LaRue, and invited a carefully chosen list of guests on the "A" list to see and be seen.

"Are you coming out?" asked Tennessee.

"No," I said. "First of all, I haven't been invited, and secondly, I'm not the kind of woman who has time enough to drop my daily affairs and jet out to L.A. merely for a party."

"Well, I can get you invited," said Tennessee.

I discussed it with my husband, and he, a wise and pragmatic man, said, "I think, if Tennessee wants you to be there, you should go out."

The invitation came, and out I went.

It proved to be a most amusing experience. People I knew out there, mostly the wives of friends and clients, who had migrated West and become very successful, were very concerned that I make a personal splash. They were concerned I might not appear chic. Wise in Beverly Hills mores, they realized I would be going to a fiesta where there would be clusters of jewelry and miles of mink, and out of the kindness of their hearts, they proceeded to offer their old Eastern friend Audrey Wood jewels and furs, even couturier gowns, so that I might not look like Cinderella at Mr. Feldman's blowout.

It really wasn't my style. I thanked them all kindly, but I wore my slightly used New York dinner dress. It would simply have to do.

Tennessee and his good friend Frank Merlo came to pick me up for the party, and we proceeded to the Sunset Strip restaurant. There, at the door, a marvelous Hollywood-type event—clichélike—took place. The maître d'hôtel would not permit us to come in. After all, this was a private party. He did not know Tennessee Williams by sight, a rather odd piece of business, considering this party was being given in Tennessee's honor!

We might have spent the entire evening out on the Strip, three wistful Stella Dallas types, outside looking in, except that Charlie Feldman, who was arranging place cards, passed by, saw us being given the bum's rush and rushed over to make amends. Instantly the maître d' began to bow and scrape, and in we went to that opulent affair.

Everyone who was anyone in the Hollywood of the forties was there that night. Dear Hedda and dear Louella, David Selznick, Sam Goldwyn, Jack Warner, phalanxes of leading men and ladies—it was a fan's dream of heaven.

But the evening's misadventures were not over. In preparation for this evening's party, Tennessee and Frank had both outfitted themselves in splendid new dinner jackets. But wherever they'd bought their clothes, they'd been advised to buy white jackets—and tonight's party was definitely black. Both of my escorts stood out amid the sea of sober formality, and in their white jackets began to be mistaken by other guests as waiters! It did not seem to bother Tennessee, or Frank. If someone at a table asked them to bring a fresh drink, they smiled graciously and agreed to be right back with the order.

And Hollywood being the nervous rumor factory that it was—and still is—my presence there that night with Tennessee and Charlie Feldman—my having flown out all the way from New York—instantly spawned gossip. Obviously, those Hollywood folk reasoned, I would not be out there, so far from my accustomed rounds, unless it was because there was some sort of a movie deal for *Streetcar* afoot.

So strenuous was the crescendo of the rumors that when three days later I left town, I had three firm offers for the screen rights to *Streetcar.*

Ultimately, we made a lush deal with Charlie Feldman for the staggering sum of half a million dollars, plus a percentage of the film's profits. When he produced the film, with Vivien Leigh giving one of her finest performances as Blanche, Marlon and Kim re-creating their roles along with Karl Malden, and Gadge directing, *Streetcar* turned out to be a triumph as a film.

Williams spent the winter abroad after *Streetcar* opened, but returned in the fall of 1948. Now Margo Jones was preparing to bring her production of *Summer and Smoke* to New York. I was not at all certain she was capable of both producing and directing this sensitive and lovely play. Even though she'd done it well in Dallas, that city was replete with her friends and local fans. The New York critics and audiences would be an entirely different breed.

I expressed my doubts to Tennessee, but he merely shrugged them off. Margo was his friend and he would remain loyal to her. In the end, he did, as usual, the gentlemanly thing. He'd promised her she could be his director, and that was that.

Several days before the play opened, I went over to the Music Box Theatre. When I arrived, the cast had been assembled downstairs in the lounge. Margo was talking to them. Quietly, I took a seat on one of the steps above and listened. Tennessee sat below me, also on the stairs. Margo made her speech, one which I referred to later as "Margo Jones's Farewell Address to the Troops."

She told her cast that without a doubt Tennessee Williams was the most important playwright of our times, *Summer and Smoke* was the best play he'd ever written, the play simply had to succeed here in New York, it was up to them to give a performance worthy of the work and she went on and on with her pep talk. Finally, she stopped to catch her breath, and looked up at Tennessee. "Is there anything you'd like to say, Tenn?" she asked.

He looked down at her, as only Tennessee could, and with an absolutely straight face he remarked, "There's nothing *left* to say, is there?"

He looked at me and smiled, and we both knew exactly what he meant.

Alas, I'd been right about the New York critics. They did not respond well to *Summer and Smoke* in 1948, and the play closed after a very brief two-month run.

But that play miraculously survived its first failure. As he has done all his life, Tennessee took his work back to the typewriter and began making revisions. When he was finally satisfied that he had improved that tender story of Miss Alma Winemiller and her brief love affair with John Buchanan, he permitted the play to be produced in London, in 1951.

It was so well received there that José Quintero and Ted Mann, who were opening a new theater, the Circle in the Square, in New York, decided to present the play as their opening attraction in 1952. Tennessee's work bore fruit. Even though *Summer and Smoke* had failed a few years before, this time the critics reversed their earlier verdicts. They raved about Quintero's sensitive direction, they were enthusiastic about Geraldine Page, who was to become a star because of her performance, and, phoenixlike, *Summer and Smoke* rose from the ashes.

Hal Wallis and Joseph Hazen bought the screen rights and turned the play into a fine film in 1961, starring Miss Page. *Summer and Smoke* has long since achieved the status as the play Margo Jones was so hopeful and enthusiastic for, so many years back in that darkened lounge of the Music Box.

In the years following, Tennessee was to work on several projects at the same time. He was in Europe in 1949, ending up living in Rome with Frank Merlo, and there he wrote his first novel, *The Roman Spring of Mrs. Stone*. Years later, that, too, would be a successful film. He and Merlo traveled to Sicily, and there Tennessee was inspired by the countryside and its people to begin writing his own version of the Don Quixote legend, a play which would eventually become *Camino Real*. He also began work on a bittersweet romantic comedy dealing with a lady named Serafina Della Rosa, a play he called *The Rose Tattoo*. (Originally, he called it *The Eclipse of May 29, 1919*, and then *Eclipse of the Sun*.) It went through five drafts before he considered it ready for production.

For the playbill, Tennessee wrote, "*The Rose Tattoo* is the Dionysian element in human life, its mystery, its beauty, its significance. . . . Its purest form is probably manifested by children and birds in their rhapsodic moments of flight and play . . . the limitless world of the dream. It is the *rosa mystica*."

The part of Serafina was originally devised for that great actress Anna Magnani, with whom Tennessee had become friends in Italy. But as negotiations for the New York production proceeded, and a deal for Magnani was being discussed, it became clearer to all of us that it wouldn't be feasible to have her play the lead in New York. First and foremost, she was a screen actress, and totally unaccustomed to the rigid disciplines of eight performances a week in the theater. Not only that, she had never before played in the English language, and it must have been a terrifying prospect for her to essay a leading role in a foreign country, attempting it phonetically. So that deal fell through.

Later, of course, she would make the film, and give one of her finest performances, opposite Burt Lancaster. But meanwhile, we still had to find a Serafina for Broadway.

At that time, Liebling had a young actress named Maureen Stapleton as a client, and he suggested to Cheryl Crawford, the producer, and Tennessee she might be right for this most important role.

I remember the day Maureen came to read for us and for Danny Mann, the director. She was uncertain and highly nervous, but she gave a great reading. When she finished she said, "I'm sorry, that's the best I can do for you. Whether you really want me is something you'll have to tell *me*."

She got the part, and she was brilliant. So was another one of Liebling's clients, young Eli Wallach, who played Serafina's improbable lover, the truck driver Alvarro Mangiacavalo ("Eat-a-horse").

In December 1950, *The Rose Tattoo* opened in Chicago at the Erlanger Theatre. Once again, as she had been with *The Glass*

Menagerie, Claudia Cassidy of the *Tribune* was most helpful. She liked the play and had several suggestions for improving it. She actually met with Tennessee to tell him what she thought. He accepted them and did rewrites. Such assistance, on a constructive basis, from a drama critic—twice, in fact—is a rare thing.

The play opened in New York in February 1951, and was a hit. Serafina's love story was awarded the Antoinette Perry Award—the "Tony"—for the best play of that season.

But Magnani returned to my life. In 1955, when the picture was being prepared, I was in Rome, and I became involved in the negotiations to secure the services of that lady to play Serafina for Hal Wallis and Joseph Hazen. She was represented by an attorney and the intricacies of working out a contract for Miss Magnani's services were endless, far more complex than any top-level diplomatic maneuvering between countries, replete with daily crises. The actual deal was on, then it was off. Problems continued to surface, and arguments raged back and forth, with every legal sentence the launching pad for further hour-long discussion.

Finally it was all, amazingly enough, settled. The day arrived on which the actual papers were to be signed. Liebling and I were on our way to the attorney's office, where the ritual signing would take place. On the Roman street, we passed a flower vendor; Liebling stopped and bought me a bunch of daisies to commemorate the occasion.

There, in her lawyer's office, sat Magnani, looking very much like a runner who had survived the Boston Marathon. Exhausted but triumphant, the lady signed the contracts. It was a moment that seemed to call for a gesture. The best I could do was to present her with my somewhat wilted bunch of daisies. It wasn't splendid, but somehow it appealed to Magnani's sense of ritual as well as mine.

We became good friends. She was truly a larger-than-life personality, exactly like the characters she portrayed. One afternoon we were up at her New York hotel suite, discussing some phase of *The Rose Tattoo,* when she received a phone call. She grabbed the phone and began to speak in Italian. Then she began to rant and rage. Whoever was on the other end had incurred her displeasure. As she paced up and down, a torrent of Italian, obviously unflattering, poured from her, building to a furious crescendo. Finally, exhausted, she slammed down the phone.

"What was that, Anna?" I asked, disturbed. "What's *wrong?*"

"Nothing," she said and shrugged. "Just my secretary."

Then there was another night that she expressed a desire to go to see the typically American rodeo, then at Madison Square Garden. Liebling and I went to work and used our influence to reserve a box. The three of us went to the Garden and sat there, only a few feet away from the horses and their Western riders.

Anna was wildly excited by the spectacle, and was obviously having a wonderful time. Suddenly, one of the riders came dangerously close, wheeled his horse and began to trot away. But at that precise moment, his horse decided to do what horses have traditionally done onstage ever since the first horse made his theatrical debut. This particular souvenir that the horse left behind flew out and hit dear Anna Magnani right in the face!

We were mortified.

But not Anna. "Very good luck!" she announced cheerfully.

And then there was *Camino Real*.

It is an allegory, a dream play, a blend of fantasy and wild comedy, the saga of Kilroy, Everyman, the little guy, and his strange passage through a dream world on the Camino Real, where he encounters gypsies, Casanova, Don Quixote, Proust's Baron de Charlus, Marguérite Gautier, Lord Byron and other legendary creatures, as they lead him, block after block.

Tennessee had written an early version of the play based on his one-act play called *Ten Blocks on the Camino Real*, back in 1946, but it did not seem to me to be ready for production in the commercial theater. After I read it, I told him so, and I asked him not to show it to anyone—not yet.

Years passed. Tennessee rewrote. Wherever he went, his work went with him. By 1953, it was ready for New York—or so, at least, I thought. I felt then, as I have always since, *Camino Real* is a wonderful, special play, perhaps his most enduring, one that will be done in the world's theater for years to come. Certainly it contains some of his most poetic and evocative writing.

Elia Kazan directed the first production of *Camino Real*, and Eli Wallach, fresh from *The Rose Tattoo*, played the leading role of Kilroy.

On opening night in New York, word came that Tennessee would have a small group of friends over at his apartment after the curtain fell. The audience at the National Theatre received the play with mixed reactions; some wildly affirmative, others far less so. A very small group of us went back to Tennessee's to wait for the reviews—Mr. and Mrs. John Steinbeck, Cheryl Crawford, the producer, Kazan and his wife, Molly, Liebling and myself—all of us very subdued.

It was quiet while we had a few drinks, and then the reviews began to arrive. They were uniformly negative. Some of the notices said whatever significance there might be in *Camino Real* was beyond their comprehension, others remarked it was hyperbole without significance. Walter Kerr's review was the cruelest. According to him, Tennessee was America's most distinguished playwright, and this was the worst play ever written by America's most distinguished playwright.

By now, Tennessee had had more than enough to drink, and certainly, on this disastrous night, having been so belabored, he was entitled. He rose to his feet and made a brief speech. I cannot remember his exact words, but I will never forget that evening. He proceeded to tell us, his good friends, that this was it. He was finished. Since no one obviously cared any longer for his writing, he did not propose to continue. His playwriting days were over. He bowed to me and thanked me for my help in the past, but after this night, he saw no reason to continue.

Silently, somewhat tearfully, we all left and went home.

Next morning, about eleven or so, I called his apartment. I'd had a very bad night. I very much wanted to speak to him, to try to counsel him to reconsider.

"Oh, I can't disturb Mr. Williams, Miss Wood," his secretary told me. "He's working."

Since that night, I've told this story to many playwriting classes. It is so much more valuable than hours of discussion as to what primary element makes one a playwright.

Camino Real closed after sixty performances, but as always with Tennessee's work, the play was far from dead. He took it back to Key West, and over the years, worked on revisions. Many years later, in 1970, it would be revived at Lincoln Center, at the Vivian Beaumont Theater.

There it was given a production by Jules Irving and Herbert Blau, in which young Al Pacino would play the part of Kilroy, with Milton Katselas directing.

When rehearsals began, neither Tennessee nor I was in attendance. He was out of town, and I was attending to my husband, who was gravely ill in the hospital. By the time I finally did get over to rehearsals, I was dismayed to find young Mr. Pacino was changing lines in Tennessee's script, making alterations in the sense of some of the scenes, and all of this with the tacit approval of his director. Katselas was being very polite to his star.

Finally, Tennessee arrived to attend the previews, and when he realized what had been done he became very upset. Hurt and angry, he felt betrayed by the producers, and perhaps also by me.

One day I came in to watch a performance and discovered that Tennessee himself had been doing some cutting. One of the speeches he had edited was the one speech which I consider to be one of his very finest pieces of writing. It is the Gypsy Daughter's prayer, which comes near the end of the play. It's when Esmeralda, the girl says:

"God bless all con men and hustlers and pitch-men who hawk their hearts on the street, all two-time losers who're likely to lose once more, the courtesan who made the mistake of love, the greatest of lovers crowned with the longest horns, the poet who

wandered far from his heart's green country and possibly will
and possibly won't be able to find his way back, look down with
a smile tonight on the last cavaliers, the ones with the rusty
armor and soiled white plumes, and visit with understanding
and something that's almost tender those fading legends that
come and go in this plaza like songs not clearly remembered, oh,
sometime and somewhere, let there be something to mean the
word *honor* again!"

When I finally got to Tennessee, I said to him, "What did you
do to that speech?" He replied, "It sounded too much like an ed-
itorial and I decided to cut parts of it."

I was nervous and very upset because of Liebling's grave illness, and I must have completely lost my patience. "You're just a
goddamned fool!" I told him. "That's one of the most beautiful
speeches you've ever written, and it was outrageous to cut parts
of it."

Tennessee was absolutely adamant. He would not put any
part back. As a matter of fact, that night after the preview,
when we walked out of the Vivian Beaumont, he would not even
let his hand touch mine when we crossed the street. It was as if
we were separated, in two different worlds.

It was a bad situation. The cast was upset; the girl who was
playing Esmeralda was miserable at the cuts. Jules Irving, one of
the producers, said to me, "I'll talk to him about this." He
wanted the full speech put back as well, and he called Tennessee the next day and pleaded his own case for restoration.
Whereupon Tennessee, who could be and can be the most suspicious of men, replied, "*Audrey* told you to call me, didn't she?"

Irving denied it vehemently, but Tennessee continued to stand
his ground stubbornly. Opening night was approaching, and still
those damaging cuts remained.

A day or so passed, and then, a miracle took place.

One night, just before his own opening, Tennessee went to see
Oh, Calcutta!, which was playing downtown. When he came
away from Kenneth Tynan's simplistic exercise in pornography,
Tennessee was so abashed by the lack of any poetic language in
what he'd seen there that he reacted by voluntarily restoring the
entire Esmeralda speech!

That is how it returned to his beautiful play, before the opening night at the Beaumont, and where it has remained in the play ever since, to my great satisfaction.

Liebling and I were in Rome in 1954 when Tennessee, who'd been living there, called to tell me that he had been working on a new play. I promptly told him that I would very much like to read it.

Even after all those years we'd worked together, Tennessee responded with great amazement. As if he were bringing me his first work, he said, "You *would?*"

He brought over to our hotel a large manuscript, typed mostly on odd pages of hotel stationery. That is another of Tennessee's work patterns: wherever he was, should he run out of typing paper, he would go right on, using pages supplied by whatever hostelry he might currently be at, uninterrupted.

This pile of pages was what he calls a "work script." Until then, I'd never read any of his vast output in that stage. This new one was mammoth, both as a script and as a play.

He'd written of two young Southerners, Brick, a football player, and his young wife, Maggie. Or, as she would be called, Maggie the Cat. In this version, if you had a scene between Brick and Maggie, the first scene would be written from Brick's point of view. Then you'd turn a page and there would be the same scene from Maggie's point of view. Page after page it went on, a massive piece of work.

I stayed up until four in the morning reading it. In that version, he had written a two-act play. I was terribly excited, and in the morning I immediately told him this was certainly his best play since *Streetcar,* and it would be a great success. He may not remember this now, but he was then overwhelmed by my enthusiasm. It was obvious to me that he didn't yet know what he had done.

"But you must have a third act," I told him.

Tennessee replied, as only he can, very definitely, "Well, my dear, I am going to write either a prologue for the beginning, or I shall do a long one-act play for the end."

"No you won't," I insisted. "This play has tremendous potential, but it has to be finished. It can't end with Big Daddy's speech, as it does. You've got to work on the story by sticking with Brick and Maggie."

Tennessee did not agree with me, and he said so. He would not go on to a third act, and by the time we left Rome he was still insisting that the play remain as he'd ended it.

Finally, after many, many letters back and forth between us, a manuscript finally arrived in my office. Rewritten, without those back-and-forth scenes he'd had, *and* with a third act.

Even so, later, Tennessee insisted that when the play was ultimately published, New Directions, his publisher, include both versions, his first version, and the revised third act as played in New York. *Cat* would win the Pulitzer Prize, gain him one of the biggest film sales he'd ever made, well over half a million dollars, and be a smash hit, revived many times over the years. But Tennessee still felt he'd been right. Such was certainly his privilege.

Cat on a Hot Tin Roof went into production, produced by the Playwrights Company and directed by Gadge Kazan. In its third act was an anecdote, perhaps it should be called a joke, later to be remembered as "the elephant story." Told by Big Daddy, it was, in retrospect, a mildly offensive story, one which in our more permissive times today would cause very little stir, if any, in a theater. But a quarter of a century ago—how quickly mores change!—Big Daddy's story caused quite a ruckus.

Briefly, the story is this. Big Daddy, who is ill with cancer, relates to his family a story about a young boy who is taken to the zoo by his parents. There they encounter an elephant, at the precise moment that the pachyderm becomes aware of a young female elephant. The male is tumescent. The young boy asks his mother just what could be that long organ rising triumphantly from the aroused elephant, and his mother somewhat embarrassed, replies, "Oh, that's nothing." Whereupon the father sadly comments, "She's *spoiled!*"

I didn't think the story belonged in the play, and I was to say so, frequently. But Kazan, who was directing Ben Gazzara and Barbara Bel Geddes, with Burl Ives as Big Daddy, didn't agree with me.

We opened in Philadelphia, and there was the customary party after the play; there were assembled Roger Stevens, from the Playwrights, Victor Samrock, the business manager, Tennessee and Gadge, as well as Carson McCullers, who had come down at Tennessee's invitation. There had already been such a controversy about "the elephant story" that it was decided to put the decision to a vote: should it stay, or be cut? Liebling and I voted it should go, but we were in a minority, since everyone else voted it should remain.

I went back to New York and sat down to write Gadge a letter, in which I tried to explain why I felt the story should be excised.

"For the millionth time—my rejection of the elephant story has nothing to do with my own reaction," I said. "I have listened to much more explicit tales than this for the last ninety years and not even blushed. I'm thinking of the average theatergoers and particularly those with the young daughters and sons who might tell this story to their own wife but who wouldn't dream of mentioning it in front of his children. What about all those people? But more important—this seems to me to come out of left field. Suddenly Big Daddy appears—and in churchlike demeanor goes back to his youth as he tells what most likely was the first suggestive story he has ever heard or told as a young man. A man facing death who has not had time to realize this is it—wouldn't he be more apt to offer an idea that brought an added illumination to his life?

"P.S. I'm sending Tennessee a copy of this so you won't have to share it with him, but can frame it right away with the theater archives as a matter of record!"

The last week in Philadelphia, there was another postperformance party, and I saw Gadge again. He announced to all of us, "If anybody has anything to say critically, you must say it now, before I 'freeze' the performance."

I looked at him and said "Well, you know exactly how I feel about one particular scene."

Gadge smiled a bit patronizingly, and did not reply.

We opened in New York at the Morosco Theatre, with the offending story still intact in the play.

Meanwhile, the odd thing was that no critic in Philadelphia, which is ordinarily a most staid community, had even mentioned the anecdote, nor would any of the New York critics, who were lavish in their opening-night reviews of *Cat*.

However, a few days after the play opened, there *were* some complaints from the audiences, and the management received a visit from the License Commissioner of New York. He informed them that either "the elephant story" would be excised or the Morosco would lose its license to operate as a theater.

Out it went.

Amazingly enough, Tennessee snipped the story out in a matter of minutes, with the most beautifully deft play surgery. It was gone by the next performance. I couldn't resist saying to Victor Samrock, "You see? I told you so."

It all seems so infantile now. So much of a commotion over a relatively harmless off-color story. But that was the first, and hopefully the last, time any play I've ever been associated with has ever brought forth a complaint to the License Commissioner.

All was far from amicable between Tennessee and myself on the opening night of *Cat*. Perhaps coming events were beginning to cast their shadows.

Years later, Tennessee was to write in his memoirs that he considered the opening night of *Cat* particularly dreadful. He did not care for what he saw, and felt it was a failure. What was on the stage, according to him, was a distortion of what he had intended.

I wasn't aware of how he felt. The curtain fell, there was great applause, and I was certain the play was a hit.

Kazan had invited Tennessee to come up to his apartment to wait for the reviews. For some reason or other, he had not invited Liebling and me. There ensued one of those misunderstandings which seem, in retrospect, to be stupid and avoidable, but in this case, proved damaging.

There was a postopening party being held elsewhere for the cast, and Liebling and I went to celebrate there.

Tennessee maintains that he said, "Audrey, we're all going up to the Kazans' to wait for the notices," and I replied, "Oh no, I have other plans."

Perhaps that's true, but I have no recollection of saying it.

But if it is so, I can well understand why he felt hurt and angry in his state of mind at the time.

Later on, at the other gathering, word reached me that Tennessee felt I hadn't come up to Kazan's because I was disappointed with his play. Which, of course, was completely untrue. I can't imagine where such a lie could have sprung into life, but the theater thrives on gossip, most of it malicious, and that night was a prime example of someone's backbiting or perhaps a confusion on the author's part.

Finally, Tennessee appeared at our party. By this time he was in such a state of anger he would not speak to me. He behaved as if he were a deserted child who'd been abandoned in a snowstorm by untrustworthy relatives, or hurtful friends.

Finally I went to Liebling and said, "I just can't take this. Let's go home."

At this point, Liebling, always warm and considerate, went over to Tennessee and said, "Come on, Tenn, why don't we all leave here? We can go out and get the papers."

Since we'd had no food at this party, Tennessee reluctantly agreed to go with us.

Outside we got into a cab. Tennessee sat far away on his side of the seat, keeping himself physically away from me, refusing even to permit his body to touch mine. He was that angry.

We picked up papers at the New York *Times* building—in those days there were still newsstands that remained open all night—and then we proceeded to a restaurant called Toffenetti's, long since gone, where we sat down in a booth to order some food.

Tennessee had brought with him a stack of opening-night wires. Those were the days when one was still able to send congratulations by Western Union, and on opening nights it was a cherished theatrical ritual. That night he'd received a lot of them, and he now proceeded to rip them open, one by one, and read them. But he studiously refused to permit us to see any of his messages. He continued to behave as if he were completely alone.

It was now 3 A.M. Finally the waiter came up to serve us.

Completely ignoring Tennessee, he stared at me, and then he asked, "Pardon me, but aren't you Audrey Wood?"

I admitted I was. Then he said, "Say, I have a friend who has written a play, and I wonder, could he send it to you?"

I'm now certain that in his overwrought state Tennessee thought I'd planned this ridiculous piece of coincidence. Certainly it added fuel to the flames.

Finally, in silence, we finished our food.

We went on to the Royalton, and he went off to his apartment. There was no conversation, barely a goodnight.

Next morning, around noon, I ventured to call him, to discuss matters of business. Needless to say, after the opening of such a hit, there were plenty. When we spoke, Tennessee seemed to have forgotten the previous evening's unpleasantness. Or so, at least, I thought, until I read his memoirs, years later.

Certainly, since he'd been drinking, I assumed he'd blacked out on what had happened. And as long as he didn't bring it up, I never again mentioned the evening.

But that ugly incident, in retrospect, seems now to mark some sort of turning point in our relationship. He'd revealed an undercurrent of anger and hostility toward me I'd never before suspected.

Later, that first breach would widen enough to become impassable.

Cat on a Hot Tin Roof was published by New Directions—that same edition in which Tennessee insisted on including both third acts—the revised one, as played in New York, plus his original version. In a statement written for that edition, Tennessee remarked that it was just possible that his first version would have done as well with audiences as the one he had rewritten under the influence of Gadge Kazan, the director.

By publishing both third acts, he went on to remark, he was thereby permitting his readers to make up their own minds on the subject.

When I received the first published copies, I was surprised

and delighted to find a dedication: "For Audrey Wood." Since *Cat* was, and remains, the only work of Tennessee's by which I was so honored, I promptly told him of my gratitude.

Sometime later, I was down in Texas. I realized I was very close to Austin, which is the home of the University of Texas, and its magnificent library. I'd had word they were having an exhibit of Tennessee's manuscripts, as well as manuscripts by my other client Bill Inge. In honor of their late good friend Margo Jones, both men had presented scripts to the library, in gratitude for the help she'd provided them at the beginning of their careers.

I flew over to Austin, climbed the stairs to that great library, and started to look through the rows of tremendous glass cases, filled with manuscripts I'd known so well since the first day they'd arrived on my desk. Finally I came to *Cat*, and there was the original manuscript on display. I saw the dedication page, and on it Tennessee had typed "For Carson McCullers." In pencil, he'd crossed out her name, and printed "For Audrey Wood" instead.

I suddenly realized how close I'd come not to getting this dedication.

And I was very proud, because ever since the night I stayed up until 4 A.M. reading it in Rome, it remains a play I respect enormously.

11

The Milk Train Doesn't Stop Here Anymore

In an interview he would give to *Playboy* some years later, Tennessee is quoted as saying, ". . . the Sixties were the worst time for me. At the beginning of one play, *Camino Real*, I quoted Dante: 'In the middle of the journey of our life, I came to myself in a dark wood, where the straight way was lost.' I didn't know then what a prophet I was. The Sixties were no good for me, even from the beginning, from *The Night of the Iguana* on, everything went to pieces for me. I told Gore Vidal that I didn't remember a thing about the Sixties—and I thought I had slept through them. And he said 'Don't worry, you didn't miss a thing.'"

Looking back, I cannot find a specific turning point that underscores precisely where and when our relationship, hitherto so mutually fruitful, began to unravel.

After *Cat on a Hot Tin Roof*, Tennessee's output continued steadily, and even though other critics have written that his work suffered because he was becoming more and more addicted to alcohol, I cannot agree.

"I work seven days a week, Sundays included," he told a

newspaper interviewer. "And I don't think it is a violation of the Sabbath. My only exception is Easter Sunday. It's a habit, an unbreakable habit. What would I do with my mornings if I didn't? Watch cartoons on TV? I don't know what I'd do without this habit. I'd probably go mad."

Could his critics make the same statement? I think not.

At about this time, he began psychiatric analysis with Dr. Lawrence Kubie, and I was quite pleased when he said he had done so. I could tell there was at least one beneficial result when I noticed Tennessee actually began to be on time for an appointment with me. In years past, he'd invariably showed up at least a half hour late.

The analysis went on, five days a week. Tennessee, as he told me, began to write letters to Dr. Kubie and to mail them to his office; then, when he arrived, Kubie would spend the hour reading Tennessee's latest missive and conducting a discussion of it. Tennessee began to feel this was not only gratuitous but expensive, and eventually ended the sessions.

Shortly thereafter, the eminent Dr. Kubie moved out of New York, and Tennessee remarked, a bit gleefully, "*I* drove Kubie out of New York!"

Sometime in the late fifties I invited Tennessee to have dinner at the Algonquin. Tennessee said he would like to have dinner but couldn't go to the Algonquin and when I asked why, his answer was, "They hate me at the Algonquin." He went on to say the last time he had been there he had ordered a special chicken entree and found when it arrived there was absolutely no white meat.

Having asked Williams for dinner, I reached the Algonquin maître d', Bennett, and explained to him Tennessee's previous displeasure. Thereupon, on this occasion, when the same dish was ordered, Bennett saw to it there was sufficient white meat to feed six full-sized playwrights. When dinner was over, Bennett appeared, and very grandly announced to us, "The Algonquin would like to serve a special liqueur, courtesy of the Algonquin."

At this point, with no humor, Williams stared at me, and with great sarcasm, announced, "Well, they certainly like *you* at the Algonquin!"

In 1956, Gadge Kazan produced and directed Tennessee's screenplay *Baby Doll*, which was based on two of his earlier one-act plays. The film was instantly notorious, largely because of the advertising campaign, which featured Carroll Baker reclining in a farm crib, sucking her thumb. Twenty-four sheets of Miss Baker were plastered everywhere. Church groups and self-appointed censor groups rose to the attack. Cardinal Spellman denounced *Baby Doll* as "an immoral and corrupting influence," and the picture was given a Condemned, or C, rating by the then powerful Legion of Decency.

Such publicity could do nothing but increase box-office grosses, and *Baby Doll* made a good deal of money.

That was the year of the stage production of *Orpheus Descending*, Tennessee's rewritten version of *Battle of Angels*. Two seasons later, there were his two new plays, one-acters, produced under the title *Garden District*. One was called *Something Unspoken*, the other *Suddenly Last Summer*.

We both felt these were special plays, and they were not truly Broadway material. So, in a somewhat experimental fashion, we arranged to have them produced in a small theater at Seventy-fourth Street and First Avenue. In those days, we were opening up a new theatrical territory, one that would later be known as off-Broadway.

The producers were John C. Wilson and young Warner Le Roy, the son of Doris Warner and Mervyn Le Roy; he's now become an extremely successful restaurateur.

That first-night opening up there, so far off the beaten path, Tennessee had assumed that since we were so far away from Forty-fifth Street, none of the customary first-nighters would show up. But just as with *Summer and Smoke*, down in Dallas, or many other Williams openings, he was wrong. Drawn by his name, the "in crowd" arrived in full flower.

Suddenly Last Summer, deals in a rather explicit fashion with lobotomy, and also with cannibalism. When the curtain fell and the lights came up, we saw our audience slowly rising, great

consternation on their faces, not knowing quite what they felt—
or what they should say—if they had anything to say at all.

Garden District had a successful run, and from it came Sam
Spiegel's film *Suddenly Last Summer,* which starred Katharine
Hepburn, Elizabeth Taylor and Montgomery Clift. Tennessee,
with his friend Gore Vidal, did the screenplay, and though he
insisted he did not care much for the finished screen version, the
picture was a hit.

In 1958, MGM, Tennessee's old alma mater, released the film
version of *Cat on a Hot Tin Roof,* with Elizabeth Taylor and
Paul Newman as Maggie and Brick. To secure the screen rights,
MGM had paid a huge price. Since the deal included a percentage of the film's profits over the next two decades, checks continued to come in.

One morning in 1956, I had a phone call from Miami. Tennessee on long distance. He had news. "I've been working on a new
short play," he said. "I haven't shown it to you yet, but it's in rehearsal down here."

"Rehearsal *where?*" I asked.

Tennessee, it seemed, had a friend named George Keathley
who ran a small theater called the Studio M Playhouse. He went
on to explain to me that he thought Keathley's place was a good
opportunity to try out this play.

I was annoyed. I remember saying "What do you mean, you
have a play in *rehearsal?* How could you possibly do anything
like that before I'd even read the play?"

It seemed Keathley had competent actors, and his theater—a
remodeled garage—was a fine place to work.

By this time, I was furious. I said, "What are you doing there
in a *garage?*"

Whereupon, Tennessee, obviously unable to cope with my
anger, said, "I'm putting George Keathley on and he'll explain it
to you."

Keathley, a pleasant young man, explained to me that in fact
Tennessee's play was in rehearsal, and he was directing it, and
they wanted me to come down and see it, but they wanted no
one else to see the play before I did. With no humor, both men

assured me, conspiratorially, that the play was such a secret in Miami that on the board outside the Studio M Playhouse it merely said PLAY NOW REHEARSING. No title, no author. No credits for the actors.

As I found out later, the genesis of this play was even more remarkable. Tennessee had begun by bringing in a one-act play and presenting it to Keathley and the cast. Then he returned to his typewriter and continued writing. Several days later, he brought Keathley more scenes, and thereafter returned with more. Finally Keathley realized that this was not a one-act play at all, but a full major work. He stopped rehearsals until Tennessee finished, and when rehearsals resumed, Keathley and his cast in that remodeled garage were preparing a brand-new Tennessee Williams play!

The leading lady was a European actress named Margrit Wyler, and Tennessee entitled the play *Sweet Bird of Youth*.

Finally, the time came when they were ready to show it to an audience. Liebling and I flew down to Miami and proceeded to the Studio M Playhouse to attend the opening performance of this "top-secret" tryout.

Of course, in the usual pattern of a Tennessee Williams venture, word had somehow gotten out that this would be the first performance of his latest work, and the audience was full of friends, fans and show business characters, all in on the secret.

It was a remarkably good first version, and Keathley and his cast had done well by the play. Tennessee's gamble on the tryout in a remodeled garage paid off handsomely. Eventually, Gadge Kazan came down to see *Sweet Bird of Youth* and was impressed enough to agree to direct it on Broadway.

But that production did not take place until three years later, in 1959. Margrit Wyler was a fine actress, but she was not sufficiently box-office to play a starring role on Broadway. Cheryl Crawford, who produced the play, engaged Geraldine Page to play the lead, Princess Pasmezoglu, the fading film star who is having an affair with Chance Wayne, who would be played by Paul Newman.

By that time, Liebling-Wood, Inc., had been merged into MCA, the vast talent agency, and I was now ensconced in a luxurious office on Fifty-seventh Street, complete with antiques and polished paneled walls.

The day *Sweet Bird of Youth* was to go into rehearsal, I got a panic call. Would I please come down to the Martin Beck Theatre immediately? Miss Page had raised a large obstacle, to say the least. Before she would sign her contract, she wished to have an assurance, in writing, that she would play the lead in whatever film would eventually be made of the play.

It was an almost impossible demand. Film producers have historically reserved the right to cast films made from plays with actors of their own choice. Miss Page simply had no reasonable grounds to make such a demand on the first day of rehearsals.

I went down to the theater and I was in control of my temper until I got to the lobby doors. But when I walked inside, and down the aisle to where a small group of people stood in a group, immobilized by this sudden dire development, I must have lost my temper completely.

Without any politesse, I said, "Under no circumstances can we accept a clause such as the one Miss Page is demanding, and if Miss Page continues to insist on it, we will have to find someone else to play this part."

On the first day of rehearsals, with the producer and the director and the cast standing there, this was a very bold statement on my part. But I'd said it, and I meant it—even though I had absolutely no idea what we would do if she refused to sign the contract.

Years ago, a playwright friend of mine, Oliver Garrett, said of me, "She's little, but you can't knock her down." I guess on that morning, I proved him to be correct.

Miss Page signed, and the rehearsal began. Another crisis had been overcome.

Remarkably enough, when the film was made in 1962, Miss Page *did* play the leading role, along with Paul Newman.

Then came *l'affaire* Pasmezoglu.

Which was caused by one of Tennessee's whimsical habits, that of naming characters in his plays after various people he'd known.

A week or so after the play opened and was a hit, I read the following letter from a prestigious firm of lawyers, addressed to Tennessee:

> . . . We are writing you on behalf of our client, Ariadne Pasmezoglu Thompson. Mrs. Thompson is often referred to as "Princess" and as "Pas," and she has used her maiden name in connection with her professional writing activities. The use of her name in the play *Sweet Bird of Youth* has resulted in substantial injury to both her personal and property rights.

The lawyers went on to urge, straightfacedly, that we move with all possible speed to arrange some sort of settlement of this matter.

I spoke about the problem with Tennessee, and later sent off a memo to Morris Schrier, the MCA lawyer who was assigned to deal with it.

> . . . I have just had a charming conversation with a gifted writer named Tennessee Williams, who informs me with great amiability that he remembers well a little girl who lived in St. Louis and played hide-and-seek with him, whose name was Pasmezoglu. He couldn't remember if her first name was Ariadne, but he thinks this was likely. . . . He tells me that when he writes names pop into his head from out of the ether and that when he wrote about Princess Pasmezoglu he must have had a fond recollection that his eight year old playmate was in the back of his mind. . . . He went on to say also that a member of the Cutrere family met him a few months ago and said he thought he should sue him—but that he didn't. You will remember that the name Cutrere figures as the nymphomaniac in *Orpheus Descending*. . . . That is all for today. AW.

An amiable settlement was shortly reached between all parties concerned. Mrs. Ariadne Pasmezoglu agreed to an arrangement whereby she would be Mr. Williams' guest at *Sweet Bird of Youth*, and henceforth the Princess would be renamed Princess Kosmopolis.

Over that period, Tennessee extended his off-Broadway activities. Long before there was much of a tributary theater, he was developing one of his own. He was the first playwright I've ever worked with who had guts enough to see the value of working on a play while it was being produced outside of the so-called big time. His first, shorter version of a new play, *The Night of the Iguana*, was played in 1960 at the Festival of Two Worlds, in Spoleto, Italy. And another new play *Period of Adjustment*, a comedy about two young couples in the very early stages of their marriages, had its break-in run at the Cocoanut Grove Playhouse, in Miami, in 1958, two years before it arrived on Broadway.

Few other playwrights in those days had the energy and foresight to do what Tennessee was doing—to mount a play, learn from the production, then rewrite it and continue to revise until he had his script in what he considered satisfactory shape. Two years after *The Night of the Iguana* was done at Spoleto, he brought over to Italy another new play, *The Milk Train Doesn't Stop Here Anymore*, which was produced there in 1962.

But before that drama arrived in New York, the Broadway production of *The Night of the Iguana* began its fabled out-of-town tour.

In an interview with Lewis Funke, Tennessee commented that *The Night of the Iguana* had been written in a period of "spiritual exhaustion," and that it seemed to be a mellow, reflective summation of many of his own "mixed feelings and attitudes." He also was quoted as having said that the theme of *The Night of the Iguana* is, "as closely as I can put it, how to live beyond despair and still live."

That was a somewhat prophetic statement.

Frank Corsaro was engaged to direct *Iguana*, and in the summer of 1961, casting began. The British actress Margaret Leighton, whom we wanted for one of the two female leads, was then married to the actor Laurence Harvey. Their marriage wasn't going too well. Along with Corsaro, Liebling and I were in London that summer, and one of our tasks was to try and persuade Miss Leighton to play the part of Hannah Jelkes.

In those days, MCA, my then employers, kept a small town house off Park Lane, in London, where they allowed executives to stay while they were in town on business. To get to this residence, one had to go through a small mews that led in, off Park Lane. Along that mews there was a photography studio, and in its windows the photographer was fond of displaying large studio blow-ups of the various celebrities whom he'd immortalized.

The day came when Miss Leighton was to stop by for tea and to discuss terms for her Broadway engagement. When Liebling and I left the town house in the morning, to our horror, as we passed the photographer's windows, we were confronted with a very large photograph—king-sized, in fact—of Laurence Harvey.

Both of us had the same idea simultaneously. It would not do to have Miss Leighton be confronted with that blow-up on her way in—or, possibly, out. We went into the shop and pleaded with the photographer to remove that photo before 3 P.M. At first he must have considered us totally mad, but when we explained the circumstances, he became sympathetic, as only an Englishman can, to the diplomatic nuances of this sticky situation.

When Miss Leighton came by for her appointment, there was no visible sign of Harvey in the mews. Our meeting went off splendidly. She accepted the part.

And then, Miss Bette Davis entered the arena.

None of us had originally thought of her for the part of Maxine Faulk, the rough-spoken expatriate landlady of the Mexican hostelry where the action of the play took place. After all, it was a costarring role, and Bette was still then very much the solo star. Who could have expected her to subordinate herself to a character role that was nowhere near the equivalent of the leads she was accustomed to, in her halcyon days at Warners?

As I recall, it was Violla Rubber, who'd also produced plays in New York, who came up with the idea to approach Bette. When she did so, Bette was receptive. She read the play, agreed to do it, terms were arranged and the contracts signed.

A long out-of-town tryout tour was scheduled, and in the early stages, there were no problems.

The opening day of rehearsals took place at the Algonquin Hotel, with Corsaro and the cast, which included Patrick O'Neal as Shannon, and Alan Webb as the ancient poet Nonno. Bette made her appearance in a very royal manner, as befitted such a star, and the rehearsal went well.

It was merely a lull before a considerable storm.

The road tour before the play arrived in New York was to become an obstacle course, replete with far more than the customary hazards and daily disasters which lie in wait for a play being birthed.

We opened in Rochester, New York. It was the first time I'd ever represented a play which opened there, and we played only three performances, beginning with Friday night. That opening night, all went well; the performances were rough, but the audience was receptive, and we were all hopeful for the future. There was an opening night party which all attended, including Bette, and we all went to bed.

At eight the following morning, the phone in my hotel room rang, and I heard the very cheerful voice of our company manager. "Did you sleep well, dear?" he inquired.

With the reflex engendered by many years of assorted out-of-town crises, I immediately asked, "What's happened?"

"Well," he said, "I just thought you should know that Bette Davis is being taken in a wheelchair to an ambulance, and then to a hospital."

It seemed our costar had fallen backstage, the night before, during the performance. Why this hadn't come out sooner, or why she had attended the party afterward, ostensibly in good physical shape, I cannot explain. But now she was, according to reports, unable to play the Saturday matinee and evening performances. At the theater we had sold-out houses for both.

What did one do now? Did one cancel both performances? While I dressed, I thought the problem over. In the case of this play, we were deeply involved. *The Night of the Iguana* was being produced by Charles Bowden in association with Tennessee's own company, Two Rivers Enterprises, and Tennessee had far more than his customary stake in the future of the play. He, and I, as his agent, were part of management.

I decided we must continue to play the show. This was the wrong time to give way, and too early an indication of what Bette might bring upon us in future. That afternoon her understudy went on, as she did in the evening, reading the part from her script. The dauntless girl had not yet had time to become "set" in the role.

The weekend over, we moved on to Cleveland. Bette, in her condition, could not take an airplane nor a train, it seemed, so a limousine was engaged to drive her to the next town.

Margaret Leighton, her costar, volunteered to sit with Bette in the limousine for that trip. She wished to show her fellow actress she was sympathetic. It was a most kind and thoughtful gesture.

What was wrong with Bette? I don't know. But I remembered that several years before, she had appeared in a musical revue for Jerome Robbins, *Two's Company,* and that there had been a similar incident in Detroit prior to the opening there. It seemed to me that if she had truly injured herself, it might have been an accident over which she had no control, something subconsciously self-willed. I also remembered when I had worked out the original bookings for *The Night of the Iguana* on tour, she'd insisted that under no circumstances would she play Detroit.

Bette recovered, and we went on. Finally, the tour brought us to Chicago. From then on, she continued to perform, and all seemed well. But it was only temporary. Between performances, she began to battle with Frank Corsaro, the director, and at one point she ordered him out of the theater, and then out of Chicago, telling him, according to reports, "Go on back to that goddamned Actors Studio!"

Tennessee had dreadful problems as well. His dog, a German shepherd named Satan, had without warning bitten him severely on both ankles, and the subsequent complications were painful. When he recovered he was confronted with the backstage problems. Suddenly, Bette might decide she would not appear for a performance, and then she might reappear and say she would. That happened so often that customers buying tickets at the box office would ask, with justification, "Is Miss Davis going to be playing in this performance?"

Every few days I'd get a call from Tennessee saying, "You'd better come back; another crisis."

I'd get on a plane and fly to Chicago. On one of my arrivals, I thought I might be able to settle this with Bette once and for all. Chuck Bowden said, "Bette has asked me to tell you she will only see you in an open meeting."

I lost my temper. I said, "You tell Bette I will not see her in an open *or* a closed meeting."

And so it went, scrimmages back and forth, all the time the play ran in Chicago.

Finally, we came to New York and opened on December 29, 1961, at the Royale. The play was a success. When Bette made her first entrance on opening night, there was a great ovation from the balcony, where many of her fans had assembled. In response, Bette turned, raised her hands above her head and clasped them in the classic prizefighter's gesture.

Then she went on with her performance.

Her pattern of missing performances resumed during the New York run. Even though the reviews had been good, for her as well as for the play—*The Night of the Iguana* went on to win the Critics Circle Award, Tennessee's third, for Best Play, and then was made into a film—there were many nights when she did not appear. Margaret Leighton and Patrick O'Neal steadily carried on.

In retrospect, I realize Bette should never have taken on that part. Maxine, her character, is for long periods offstage during the play, while Shannon and Margaret Jelkes play out their dramatic conflicts. The initial error was ours, in casting her in a somewhat unrewarding role. When you have been a great film star, it must be difficult to sit backstage in your dressing room for protracted periods, in which there is nothing to do but to wait for your next entrance.

Weeks passed. Bette's understudy was playing her role more frequently. One day, Bette's representative, a gentleman named

Tom Hammond whom I'd known for many years, came to see me. He explained that Bette wished to leave the play, even though she'd signed a run-of-the-play contract.

By that point, there seemed no advantage to be gained by forcing her to adhere to the terms of her contract. She was obviously most unhappy with the way things were going. I inquired if there was a particular date when she would like to leave.

Tom gave me a specific date. And I, like an innocent child, asked, "Why must it be *that* day?"

His reply, very straight-faced, was, "Because it's Bette's birthday."

Since we needed a replacement for her, we began to cast. One afternoon, I ran into Shelley Winters, and the thought came to me that she might be right for Maxine.

Not that Shelley did not present problems. In 1955, she'd played one of the leads in a play by my client Mike Gazzo, *A Hatful of Rain*, and the experiences we'd had then with Shelley had been far from pleasant. But after inquiring, I learned Shelley was lately behaving in a far more professional manner. So we began negotiations with Shelley to replace Bette.

I really had no idea of the intensity of the tensions that were building backstage at the Royale until one memorable day when I arranged a meeting with Tennessee, Corsaro and Patrick O'Neal to discuss with them the change in the cast.

We went to a restaurant near the MCA office on Fifty-seventh Street and we all talked quietly about Shelley. I thought it had all been worked out satisfactorily, and Tennessee began to leave. Moments later, without warning, Patrick O'Neal suddenly lost his temper, over what I don't know. Without warning, he literally blew his top—took a very large table in that restaurant, flung it into the air, with china and glassware flying in every direction!

Frank and I sat there, astounded. O'Neal had caused such a ruckus that Tennessee, who was outside, heard the noise and returned. O'Neal continued to rage. The restaurant's owner looked at me with great dismay. Luckily, nobody was hurt. Finally, Patrick, still furious, left.

That night, unaware of what had happened, Liebling

suggested that we have dinner out, at that same restaurant. I suggested we dine elsewhere. Later I explained why.

Later on, we found out O'Neal was being treated by Dr. Max Jacobson, the same "Dr. Feelgood" who had begun providing Tennessee with those notorious shots designed to induce instant mood uplift. Perhaps that medication had caused his rage. Whatever it was, he did not play that night, and remained out for several days, pulling himself together. Finally, he returned.

Our troubles were not yet over. Shelley replaced Bette, and for a while all seemed placid. Then I began to get reports that Shelley, also bored and impatient with those long waits backstage between her scenes, had taken to leaving the Royale and going across the street, in full makeup, to have a drink with the boys at a small theatrical bar. That was another situation which called for my attention.

One final anecdote about that long and unpleasant experience.

I went backstage one night to visit Margaret Leighton, in the days before Bette left the cast. Bette had just returned from one of her protracted absences, and I asked Leighton, who had remained stable throughout, without temperament, "Has Bette spoken to you?"

"Oh, no, dear, not a word, not a word since she returned." She paused, and then she said, without the slightest trace of a smile, "You know, I believe Bette thinks I should have sent her flowers."

It was not a good period for Tennessee. By his own later admissions, he was drinking heavily, and even though he was being lauded with critical acclaim here and overseas, he was depending more and more on liquor and various pills.

Frank Merlo, his dearest friend, was to die of cancer in 1963, and the shock of Merlo's passing would cause him deep despair. Once, Tennessee admitted to me that he was unable to rise in the morning without reaching out a hand to feel the wall of the room, to make certain that it and he were still there.

But our relationship was not threatened by any rift, not yet. He wrote an article for *Esquire* in which he defined me, with affection: "She is a cross between a flower and the rock it sprang from." Later, in the same article, he commented, "And yet I know that if someday our professional relationship should come to a close, it is she who would close it, not I, and that her reasons would be the reasons of both a rock and a flower."

As yet, neither of us knew how prophetic that statement of his would prove.

In 1962, MGM released the film version of *Sweet Bird of Youth,* and later, George Roy Hill's film of *Period of Adjustment.* That summer, Tennessee's next play, *The Milk Train Doesn't Stop Here Anymore,* in its earliest version, was done at Spoleto. The starring role of Mrs. Flora Goforth, the doomed lady stricken with cancer, was first played by that excellent British actress Hermione Baddeley.

The following year, when Roger Stevens produced the play in New York, with Miss Baddeley repeating her performance, we ran into a newspaper strike. What reviews there were to be printed were not favorable, and the play closed after a very brief run.

As always, Tennessee retrieved his script and went to work to make changes. The legendary David Merrick was very anxious to produce a play by Tennessee. Tennessee said he'd like to see his revised script produced somewhere away from Broadway. Merrick and I discussed this possibility and it seemed to him to be a sound way to proceed.

Somehow, Tennessee and I both thought of the Barter Theatre, a small playhouse in Abingdon, Virginia, which had been operating for many years through the efforts of a delightful actor-producer named Robert Porterfield. It was named the Barter because in its early days, during the Depression, Porterfield had originated a policy of permitting his cash-poor audiences to gain entrance to the theater by literally bartering their way inside with food or produce from their neighboring farms.

When I discussed *Milk Train* with Porterfield, he was all for doing it, but he told me that the Barter had a unique situation.

It was subsidized by the state of Virginia. (I doubt if there is another such operation in the U.S.) He simply could not afford to bring in outside actors from New York for such a production.

I went to Merrick and asked him whether he would put some money into such a tryout in Virginia; as I recall, he was about to go abroad. Without any discussion, David did what was for him —or for any other producer—a remarkable thing. He gave me a check, signed by him, with no amount filled in. Such was the extent of his faith in the project.

We proceeded with the production at the Barter, this time with Flora Goforth played by an excellent actress, Claire Luce. Less than a year after its first failure, Merrick was sufficiently impressed with the revisions Tennessee had made to bring the play back to Broadway.

This time, Tallulah Bankhead was cast in the lead. Tony Richardson, the brilliant British director, was hired to stage the play, with Mildred Dunnock and Tab Hunter.

I remember the first time Tallulah called me, to ask me to come over to discuss the role she would play. That remarkable lady suggested we meet at her apartment. "It's on Fifty-seventh Street, darling," said that familiar rasping Southern voice on the phone. "It's a two-way street, my dear. The story of my life."

Came the first day of rehearsals. Tony Richardson had some sort of complex about starting them in the theater, so it was decided to hold the first reading in Tallulah's apartment.

I went over that morning. The company was assembled, but no Tennessee. Finally, we did not wait any longer. Tallulah moved over to a sofa and sat, script in hand, very much the star.

Above her on the wall hung a famous portrait of her, done by Augustus John many years ago. I believe it now hangs in the Washington's National Portrait Gallery. It was the most touching contrast: on the wall, a radiant young woman of the twenties, and, seated beneath it, the fragile, aging beauty, four decades—and many experiences—older.

We could not start preparing a play which dealt with the imminence of death with more ironic impact than that tableau provided.

Finally, Tennessee appeared, bearing his contracts for the production—which he hadn't signed yet. We attended to that slight detail, and *Milk Train* started on yet another journey.

Tallulah worked extremely hard to bring Mrs. Flora Goforth to life. There were none of those legendary scenes, no temperament, merely her constant effort to do her very best. She behaved extremely well, but obviously, as we continued, one could tell that the lady no longer had the energy and fire she had once possessed. There are scenes of high drama in *Milk Train* which call for a virtuoso performer, and Tallulah had serious problems, undoubtedly due to her fragile health, in rising to them.

Then we had another problem. Before we'd gone into rehearsal, Richardson had told us he'd promised his wife, Vanessa Redgrave, he'd be home in England for Christmas. When this was originally proposed, it had made sense, but the rehearsals had been delayed. When we finally opened in Wilmington in December, Tony shortly departed. Hardly the best time for a director to leave a production, but according to Tony, unavoidable.

So there we were, in Wilmington, with Tallulah doing her best, which wasn't enough, as we could all see, and Tennessee, ever suspicious, convinced that Richardson had used Christmas in England as an excuse to leave a faltering production and not to return.

The show struggled along without Tony. As we approached New York, his return was delayed. That winter, there were Atlantic storms raging on both coasts, and while Tony tried to get back on time, the airlines couldn't oblige. By this time, you may well imagine the agonized condition Tennessee was in, sans his director.

Finally we came to New York, with Richardson blessedly back. We opened at the Brooks Atkinson. We had two previews, and then Tallulah stepped forward on opening night.

It was tragic. All over the theater there was a vast coterie of Tallulah's so-called fans, a galaxy of boys of all ages, who'd come to have themselves a hoot of a time. They laughed in all the wrong places because there she was, their darling Tallulah, up there, and they obviously believed such a reaction was what she expected from them.

She carried on bravely. But when she came to her big scenes, she simply could not rise to them.

We closed on Saturday night, after only five performances.

Once, out of town, I remember Tallulah confided in me, "I hope I'll play this play for the rest of my life!"

Ironically, it would be the last Broadway play she was ever to do.

Our relationship was becoming strained. Tennessee was now in what he would later refer to as his "Stoned Age." Those daily shots that Dr. Max Jacobson was providing him were having disastrous effects. He was not writing with the fervor he had previously possessed.

His attitude toward me was becoming quite different from what it had been during earlier years. He wrote me a letter after the failure of *Milk Train* and my reply may indicate the stresses between us.

February 23, 1963

My dear Tenn:

I have read and re-read your letter of February 6th in which you discuss your present state of mind.

I must admit it is difficult for me to understand why you have come to believe my attitude toward you in the last years has, to quote you, "chilled, hardened—sometimes to the point of downright hostility." If this is truly the impression I give you, my basic intent toward you as a man and your work has been completely misunderstood.

God knows, I am well aware how troubled you are now and have been during the last few years. Because you have admitted to me your distrust of everyone, I am conscious I am not excluded. . . . Being human, I do not make any claim to perfection. I am not infallible. I do know my attitude toward you professionally has not altered and I have constantly tried to work for your maximum good as a creative writer. I have tried to give you friendship whenever you allow me to get that close to you. It is not easy to reach you on that level. You are even suspicious of what could be a healthy association between two old friends. . . .

. . . We have had a crowded, stimulating, rewarding period of years together. From the very beginning, I have taken great pride in representing you. You cannot have forgotten I was elated about your work long before you enjoyed your now much deserved popular and critical success. My job has been to carry your work like a banner throughout the world and this I have done and continue to do with gusto and enthusiasm.

I pray one morning in the near future when that angry old lion, the sun, shines at his golden best on you in Key West that the truth of all the above will become clear to you again and that you will recapture the glow of a splendid business relationship and a friendship that is staring you in the face if you will only open your eyes, see it and take it by your hand. . . .

Affectionately . . .

Audrey.

Later I would get a wire from Key West which read:

DEAREST AUDREY PLEASE DON'T WORRY ABOUT ME HAVE GONE A LONG WAY TOGETHER AND HOPE HAVE A LONG WAY TO GO. LOOK LIKE JACK A LANTERN TRUST TO BE HANDSOME AS EVER WHEN I SEE YOU SOON IN NEW YORK LOVE TENN.

For the nonce, our relationship continued as it had been, or so I thought, and I fervently hoped I was right. But there continued to be differences between us, and again, I tried to reassure him.

In January 1964, I wrote:

. . . I hope you are not feeling any sense of failure as a writer. Your ability as a craftsman, your knowledge of human beings, your poetic mastery with words—all are still yours, and will be as long as you live and write. There is no other American playwright whose work approaches your level of human understanding and compassion. You are an acknowledged artist whose accomplishments in the theatre are not matched by any other American dramatist, with the possible exception of O'Neill—and with all his greatness, he lacked your magic with theatre dialogue.

Your failure is a human one. You make decisions which are ill-timed and often occur out of a deep desire to help someone other than yourself—to give an actor—a director an opportunity, when the risk may well endanger your play. Plus that, your being unable to wait for the moment that would be safe for you and your work—leads you into dangerous waters and when the heavy seas are rolling (before you are prepared for it) your ship of words founders. This does not mean the ship might not have been saved and made to endure *if—if* you had waited until in your opinion the work was as shipworthy as you could make it and all the passengers and crew were the best possible for each and every chore.

This last production of *Milk Train* I knew you wanted very much. Merrick came to you. He is a successful producer. He gave the script to Bankhead. He gave the script to Richardson. All this happened with the speed of Broadway-today. But all this as exciting as it was did not mean it was right timing for you or your play. You knew you were running a great risk. This had never happened before in our theatre. But—should it not come off—the one who would get hit the hardest had to be you. For all the reasons we both know, the play failed, and the chance to redeem a play was lost. This does not mean you dared to gamble with stakes which could put you out of the game with one throw of the dice coming up with the wrong combination.

What I hope can happen in the future is that you and I can get back to a basis of understanding where you will let me give my opinion, as I used to be able to do in the past. In the happy past you have called my judgment "infallible"—can you remember that far back? On this production, I felt strongly if I had said—wait—don't rush—there's no hurry, you would suspect for some reason or another I didn't want this producer, or something else—or I was not standing by you when you wanted to move forward. Your suspicion is so strong even the best of motives can be mistrusted by you and this does not make it easy to reach you on any solid ground of experience. Shall we try to find each other again—in understanding as well as deed?

Tennessee finished his next—*The Two Character Play*—in 1967. As I have said before, it is one of the plays he's written which impress me the most.

Originally, it would be produced in London, at a very small experimental theater near Swiss Cottage, the Hampstead Theatre Club, in 1967.

The year before, he had completed two plays, both short, one called *The Mutilated,* and the other *Gnädige Fraülein.* They were produced in New York under the title, *The Slapstick Tragedy.* By now, Tennessee was obviously totally addicted to those "speed" shots which Dr. Max Jacobson supplied, and both plays were written under their influence. Even though he felt both were good, the New York critics did not agree. *The Slapstick Tragedy* closed after a run of seven performances.

And so, when he brought this next play to London, he was obviously in a very depressed frame of mind. He had been waiting some time to get *The Two Character Play* this far, and was very anxious about its production. Hopefully, it would serve to change his recent fortunes.

I flew to London to be there with him for the opening. The female lead was played by the late Mary Ure.

Tennessee came to the opening with his good friend Lady St. Just.

We drove back from Hampstead to his hotel. It must have been 3 A.M.; by this time, Tennessee was quite drunk. When we got to his hotel, he began to say, over and over again "I want to die. I want to die. . . ." Nothing but this, over and over. He was totally submerged in his own misery.

Finally, out of a clear blue night sky, I heard myself say, "Well, I'm terribly sorry, you may want to die, my friend, but God is not ready for you. God is not strong enough to take you, it's impossible. You cannot die yet."

Somehow, this broke through the spell of his self-pity. Miraculously, he began to laugh. The litany, at least for the moment, was ended . . .

The most ironic aspect of that dreadful evening for me is how it was later reversed in his mind and used against me.

Years afterward, when the play was produced in Chicago, under the title *Out Cry,* Tennessee would announce to the world that this was the one play he'd written of which I'd never approved. So totally untrue! I was completely aware of the effort and work he'd lavished on that haunting piece of work. How he could deduce that I didn't care for it remains a puzzle to me.

In 1968, David Merrick produced Tennessee's next full-length play on Broadway. There was controversy about the title, which was originally *The Kingdom of Earth*. Everyone connected with the production agreed it presented too much of a religious connotation for an earthy work which dealt with the improbable love story between an ex-cheerleader named Myrtle, and a Mississippi farmhand named Chicken, both of them coming together in an abandoned farmhouse threatened by a flood.

It was Tennessee who retitled the play *The Seven Descents of Myrtle*. I am sure that if anybody else had brought up such a title he would have rejected it, but at the time he was well pleased with it.

At Tennessee's insistence, David Merrick had brought the talented José Quintero in to direct, the same Quintero who had done so well by *Summer and Smoke* in the off-Broadway theater and the film version of *The Roman Spring of Mrs. Stone*. Estelle Parsons played the lead, opposite Harry Guardino. I remember, at the first rehearsal, when we were all there at the theater; I was worried whether Quintero could really direct this play. I knew he was having problems of his own at the time. In the midst of the first rehearsal, Tennessee turned to me and in his most sibilant whisper, said, "José is a very troubled man."

I whispered back, "I'm sure, but this is not your problem; that's *his* problem."

It turned out to be ours as well. José is a brilliant director, but he was not then at his best. There were strange lapses during the rehearsals, and later, during the Philadelphia tryout. I well remember one night when he sat during a performance with his secretary, taking copious notes to give his cast. Then, when the curtain fell, he proceeded backstage to tell his actors how marvelous they all were. He left without giving a single note.

Later, there came a time when Tennessee and Quintero discussed an additional scene which they both agreed would be helpful to the play. Tennessee went off, wrote the needed scene and brought it to Quintero, fully expecting it would be immediately rehearsed and put into the play. Two or three days later, he returned, expecting to see his new scene. The scene was not played. When he asked José where it was, the director had completely forgotten it existed.

David Merrick was quite disturbed because of the behavior of his director, and offered to replace Quintero. But Tennessee prevailed, and Quintero remained. After a very brief run in New York, *The Seven Descents of Myrtle* closed.

Later that year, Universal released the film version of *The Milk Train*. It had been directed by Joseph Losey, with a screenplay by Tennessee, and the film starred Elizabeth Taylor as Flora Goforth and Richard Burton as Chris, the ascetic who comes to comfort her in her final days. The film title was *Boom*.

While the film was being made in Sicily, there was some confusion over the casting of one of the lesser roles. In the play, the character was known as the Witch of Capri, and had been originally played by Mildred Dunnock, later by Ruth Ford. The Witch was an aging storyteller, malicious and sly, bringing gossip and rumor concerning all her fashionable acquaintances. There'd been problems in finding the right actress for the film.

One day in Westport, I received a cable from Tennessee, which said, as I remember, "WITCH SOLVED. SHE NOW A HE. TO BE PLAYED BY NOEL COWARD."

Sadly, this decision, startling as it was, did not help *Boom* to be much of a success with audiences.

By 1968, Tennessee was in very bad shape, so much so that I was dreadfully worried about his physical condition.

Liebling and I had taken a winter place in Sarasota, and during that winter, I decided we must go over to Key West and meet with Tennessee, to see if we couldn't persuade him to leave Dr. Jacobson and go elsewhere for some sort of treatment.

I called him to ask if he would permit us to come. He seemed very pleased that we'd leave Sarasota and come all the way to Key West. He knew, as we were to find out, that while it seemed a simple journey, it involved flying down to Miami, changing planes, and then taking a second flight to Key West, all at a time when Liebling was far from well himself.

We made a hotel reservation in Key West; when we arrived, we had a date to meet Tennessee for dinner at a local restaurant.

We arrived ahead of him, and sat down to wait.

When he finally arrived, I was shocked by what I saw. My old friend was being led by a dog, a bulldog, on a leash. He came into the restaurant, blood dripping from his forehead. Somewhere along the way to our appointment, he had fallen in the street.

The restaurant owner would not permit the bulldog to stay inside, so we had to take the dog outside and tie him to a nearby tree. While we repaired the damages to Tennessee's forehead, mercifully not serious, the poor animal, miserable at being separated from his master, yowled and cried outside.

We ordered some wine to go with the meal. Tennessee had a good deal of it. I very carefully took the wine bottle and put it to my left, away from his reach. Tennessee would lean over to take some more, and since I thought he'd had quite enough, I kept blocking his hand.

Liebling made some sort of small joke which had to do with Tennessee's possibly hitting me with the bottle.

With no humor at all, Tennessee blinked and inquired "Bill, do you think I would ever strike Audrey with a bottle?"

The conversation was awkward and dreadfully strained. Finally, we came to the heart of the matter. Liebling, with great courage, launched into his plea, very directly. Dr. Max Jacobson. "Tennessee, you must stop seeing this man," Libeling insisted. "He's lethal."

Liebling had known Tennessee as long as I had, all those years, and truly loved the man. He spoke from his heart. "The man is killing you, please believe me," he said. "The two of us cannot stand watching what those shots are doing to you!"

Tennessee shook his head. "No, Bill," he said, his speech slurring. "He is a *lovely* man . . . a *lovely* man."

Which was all he would say, over and over again, until the repetition made it obvious he was far from rational. "He's a lovely man, a lovely man," continued his chant.

Finally we took him home. There was a marvelous black lady

there who'd worked for Tennessee for many years, and when we reached his house, she heard us coming, came to the door and greeted us warmly.

Tennessee stood there, impassively, and then he said "These people have given me a bad, bad time tonight . . . a bad, bad time."

She looked at us, and we looked at her, and we both realized the trip to Key West had been a total waste of time.

Shortly afterward, Tennessee converted to Catholicism.

Then, in May of 1969, there would be a production of his new play, *In the Bar of a Tokyo Hotel,* in New York, at the Eastside Playhouse, directed by Herbert Machiz.

It was not well received and while the play was running Tennessee wrote a rather ominous piece which was published, for the world to read, in the daily papers, as an advertisement for his play. Referring to the artist—himself—he wrote: "His youth passes. The health of his body fails him. Then the work increases its demand from most of him to practically all of him. At last it seems to him like an impotent attempt at making love. At that point he is sentenced to death, and as death approaches, he hasn't the comfort of feeling with any conviction that any of his work has had any essential value. . . ."

There was more, but all in the same mood of despair.

It was while this play was in rehearsal that I was called by Tennessee's brother, Dakin, who was in New York for the opening. He told me that he wished to see a matinee of some other play this day. But Tennessee had promised to buy his mother, Edwina Williams, a fur coat today, and Dakin wondered if I'd be good enough to substitute for him at that task.

I promptly canceled all my appointments, went over to the Plaza, where Mrs. Williams was staying, and took her to lunch. We had a friendly reunion. Then we proceeded to Bergdorf-Goodman, to the fur department, where an appointment had been made for her.

She spent time trying on various coats, and in the manner of most shoppers, she decided the first one she'd tried on was the one she truly fancied. When we asked the price, it became clear

is is how the *Esquire* artist decided I looked, in 1962. (COPYRIGHT ©1962 BY DAVID VINE).

Laurette Taylor, unforgettable by those who saw her in *Outward Bound* or Tenness Williams' *The Glass Menagerie*.

Eva Le Gallienne,
my neighbor in Connecticut
and only acting client,
recently on Broadway,
and the recipient of an Academy
Award nomination for Best
Supporting Performance in
the film *Resurrection*.

Anna Magnani, my Italian friend, with a friend from the countryside.

Young Marlon Brando as Stanley Kowalski, with Jessica Tandy in *Streetcar*.

to me that one did not discuss price when one ordered a coat from Bergdorf's. Since it would be made to order, the store would send fitters to her St. Louis home, to make certain the coat fit properly. However, I was insistent on learning the price. I also made the point that Mrs. Williams was a small lady—no taller than I am—and there would be fewer skins used in her coat. I hoped Bergdorf's would properly adjust the price. Not for nothing have I spent most of my life bargaining over such matters.

Whatever the exact price was, I do not remember, but it was in four figures. Mrs. Williams was delighted. She gave her home address, and the salesman informed her that on a day to be selected, the store would send a fitter to St. Louis.

When I arrived at the Eastside Theatre that night for the opening performance, I found an outraged Tennessee waiting for me. He was quite certain I had selected the most expensive fur coat Bergdorf's had ever sold, and persuaded his mother to buy it as a malicious act toward him.

The play wasn't going well, and in his near-paranoiac mood, he'd decided I'd done what I'd done that afternoon merely to cause him further distress. The accusation was so outrageous I could hardly reply to it. He spent the entire evening avoiding me as if I had some contagious disease.

It was a sad experience. Mrs. Williams had been so pleased by her son's generous gesture, and what I believed had been so pleasant was now totally destroyed by his irrational anger.

That summer, I continued to pick up the cudgels on his behalf. I was in Europe and I returned to find a full-page ad in the New York *Times,* placed there by *Life* magazine, which announced that Tennessee was not only "played out" but that his "early demise" was foretold.

Almost on reflex to find such a demeaning forecast, so gratuitous, I wrote a protesting letter to *Variety,* where I was certain it would be read by his professional confreres. I rose to his defense and said, "Only two months ago, the National Academy of Arts and Letters awarded Williams its highest honor, its Gold Medal for Drama. Lillian Hellman, in making the presentation, said in part, 'There are many good writers who do not influence men who came after them—influence is not the only measure of worth—but I think it is safe to guess that Williams' influence on the theatre will be there 100 years from now because the mirror he held in his hand announced a new time, almost a new people, and the mirror will remain clear and clean.'

" 'An artist has to lay his life on the line,' Williams wrote, in his last play, *Out Cry*. He has continued to do that in every play he has written. Remembering his consistent contribution to the contemporary theatre, it is appalling to find a newspaper of the stature of the New York *Times* accepting an advertisement of the sort it did."

Nineteen sixty-nine was a dreadful winter. My dear Liebling, so ill by now, died in December. At about the same time, Dakin, as disturbed by his brother's physical and mental state as we had been, had him hospitalized in St. Louis at the Barnes Hospital. Doctors there decided to go the "cold-turkey" route, taking Tennessee off liquor and those shots simultaneously. The treatment, so abrupt, caused Tennessee dreadful reactions. He went through periods of convulsions, delirium, and what is called a "silent coronary" during his three months at Barnes.

But he recovered. For years, Tennessee had gone to our doctor, Irving Somach, and Irving used to tell me Tennessee had one of the best hearts he'd ever listened to. Irving's diagnosis was proven correct. Tennessee would come out of Barnes fit and ready to resume his writing.

But as to Dr. Max Jacobson, later Tennessee would write a letter to the New York *Times*, and would somehow gallantly comment: "As for the doctor himself, I am inclined to believe that he was a brilliant experimenter but that in certain cases, including mine, the experiments—perhaps like all medical experiments, happened to involve a good deal of hazard. . . . I think his motives are humanitarian. . . ."

There are others of us who continue to disagree.

Finally, there was a revision of *The Two Character Play*, now retitled *Out Cry*.

It would be produced in Chicago, in July 1971, at the Ivanhoe

Theatre, directed by George Keathley, the same man who'd originally directed *Sweet Bird of Youth* at its first tryout in that renovated Florida garage. The new cast was carefully chosen. Eileen Herlie and Donald Madden were to play the leads, and since Keathley and Tennessee had had such a good professional relationship over the years, we had high hopes for the outcome.

Lady St. Just, Tennessee's friend, had come over from London to be with him for the opening night in Chicago. We three had dinner before the first preview. Tennessee seemed quite sober and far less tense than he had often been at other openings over the years.

I had memories of other opening nights in times past, when Tennessee, preparing to face that packed house of tough first-nighters, would hire a limousine and a driver to stand by outside the theater. The car would be waiting, ready to take him away at a moment's notice, to enable him to make his getaway, to some other town, far from Broadway.

The curtain would fall, there'd be applause, bows, affirmation, congratulations, and Tennessee, his ordeal ended, would come out to his car, cancel his getaway to another town and instruct the driver to take him to whatever place the opening-night party was being held.

The audience that night was not the usual group of Chicago theatergoers. Instead, it was a cross section of people who had come to enjoy the adventure of witnessing a first performance of a new play by a major American playwright. They knew nothing of the play's content. And they had no idea Williams was once again bravely reentering the theatrical arena with highly subjective material no other playwright would dare to dramatize. Tennessee has always been willing to take chances, to dare. It remains one of his great gifts.

During the intermission, I policed the lobby, as is my lifelong habit. I eavesdropped. There were some words of concern from a few of the people; there were the usual quiet ones who said nothing, and then there were those who commented to the effect, "I want to read the reviews before I give my opinion." In other words, a typical audience. At the end of the play, when the curtain fell, the audience reaction had become enthusiastic.

Miss Herlie and Mr. Madden received long and loud applause for their first-rate performances.

When the house lights went on and the audience began to file out, Tennessee was nowhere to be found. Of course, I thought, he has gone backstage to thank the cast. There he was, indeed, in Eileen Herlie's dressing room, talking very excitedly to George Keathley. Lady St. Just was also there, listening silently. I went inside. Suddenly, Tennessee swiveled about to stare at me, and with the vigor only he possessed, shouted at me, "And as for you, you have wished I was dead for the last ten years!"

Later, he would write in his memoirs that it was because I didn't care about him any longer, that he cared for me, and still does, but that the extent of his affection was diminished by a decade of neglect on my part. He'd been sympathetic to the dreadful time in which Liebling became ill and died, but he felt I'd paid too much attention to others, the new playwrights I represented, and that I'd begun to consider him a man of declining fortunes.

I knew none of that. For the first time in all our years together, instead of protesting the utter lack of truth in his accusation, I wanted only to strike him hard on the face.

But then, wisely, I realized he would enjoy such a scene, and perhaps even use it someday in a future play. The only other action left to me was to get the hell out of that dressing room, one, two three! But even though the exit was quick and perfectly executed, Tennessee would have the final curtain line. As I exited, I heard him say, "That bitch! I'm glad I'm through with her!"

After such a trauma, one needs to find a chair and a stiff drink in the bar of the nearest hotel. I found both. Tennessee had the same idea. Soon afterward, he came rushing in with Lady St. Just. When he saw I had arrived before him, he went charging out in a further rage.

Now it was well after midnight. When I reached my hotel room, the red message service light was madly blinking, on and off. Breathing deeply to calm myself, I decided the safest thing to do was to do nothing. The red light continued to blink, on and off. I went to bed, where I proceeded to talk to myself. The dialogue went like so. "I have been through similar Williams scenes through the years. I am strong. I have humor. The play will open. I can get by for a few days more. I will see him as little as possible. . . . I won't talk. I will stay here and wait."

Finally, I fell asleep. Nothing happened during the rest of that night. However, when I awoke in the morning, I knew I had to get out of Chicago at once. I couldn't wait for a train or a plane. A car with a driver was the only escape . . . but where would I go?

To Wisconsin—to Milwaukee—where my mother had been born and where the Wood family still lives. I made no phone calls to anyone in Chicago, except to order the car. An escape in the early morning to my Wisconsin family seemed the perfect reason to leave town.

As the car arrived in Milwaukee, I asked the driver first to stop at a cemetery where I might visit the graves of my mother and father, somehow feeling certain both would want to congratulate me for having—at long last—dared to be free.

Later, I heard from others that, on the night *Out Cry* opened officially in Chicago, with absolutely no humor, Tennessee said to Keathley, "Well, at least Audrey could have sent me a *wire*."

Looking back now at the sixties, I had continued to work with Tennessee through his troubled experiences, through his unfailing devotion to a doctor whose chief remedy for one and all was amphetamines, through all of his many disasters, never questioning why. But now I could see that what led to our permanent estrangement—whatever the detonator that exploded—did not actually come as any surprise. It was a collision course for both of us.

I had thought it would be possible, despite our professional breakup in Chicago, to remain, if not actually friends, perhaps acquaintances. However, what I did not foresee in the future was my total lack of emotional control, if and when either of us would suddenly enter the same arena again.

My final proof that we could not ever continue occurred at a chance meeting, many months after that dreadful night in Chicago.

Sidney Sheldon, the very successful novelist, who's been a

friend ever since I represented one of his plays, years back, was in New York and wanted to talk before returning to California.

I suggested Sunday brunch at the Algonquin, even though most Sundays I'm usually up at my Westport home, enjoying the country while I plow through that ever-present stack of scripts I've brought up from the city.

Sidney and I met, were given a table and ate and talked. Sidney has reminded me since that most of what I said that day dealt with my unhappiness at the recent break with Tennessee.

Because I am nearsighted and was not wearing my glasses, I was not aware Tennessee had entered the dining room and was walking down the aisle toward our table. Suddenly, a hand was thrust out to me, and a voice above said, "Hello, Audrey."

Before I saw the face above, my hand went out in response.

Then, something happened over which I had no control. My hand involuntarily withdrew.

The seconds seemed like hours, until Tennessee angrily stalked to his table. I could hear him making a vocal condemnation of the bad manners of women.

I explained to Sidney I had to leave the table quickly. I went out to the lobby, sat down, asked for water, and took a tranquilizer. I began to breathe deeply, and I prayed my heartbeat would be less violent.

This was the first time I realized how much I cared for this man, and also obviously why I could not enjoy even a casual friendly relationship with him in the future. The wound was too deep. Only now, years later, has some scar tissue formed.

Tennessee's perceptive prediction, all those years ago in *Esquire*—that I would be the one who would end our relationship —was, alas, true.

Survivor that he remains, he has continued to write during the ensuing years. Perhaps some of his work has been less successful than the ones he so masterfully wrote previously. No matter. I am as certain as Lillian Hellman was ten years ago that in this peculiar so-called business called the theater Tennessee's body of work is the most important we have had, or will have, in this century.

It's now 1980. A few months ago, dear Mrs. Williams, his

mother, passed away, and I was deeply moved. I broke our silence of the years passed, and I wrote Tennessee a note of condolence.

He wrote back a warm and friendly reply.

Meanwhile, I am proud to have played some part in helping to bring him to the place he has so richly deserved in the cultural history of our time. Ours was a relationship that went steadily forward for a long and fruitful time, ever since that day, so long, long ago, when he first stepped into the Liebling-Wood outer office . . . and into my life.

12

Night and Day—at MCA

It's very tough to get people—creative people—to stay with the legitimate theater. A few months back I was on the phone with George Roy Hill, who was a very good theater director, and I said to him, "George, I really wish we could lure you back to the theater; we need people with your background." His reply was quite frightening. He said, "No, Audrey, too much work for too few people."

And I know what he means. When you do a film, millions of people will see it, and in the theater, you go on a night-to-night basis—and if you have a success, you have more nights than usual, but it can't begin to compare with what happens to a play produced on television. That is what makes it so difficult to keep authors writing—serious plays, especially—for the commercial theater.

Then came the time, in 1954, when Liebling-Wood sold out.

Our small firm at 551 Fifth Avenue had prospered in the years since 1937. Our client list was impressive, business was good, we'd been functioning for seventeen years—in show business truly a long run—and it was tough to close.

But we were still small, very much a two act, and my husband felt—I must admit I was the first to agree with him—we desperately needed some time to ourselves. Since we were our own bosses, we'd found it was difficult to get away, even for a summer holiday, together. If one of us were out covering an out-of-town tryout, the other always had to stay in the office. If we both disappeared, who'd mind the store?

Liebling as usual was right. He suggested that the only way to make any sort of escape from our constant responsibilities would be to sell our business to another, larger firm. He went off to see what he could accomplish.

At that time, the fastest-growing agency in the business was MCA. It had been started in Chicago in 1924 by Jules Stein, an eye doctor and part-time musician, who decided there was far more future in booking bands than there was in sitting on a bandstand every night. Along with Lew Wasserman and Sonny Werblin, Taft Schreiber and Charlie Miller, Stein had built MCA into a formidable enterprise, an international business with an illustrious client list.

Liebling reasoned that MCA would offer the best deal for our client list, and he approached Lew Wasserman—who is today the head of MCA-Universal in California—with the idea of a buy-out. Eventually a deal was made which would provide us with a good sum of money, one that would provide for our future, and MCA bought Liebling-Wood.

Since Liebling had decided he wished to retire from the agency business and try his hand at producing on Broadway, in the final deal he stipulated only I would make the transfer to MCA, along with my list of playwrights and authors. That way their future and mine would be assured. But in the process I would also see to the affairs of some of Liebling's acting clients —such talented people as Ben Gazzara and Lorne Greene, who came to MCA when I did.

I can still remember the day we closed Liebling-Wood. At noon I took our faithful small staff downstairs to the restaurant at 551 Fifth Avenue and we had a farewell party. All of us were trying to be merry and bright, but it wasn't truly gay. We all realized that from that point on things would never quite be the same. It really was very much like a scene from some old tear-jerker melodrama in which the old homestead is sold, and the family knows it can never return.

My clients and I were promptly invited to a lavish welcoming party at the MCA offices at 595 Madison Avenue, N.Y. The contrast of my new surroundings took some adjustment. Jules Stein and his wife Doris had furnished several floors of that building with exquisite English antiques, paneled walls, deep carpeting and tasteful drapes. There was an equally opulent MCA establishment in Beverly Hills.

The party was a big one; it was as if we were being welcomed into a highly exclusive club. Clients came, a solid phalanx beside me—Tennessee, who was in town, Bill Inge, Bob Anderson, Truman Capote, whom I was representing at the time—like some staunch army following its leader.

I needed time to become accustomed to daily life at MCA. The firm was such a vast organization—floor after floor of offices of all shapes and strata, each inhabited by agents of the stature of Kay Brown, whose clients included Arthur Miller and Ingrid Bergman; Phyllis Jackson, who headed the MCA literary department; Phyllis Anderson and her playwright clients; Maynard Morris and Edith Van Cleve, who specialized in representing legitimate actors; Dorothy Kilgallen's capable sister, Eleanor, who, along with Monique James, handled casting for films and TV.

The MCA talent list was remarkable. On it were such names as Jimmy Stewart, Henry Fonda, Fred Astaire, Ingrid Bergman and Gregory Peck. Playwrights, directors, producers—you name them, MCA could supply them (at a hefty price—you could be sure of that).

In order to find out what went on all over the various floors, I initiated a weekly meeting to get the heads of the various departments together. Even if they didn't want to know what anyone else in the firm was doing, I did.

For several weeks we met in my small office, jammed together for several hours, until one day Jules Stein, who had started this entire worldwide enterprise, came by and peered in. At the sight of all his high-priced agents bunched up in my office, he did a take. He came back later. "Audrey," he said, "wouldn't you be more comfortable using the main conference room for a meeting of that size?"

From then on we held our weekly meeting there, surrounded by elegant Chippendale and Sheraton furniture.

A few days later, Mr. Stein came in again. He'd heard I had numerous originals of Pulitzer Prize awards, various Critics Circle citations, framed certificates honoring plays I'd handled, and knew I wished to hang them on my office wall.

In the overall design scheme for MCA, every office had not only been done in exquisite antiques, but the wall decor throughout each floor consisted of elegant original British hunting prints, landscape paintings and one-of-a-kind caricatures.

Mr. Stein was a quiet man, gentle and friendly; he treated me as if he were my grandfather. "Audrey," he said, "I hear you have all these awards and you wish to hang them on your wall."

I took the framed awards out of the closet and showed them to Mr. Stein. He looked at them and then said, "Now, Audrey, I'll tell you what we're going to do. We'll get you a beautiful antique stand and on it we'll put a hand-tooled leather portfolio. We'll take these out of their frames, we'll put them in the portfolio and then, when people come in, they can stand here, turn the pages and look through your portfolio."

I looked at him with no humor and I said, "Mr. Stein, this is what you *bought*. This is Liebling-Wood."

He nodded. To his credit, he promptly regrouped his forces. "All right then, here's what we'll do," he said. "We'll send them out to California, have them reframed, and then at least the frames will match the wood paneling of your walls."

When they were all reframed in California, back they came and they were hung on my office walls in their elegant new antique frames.

One day Tennessee Williams came to see me. He rarely came to my office, either at Liebling-Wood or at MCA, but on this particular day he was sitting on my sofa when Mr. Stein happened down the hall. Mr. Stein hadn't seen the awards since they'd been reframed. He looked in my doorway, stared critically, and then he said, "Yes, yes—they look very well, Audrey."

Tennessee looked up and said, "They look a lot better than those old hunting prints she had when she first came here!"

Astonished, Mr. Stein hurried away.

He didn't know it was Tennessee, and Tennessee didn't know it was Mr. Stein and that was the way I left it.

One of my very talented clients was the playwright Maurice Valency, who has a unique gift: he is able to translate French playwrights and adapt their works for the American stage with great success. In 1949 he adapted Jean Giraudoux's brilliant play *The Madwoman of Chaillot*. It was produced by Alfred de Liagre with Martita Hunt in the lead and was a great success. A year later, Maurice adapted Giraudoux's play *The Enchanted*, and it was produced and directed by George S. Kaufman, with his wife, Leueen MacGrath, in the lead. Later on, in 1958, he adapted Friedrich Dürrenmatt's *The Visit* for Alfred Lunt and Lynn Fontanne.

Earlier, in 1954, Maurice had another Giraudoux adaptation ready for Broadway, this one a lovely play called *Ondine*.

It was not an easy play to produce; it was the story of a mermaid, a beautiful creature from the sea, and the prince who falls in love with her. The Playwrights Company decided to produce the play and there our problems began. Who could play a mermaid? No one at the Playwrights Company had any suggestions that seemed right; we spent weeks going around in circles trying to solve the dilemma.

Then, in the magical way things happen in the theater, one day I had a call from abroad from a gentleman named Mel Ferrer, announcing that he and Audrey Hepburn wanted to do a play together. "Do you have any ideas?" he asked.

I thought how wonderful it would be if that beautiful star could play the lead in *Ondine*, and I promptly sent off the script. They both agreed to do it.

Which catapulted me to a never-to-be-forgotten experience. Not only was I the adaptor's agent, but I was also asked to represent Mel Ferrer.

Alfred Lunt was engaged to direct *Ondine,* and rehearsals began.

Ferrer began to throw his weight around. At that time he and Hepburn were very much in love, which may have accounted for his frenetic behavior. From the very first day he behaved as if only he mattered. He made demands which were outrageous. During rehearsals he would disregard Lunt's authority as a director—something which is sacrosanct during a production.

One of his demands was that his costumes be the exact duplicates of authentic coats of armor on display at the Metropolitan Museum. He had ideas about the scenery as well.

I tried to explain to my new client Ferrer that he had no artistic control over such matters, but it was no use. He continued to assert himself.

Since Kay Brown was representing Audrey Hepburn—then an MCA client—the two of us struggled to keep the lid from blowing off this touchy situation. None of the Playwrights Company founders nor Roger Stevens, with whom they were now in partnership, were very visible out of town, so Kay and I worked out a schedule that one or the other of us would always be standing guard at the theater in Boston, in order to cope with whatever fresh daily crisis might arise.

We kept it up all through the out-of-town tryout, where *Ondine* was a critical and financial success, mainly because of Audrey Hepburn's star name, as well as the allure of Lunt and Giraudoux. Audiences weren't flocking to see Ferrer, but he obviously believed they were.

The company returned to New York and prepared for the opening at the Forty-sixth Street Theatre. Forty-eight hours beforehand I had a call from Mr. Ferrer summoning me to meet him at the theater. A new crisis had developed, one which he could not discuss over the phone. I had other things of importance to deal with but he refused to take no for an answer. Eventually I walked over to the theater, where I met Ferrer, who was waiting with Louis Lotito, the theater's manager.

Ferrer led us backstage to Miss Hepburn's dressing room.

Then he led us upstairs to show us his dressing room, which was furnished and decorated in far less opulence.

"We are costars," he said. "I insist that my dressing room be exactly the same as hers."

His implication was clear.

To my utter astonishment, the producers agreed. Within hours, painters had moved in and refurbished Mr. Ferrer's room!

The Broadway theatrical community is such a small one; by now the rumors of Ferrer's behavior toward his director had spread. Obviously Ferrer himself had heard the extent of the gossip. He decided to take steps to pour oil on troubled waters.

On opening night, at the curtain, there were cheers for Miss Hepburn. Then Ferrer held up his hands for silence. He proceeded to tell the audience he wished to thank Alfred Lunt for having been such a splendid director, he lavished praise on Lunt for his efforts and added that he and the entire cast were in Lunt's debt.

But his beau geste was lost on those to whom Ferrer obviously directed his remarks—the New York critics. By that time they were gone, having left the theater in a rush to make their morning deadlines.

However, the following week's *Variety* carried the entire story, reporting it as a front-page news item, mentioning the bad feeling behind the scenes which must have prompted Ferrer to take such an extraordinary opening-night step.

The next day I had a call from Ferrer, who summoned me to a meeting at the Plaza. With no humor whatsoever he then instructed me he wished the story properly reported, he wished an official apology from *Variety* and I must take charge of rectifying the situation.

I took a deep breath and I said, "Mel, let me tell you all the things you've done since the play went into rehearsal which you should never have done." I held up my ten fingers and began to tick them off, one by one, each instance of his unprofessional behavior.

To his credit, I must say he listened. And never again mentioned *Variety* or a retraction.

Ondine ran for 146 performances. While it was running, I took

Roger Stevens to lunch at the Algonquin. I said, "Roger, you must never again produce a play without someone in authority being there at all times. This one could have been a disaster had it not been for Kay Brown or me staying with it constantly." I still firmly believe I was right in making that statement.

Later in the conversation I asked Roger, "Where *were* all the Playwrights?"

"Off writing plays," he said.

About a year later I was in California, in the dining room of the Beverly-Wilshire Hotel. Who should come in but my former client, Mel Ferrer. He spied me, came over, embraced me fondly as if I were one of his dearest relatives, sat down and chatted with me. There was no mention whatsoever of *Ondine*. It was as if he'd entirely forgotten the play. And, certainly, I wasn't about to bring it up.

There was another time at MCA when I inherited Jerome Robbins. I had never worked with a choreographer before. I didn't really want to take him on as a client; I didn't feel my background was the right one for him. But the MCA executives in New York disagreed. Morris Schrier, one of the officers of the firm, proceeded to sell me the idea that I would be absolutely right for Robbins; he insisted it would be the ideal marriage of talent and agent.

Robbins agreed to have lunch with me. I'd never met him before and we made a date to eat at Dinty Moore's, which was a famous theatrical restaurant, then still open on Forty-sixth Street, across from the Lunt-Fontanne Theatre, where Robbins was in rehearsal.

Jerry had by this time become one of the major forces in the American musical theater. He had choreographed *Call Me Madam, The King and I* and *Peter Pan,* and his memorable Mack Sennett cops-and-robbers ballet in the second act of *High Button Shoes* was a classic work of high comedy. His direction of *West Side Story* in 1957 will always remain one of the creative landmarks in theater history.

I arrived at the Lunt-Fontanne a few minutes before our appointment. Jerry was rehearsing his ballet troupe for their trip to Spoleto, Italy, where they would be presenting his *Ballets U.S.A.* I sat down in the empty theater and waited while he rehearsed. After a bit, he turned around and saw me sitting down there. He waved a hand but so rapt was he in his work that he didn't break the rehearsal, nor did he come down to say hello. The rehearsal continued for some time, well past our date. I thought to myself, well, this is hardly the way to begin working with Mr. Robbins, is it? Finally I got up, went to the stage doorman and said, "When Mr. Robbins is finished, tell him Miss Wood is across the street—if he still wishes to join her."

I went over to Moore's and began to eat. Finally, Jerry came over. He was by then quite late, but he did come. While we ate I told him frankly I had no idea whether this would work out or whether he would enjoy having me for his agent, or I having him for a client. However, I assured him I would be willing to try, if he would. Jerry smiled and agreed. Then he went back to his ballet troupe.

At MCA I discovered his representation contract with the agency had actually expired; he was only signed on a yearly basis and the year had expired. So I had a set of new contracts drawn up and sent them up to his office and I called his secretary to say, "Now, please, let's not have any fooling around; if Jerry's not going to sign I don't wish to play games in which I have to call you once a week and ask, 'Where are the contracts?' Please have them signed *now*."

"Oh, *no*, Miss Wood," his secretary insisted. "He's going to sign!"

I knew Robbins was very much his own man, often mercurial, difficult to pin down, accustomed to total authority in whatever project he took on. I wasn't at all certain he would accept our proposed relationship.

But back came the contracts, signed, accompanied by his card —and a box of yellow roses. It was the talk of MCA: not only had I re-signed such an important client—but to receive roses from him as well!

I sent back his copy of the contracts, signed by me, and I sent roses as well, this time red ones. I added a note which read, ". . . Red is for blood, you know."

The time came when *West Side Story* was to be produced as a film and the producers, the Mirisch brothers, offered Robbins the task of transferring his brilliant choreography to the screen. We had several discussions about this. I could sense he was reluctant to make the commitment. MCA had California executives close to the film company. Even though Robbins had never choreographed a movie, a huge deal was negotiated by which he would take over the entire job. Robbins merely had to agree.

One day he came to see me and said he'd been talking with his good friend, Leland Hayward, the ex-agent who'd turned theater producer. Shortly afterward, Leland would produce *Gypsy* on Broadway and Robbins would direct it; but at this point Leland was advising Jerry not to work on the film of *West Side Story*. He argued that Jerry was a perfectionist—which we all knew—and for him to work on a film might well be the wrong move. Movie production costs would simply not permit Jerry to indulge his passion for perfection. In the end, such a venture could cause Jerry great artistic frustration.

I listened to all of this. Finally I said, "Jerry, if you really feel you cannot go through this sort of anxiety—if you really feel you can live through someone else reproducing your choreography on the screen, it's fine with me. Obviously, you don't need the money, you're well off, so if you decide against it, I'll go along with your decision."

A day later he advised me he would do *West Side Story*.

I have always understood his reasoning; he would have suffered infinitely more if he had not done the work himself.

Very soon after that, *West Side Story* went into production as a film. A good deal of it would be shot in New York. In the customary fashion of the motion-picture business, things had moved so rapidly Jerry was actually shooting sequences with his dancers before he signed his employment contracts.

The contracts finally arrived in my office, agreed to by both sets of lawyers, the producers' and Jerry's, and I took them uptown to him. That particular day he was working in the area which was to be the site of the new Lincoln Center. On all sides there were razed building sites, vacant lots piled with rubble, city blocks which looked as if they were part of bombed-out London—and, in their midst, on one block, down this ruined street, Jerry and a huge crew were rehearsing a scene in which the Jets street gang come dancing down in search of the Sharks, their rivals.

Jerry was perched high on a camera crane, surrounded by lights and sound equipment; off to one side a recording was playing, the Bernstein music echoing across the empty lots, while below the dancers performed steps for Jerry's camera. Again and again he rehearsed them, over and over, until the very last detail was perfect and—not until then—finally he made a few feet of acceptable film.

The company broke for lunch. Jerry came down from his perch to join me. We stood in line at the catering table and we each were given a box lunch. Then we went across the street to find a place somewhere to sit down and go through those voluminous contracts.

There was an old public school building on that block, long since closed, due to be demolished because of the oncoming building of Lincoln Center. I managed to get us through the front door. Inside we found an empty schoolroom with a few rows of abandoned desks. For years school children had sat here, possibly to eat their lunches, too. Nobody was there today, just Jerry and me. I spread out the contracts on one desk, our box lunches on another, and while we ate we went through the endless pages to discuss what they contained.

Since the contracts had been negotiated by our office in California, all I could do was to explain the terms as clearly as I could, and then I suggested he had better sign, to protect his own interests. Finally he signed all the copies. We finished lunch and he returned to work.

Sometime later Jerry left MCA to be represented by his attorney.

I never worked for or with him again. I've always regretted our professional relationship was so brief. Perhaps one day we'll

work together again. I would be proud to work once more with
so gifted an artist.

Toward the end of my days at MCA I operated out of a very
large office. It hadn't always been so. The longer I stayed with
that firm, the more complex the job became. Hardly a day
passed without someone appearing in my office doorway asking,
"Audrey, could we have a meeting about this? It's a crisis." The
work days grew longer; the interruptions kept pace. I had less
and less time to do my own work.

Finally I went to see Lew Wasserman himself. Lew, a tall,
quiet man, is the sort of executive who sits at a desk on which
there is not a single piece of paper, not a pencil or pen, not even
a note. He listened to my problems, how my workload was complicated by the foot traffic on my floor, and then he nodded and
smiled. "Very well, Audrey," he said. "Go find yourself another
office. Anywhere in our building you see one you like, move in
and take it."

So I'd ended up in a large suite on another floor, very much
by myself, only available through an outer office.

Such isolated splendor was welcome. But it soon came to an
abrupt end.

In 1962, the U. S. Government moved against MCA. The Department of Justice maintained that MCA was a monopolistic
entity, operating in restraint of trade. The government's case was
based on charges that while MCA represented hundreds of clients on a commission basis, the firm was also busily engaged in
the film and television production business, operating as a
"packager," and often employing its own clients.

Just before that time, in 1962, Liebling and I were going
abroad for a vacation. Before we left, Charlie Miller, then one of
the heads of MCA, told me MCA did not know what was going
to happen; the government ax had not yet fallen, but he and
some others were thinking of opening a small agency and they
hoped I'd join them. I said, "I'm going to London; can we discuss it when I get back?"

The rumors of what might happen had reached MCA's London offices. All the British executives there—Robin Fox, Laurence Evans, Cecil Tennant and the others—were completely puzzled and distrait. How could such a thing happen? In England no such problems exist; legally, most big businesses there function as monopolies. No government, either Conservative or Labour, would dream of challenging their right to do so.

While we were in London I received a call from Ted Ashley, an aggressive young agent in New York, who'd begun his own agency previously with Ira Steiner. Ted told me he hoped I'd join Ashley-Steiner and bring over my clients. "I'm sorry," I told him, "but I have a contract with MCA."

Quietly, Ted said, "Well, Audrey, you won't have it much longer."

By the time Liebling and I returned to our apartment at the Royalton in New York, on a weekend, there were dozens of phone messages waiting for us, clients who'd heard MCA might close and wanted to know what to do, fellow employees at MCA seeking information, other interested parties such as our lawyer, Eddie Colton. I had no answers.

Monday morning, I went to my office and began to go through the various items of business piled up in my absence.

At 5 P.M. we were all officially notified that MCA no longer existed. The federal courts had handed down a decision. MCA must divest itself of its agency business.

It was the strangest experience of my life. Within a matter of minutes, a large, thriving enterprise had abruptly closed. Gone out of business, ceased to be. We were given until the end of that week to wind up affairs.

All our clients, that roster of talented people, were from that moment legally free agents, unrepresented. And the MCA staff—all those experienced agents, some of whom had spent years with the firm, plus all the younger secretaries and assistants, readers and office boys who'd joined the firm with stars in their eyes—were out on the street, unemployed. People wandered from office to office, literally in shock.

Meanwhile, we encountered another unpleasant experience. As we left the building at night, we encountered government agents stationed in the lobby by the elevators, searching MCA employees as they left, to make certain no company papers or official documents were removed.

Such a situation caused me grave difficulty. In my own office there were contract files which went back many years. They covered rights for foreign productions, for stock and film deals. For Tennessee Williams alone there were bulging folders. I didn't know where I would be going but I was certain most of my clients would be going with me. It was vital to get all those papers out of the MCA offices.

My handbag was searched as I left in the evening. Friends in MCA management, especially my good friend Morris Schrier, did what they could eventually to get the rest of my valuable files returned to me.

A meeting was called at which we MCA executives were given a release form to sign, one which legally made us all free agents, no longer bound by our employment contracts. One of the MCA officials took me aside and counseled me not to sign. He knew my contractual situation well. When we had sold Liebling-Wood to MCA, eight years earlier, MCA had contracted to pay us over a period of years. We still had several years to go on that contract. Had I signed the MCA paper I would have been free to operate on my own, no longer as an MCA employee, but MCA would no longer be legally bound to make any further financial payments to what had been Liebling-Wood.

The final week went on, day after depressing day. Most of my young staff were still with me, working valiantly away, on a floor where other offices were vacant, and phones went unanswered. It became more ghostly each day.

The situation was so lugubrious I went home one night and said to Liebling, "I can't stand this. I have to give a farewell party for all those people. Everyone on my floor."

Liebling agreed. The next day I thought about it and went home and told him, "I have to serve champagne."

Liebling said, "All right, all right—champagne it is."

"Not merely champagne," I said, later. "Good French champagne!"

And Liebling said, "Why not? Who's telling you you can't?" He understood how I felt.

By Friday morning of this last week, the party was arranged. That afternoon, the last day at MCA, we all assembled. Not only the staff on my floor, but their wives and husbands and children. Someone found a stereo in one of the empty offices and music began to echo through the empty halls, resounding through all those offices with their antiques and expensive furnishings and shelves full of old English leather-bound books.

We tried to make it gay but it was difficult. I went out of my office to do a final errand downstairs and when I came back I was confronted with the sight of all those young people, now in pairs, dancing to the music in that long dark splendid MCA hallway . . . dancing a final farewell to MCA.

It was like a scene from a sad Russian novel. When I left for the last time, and the government man downstairs searched my purse, I had trouble holding back the tears.

Liebling and I flew out to California immediately to meet with Ted Ashley. He'd made his offer again, and we'd decided to accept. While we waited to confer with Ted we stayed at the Beverly Hills Hotel.

That venerable establishment was buzzing with activity, there was action everywhere. Meetings and kaffeeklatsches surrounded us, people came and went, huddling and making deals all over the hotel. Since all those valuable MCA clients were now free, they were literally up for grabs. The big trick for other agents in the business was to see which stars they could pick up fast.

In the midst of all this speculative action I was secure; most of my clients had firmly agreed to stay with me wherever I went. While Ted Ashley and I held our meetings, I called my old friend Jules Stein at home. Mrs. Stein answered and told me her husband wasn't feeling well, which, under the circumstances of the past weeks, was certainly understandable. But they did want to see us so she sent their car and we went over to visit the Steins at home.

Jules Stein came downstairs from his bedroom wearing his

dressing gown, looking sad and plaintive. We sat together and I told him about the last week at MCA in New York and the final closing party, and we both wept a bit together.

We went back to New York with a deal by which I would promptly join Ashley-Steiner. Ted and Ira had moved with great acumen and speed. They'd also acquired the considerable services of Kay Brown and her clients, Phyllis Jackson, who brought along a formidable list of authors, and Jay Sanford, who had many talented clients writing for television. Overnight, Ashley-Steiner had literally exploded into a major agency. So quickly had the firm expanded that there was no office space in which to house all the new agents.

Resourcefully, Ted immediately rented hotel rooms in a small establishment on Fifty-sixth Street between Madison and Park avenues. There each member of his new staff was provided with temporary rooms. Each morning I went uptown to an office which consisted of a small double bedroom from which the beds had been removed. There my secretary and I worked.

Those improvised quarters were quite different from my lavish establishment at MCA. But after all my years in show business, I had long ago developed the ability to adjust. Where you work isn't important. What you do is.

Ashley-Steiner shortly became Ashley Famous, Inc. Later it became International Famous and, after its merger with C.M.A. (Creative Management Associates), the firm is known as International Creative Management. It is now as vast as the former MCA and it has been my home ever since 1962. More important, it's been a home for my clients as well.

MCA went on to become MCA-Universal, a mammoth enterprise involved in film production, TV shows, book publishing and even banking, on a worldwide basis. The corporation is enormously successful; Lew Wasserman still holds the reins of power.

But I am certain MCA-Universal can't be as exciting a place to work as it was for me back in those days amid the antiques, the paneling and the hunting prints on Fifty-seventh Street and Madison Avenue.

13

Come Back, Sweet William

Bridget Aschenberg, my very efficient coworker at International Creative Management, appeared this morning in my office, with several bound volumes in hand.

"I think you will be happy to see these," she said. "They just arrived from the publisher."

I opened one and glanced at the writing there, but I could make no sense out of the title. "What is this?" I asked.

"This is an African-language version of William Inge's play *Come Back, Little Sheba*," said Bridget. "It was sent to me, but I think both of us should have it on our shelves, don't you?"

How remarkable.

After all these years, from so many thousands of miles away, an African version of my client's—*our* client, for Bridget was deeply involved with his affairs too—first produced play. His first success, in fact.

How sad that he could not be here to have one.

"We must send some of these to his sister," I said.

She would be so pleased to have them.

Almost as pleased as we were. Pleased, and also, quite touched by this tangible evidence that Bill's work is still being performed, so long after the first opening night, over three decades ago.

Despite what you may have heard, or read about us, we agents are not totally without our own emotional responses.

Bill Inge was tall and quite shy, soft-spoken and enormously gifted. He was modest, often inarticulate. For over a decade, from 1950 until the mid-sixties, critics and playgoers applauded his work. At the time, he was considered one of the most successful young playwrights of the American stage.

His deeply empathetic observation of small towns and their inhabitants afforded his sophisticated metropolitan audiences an entirely different and possibly more sympathetic attitude toward their neighbors in the heartlands. On the screen his plays proved just as successful as on Broadway, often more.

Then he went into an eclipse, both professional and personal, almost a total one.

His tragic suicide, several years ago, was a profound loss.

William Inge came into my life through the very good offices of my client—my then client—Tennessee Williams.

In the autumn of 1944, while his play *The Glass Menagerie* was being staged for its eventual premiere in Chicago, Williams returned for a visit to his former home in St. Louis. The local newspaper, the *Star-Times,* long since gone, promptly sent its young drama critic to interview the prodigal native son. That critic was Inge.

Bill was a native of Kansas who had been a teacher at Stephens College in Columbia, Missouri, during those years when that institution's drama department was supervised by the dramatic actress Maude Adams.

He and Tennessee became good friends, and several weeks later Inge went to Chicago to attend a performance of Williams' new play. Something within Bill responded powerfully to the seemingly artless manner in which Williams had fashioned his lovely play out of the inner emotion and aspirations of such highly unheroic characters. And he was—as we all were—stirred by the leading lady, Laurette Taylor, who was certainly giving one of the greatest performances those of us who were fortunate to witness it can remember.

After seeing *Menagerie* in Chicago, Bill wrote the following in a still unpublished journal:

> I rode the train back to St. Louis and gave my experience in Chicago deep thought. Tennessee had shown me a dynamic example of the connection between art and life. I could see, from what he had told me of his youth and family life, how he had converted the raw material of his life into drama. I had been wanting to write plays myself, but I had never known where to look for material. I always tried to write like Noel Coward, with each attempt an embarrassing failure. Now I knew where to look for a play—inside myself.
>
> That spring in St. Louis, when the symphony season was over and my work on the paper had lessened, I sat down to write my own play, garnered from my memories of childhood. I had seen enough plays at the American Theatre, both good and bad, to have the courage to fail. What if it didn't turn out to be another *Menagerie*. I would at least write it. The play was a domestic comedy, based upon my early memories of my family and relatives. I called it *Farther off from Heaven*, from the sentimental little poem of Thomas Hood's. I dared to think that it was pretty good. I sent a copy off to Margo Jones in Dallas. I had met Margo when I was with Tennessee in Chicago and she had told me of her plans to start a professional theatre in Dallas. Tennessee happened to be visiting her at the time. They both read the play and telephoned me to tell me they liked it. Margo said she wanted to open her theatre with it. I was ecstatic. I now felt myself to be a playwright and to have a future.

Eventually, Bill left the newspaper and began to teach English at Washington University.

Margo gave Bill his first production, and Tennessee saw to it that Inge's play arrived on my desk.

I read it, and didn't think it was salable, so I sent it back to Bill with a note in which I told him so. But I truly didn't wish to discourage him from continuing to write; his script showed unmistakable talent. I suggested he do another play, and hoped he'd permit me to read whatever work he did in the future.

Luckily for me, and for the American theater, Bill was not discouraged. He went back to work.

What was to be his first Broadway play was a sensitive and well-written drama about two very ordinary people, a middle-aged chiropractor named Doc, with an alcohol problem he was fighting, and Lola, his mild, somewhat disheveled sympathetic wife. The name of the play was *Come Back, Little Sheba*, and once again, Tennessee made certain it came directly to me, with a strong recommendation.

He was absolutely right.

Now the difficulties began. First, I had to find a producer with as much faith as I had to give this unknown playwright his first Broadway production. Under the best of circumstances not a simple task.

We were lucky. I sent the play over to a very perceptive and bright lady, Phyllis Anderson, who was at that time working for the Theatre Guild. Phyllis, married to my client Robert Anderson, promptly responded to Inge's drama, and was most influential in helping me arrange for the guild to option *Come Back, Little Sheba* for Broadway.

As always, the path to the eventual production was littered with all sorts of frustrating obstacles. Theresa Helburn and Lawrence Langner of the Guild were, to say the least, uncertain about Inge's play and its potential with audiences. For many months, they dragged their collective feet. In fact, if Phyllis hadn't been at the Guild and hung in there, pressing and pushing to get *Sheba* into production, there might well not have been a production at all.

At last, it was decided to give the play a week's tryout run at the Westport Country Playhouse, toward the end of the summer of 1949. But the exact date for that run was not settled for many weeks, and when it finally was set, it turned out to be for an extra week's booking after Labor Day, following the Playhouse's regular subscription season. Not precisely an auspicious time. The summer audiences would have departed; if it was a hot night, there would be no air conditioning, and—more important, as it turned out—no heat in the theater if it proved chilly.

But we went forward. Phyllis and I worked together on the project, and we secured Daniel Mann as the director. He had done some B films in Hollywood and worked in New York at the

Actors Studio, but as yet he hadn't done anything important on Broadway. For the part of Doc, one of the two major leads, Sidney Blackmer, a very fine actor, was cast. For his wife, it was Lawrence Langner's suggestion that we try for Shirley Booth.

Heretofore Miss Booth was known primarily as a fine comedienne. On radio she was "Miss Duffy," and on the stage she'd appeared in such comedy hits as *Three Men on a Horse, My Sister Eileen* and *The Philadelphia Story*. She herself was not at all certain such a major dramatic role was right for her. She kept Inge's script for quite a while, and didn't respond to the Guild's inquiries. Finally she called Langner personally and told him she didn't think the part was right for her, and she was returning the script.

At this point I'd become convinced she was absolutely right for the part, and after consulting Langner on the protocol of this situation, I called the lady up myself. Years before, when I was a young girl, Shirley had been the ingenue in my father's stock company in New Jersey, and I believed I knew her well enough to make one last college try to change her mind. When I reached her at her farm in Pennsylvania, I made a long and impassioned speech on behalf of my client and his play. I told her how important this first production was to William Inge's future, and I suggested that if she didn't do the part, *Sheba* might well not be produced at Westport this summer, which was certainly possible, and if not, *Sheba* might not ever get on at all.

Shirley listened and made no comment until I was done. "I'll think it over," she said, and then hung up.

A couple of days later, miraculously, she called Lawrence Langner and said she'd changed her mind. Even though she had a commitment to another play for the fall, she was ready to do *Sheba*.

Finally, all the pieces were together and we went into rehearsal, with our date in September. I am certain it was the latest postseason date the Guild had ever played at the Country Playhouse, and I will never forget our first and only dress rehearsal, on the Sunday night before the Monday opening.

The Guild, lacking its regular subscribers, had asked various Westport businessmen and other friendly locals to come sit in the theater for the Sunday-night preview. They'd in effect "papered" the house so the actors could get a sense of someone being out there.

It turned out to be a very cold September night. Liebling and I went to the theater and took our seats, and never have I been so chilled as I was in that drafty auditorium. I remember my husband taking off his jacket and putting it around my shoulders, and there we were, huddled together in the dark like refugees on a sinking ship, surrounded by other equally frigid spectators, all of us shivering.

There is one climactic scene in the second act of *Sheba* in which Doc, a usually quiet man, suddenly goes off the wagon, and in his demented drunken state threatens to kill his wife with a hatchet. Coming as it does after a long and quiet series of scenes between the two characters, it is highly melodramatic and something of a shock to an audience. I'd always felt, in reading the play, that this was the crucial scene. If it worked for the audience, if it held them, then I was certain Inge had written a viable piece of theater.

To my utter joy, this cold night in Westport, with an audience of complete strangers who weren't really theatergoers and had no idea whatsoever what they were going to see, when we came to that startling scene between Blackmer and Booth, you couldn't hear a sound from anywhere in the drafty theater. We knew. *Sheba* worked!

The next night, the official opening, was almost an anticlimax for us. Not for the audience, however. When the final curtain fell, there was wild applause. Two performers cast against type, a director given his first major job, a play by a hitherto unknown author . . . it was a marvelous feeling to know that we had something wonderful here.

In the usual way of the theater, which is a small business, the good news traveled very fast. By the end of that first week's run in Westport, all sorts of theater people had heard about Bill's play and made the trip to Westport to see it. The excitement was contagious; it always is when a play and a cast come together so excitingly.

But . . . we were far from being solidly established.

Shirley Booth had a prior commitment to producer Brock Pemberton to do a new play called *Love Me Long,* coincidentally written by my old friend and ex-partner, Doris Frankel. There was no way Shirley would be free to do *Sheba* on Broadway until the other play had opened, and she'd fulfilled her contract. As much as I didn't wish Doris to fail, I couldn't help being torn about the prospects for her play. Nobody else but Shirley could play Doc's wife.

Eventually, *Love Me Long* opened. Sad for Doris, but marvelous for Bill, it failed.

Finally, in midwinter, we went back into rehearsal, this time for Broadway, with Shirley and Sidney in their original roles. We went out of town to play our first tryout in Wilmington, Delaware. For several reasons, the engagement was an interesting experience.

To begin with, on that opening night, nobody from the Theatre Guild's upper echelon appeared. Theresa Helburn and Lawrence Langner and their cohorts were all off elsewhere, attending to the opening of Katharine Hepburn's production of *As You Like It.* So there we all were, alone in Wilmington, Phyllis Anderson, Danny Mann, our author and our cast, on our own. I remember we sent a congratulatory wire to the Guild for their other opening, and collectively we signed it, "From the Dark Horse."

Looking back now, it was fortunate for all of us that we were there without them all. Their absence spared us all the customary frenzied second-guessing, lobby conferences and late-night free advice, a ritual and tiring part of most out-of-town openings.

But there was another, serious problem for us. It was Bill Inge's alcoholism, and it had surfaced in the past few days. I'd come to realize that when Bill was under tension, he, like his character Doc he'd so brilliantly created, resorted to the bottle.

Before, he had been able to relieve some of those tensions by compulsively rewriting his play. During the months before *Sheba* was finally produced, it seemed he did a new rewrite every week. I remember once I wired him, "NOW JUST STOP. I CAN'T BEGIN TO READ YOUR PLAY EVERY WEEK."

But now, in Wilmington, as the time for the curtain to rise approached, his tensions began to take over. Bill was suffused with fears he could not articulate.

I'd already seen what liquor did to him. A warm and shy man, under its influence he became almost mute. Thus tranquilized, Bill would look at you and you could smile at him, but he had no conversation. You could take his hand and hold it, and he'd hold yours, but you got no verbal response. It was almost like dealing with a shadow, not a man.

Come the morning of our opening night, and luckily there was a man with us, Paul Bigelow, who was working for the Guild, who was well aware of Bill's problems. Paul improvised a brilliant way to ensure that Bill did not wander off somewhere and go on an alcoholic binge. Early in the morning Paul managed to take all of Bill's clothing out of his hotel room and send them to the hotel tailor to be cleaned and pressed. Unable to leave his room, Bill stayed sober. When the curtain went up that night, he was in control of himself. When it came down, and the Wilmington audience applauded the cast, it was truly a happy time for all of us. *Sheba* was even better in Wilmington than it had been that first week in Westport.

We opened in New York on February 15, 1950, and the New York critics were full of praise. Shirley Booth and Sidney Blackmer won raves for their dramatic performances. The simple, honest play which dealt with two ordinary people and their problems established Bill Inge as an important American playwright. When the Tony awards were handed out that spring, one went to Shirley, the other went to Sidney.

Sheba had a long run, and I promptly sold the film rights to Hal Wallis and his partner Joe Hazen. They had a script written for their proposed film by Ketti Frings. When the time came for casting, they gave the film script to practically every one of the available great Hollywood ladies who were then box-office names. In practically every instance, those film stars turned down the role. I understood that in one way or another, they all said the same thing: "The only actress to play this character is Shirley Booth. Nobody else could do it."

Finally, very bravely, Wallis and Hazen gave Miss Booth a contract to re-create her original part. But having done so, they became nervous about the lack of marquee attraction, and their potential box-office return. To play Doc, they insisted they needed an established "draw." Thus, when the film reached the movie theaters, it was Burt Lancaster playing opposite Miss Booth.

Life being far more interesting than fiction, it was Miss Booth who won the Academy Award for her performance in the film of *Come Back, Little Sheba.*

In the following decade or so, Bill's career was spectacularly successful. His next play, produced by the Theatre Guild and Joshua Logan in 1953, was *Picnic.* It was a great success, and was eventually made into a major film hit by Columbia.

Once again, Bill's vivid dramatization of the love affair between the virile Hal Carter, who drifts into a small Kansas town, and Madge Owens, the proper girl he meets there, was a sensitive and moving evocation of his own Midwestern background. *Picnic* was a prime example of the sort of play which Brooks Atkinson of the New York *Times* referred to as "Inge's beguiling dramas about the private dilemmas of obscure people."

But the preparatory work, the behind-the-scenes stresses and tensions that preceded the triumphant opening night in February 1953 at the Music Box Theatre were enormously difficult and taxing for Bill.

Joshua Logan, who also directed the play, and who, in his book *Josh* refers to *Picnic* as "my biggest dramatic success," gives a vivid account of the torturous process of writing and rewriting that took place, throughout the rehearsals and on the play's out-of-town tryout run.

It certainly wasn't the casting that caused problems; the producers did a wonderful job of populating the stage with Inge's characters. Ralph Meeker played the swaggering, virile Hal, and Madge, his conquest, was played by the lovely and talented Janice Rule. Eileen Heckart gave an unforgettable performance as Rosemary, the spinster schoolteacher who finally breaks down, and in a highly dramatic scene, literally on her knees, pleads with Howard, her longtime boyfriend (wonderfully played by Arthur O'Connell), to marry her so she will not live out the rest of her days as an old maid. Kim Stanley, who would later play the lead in Bill's next play, *Bus Stop*, made her Broadway debut in *Picnic* as Madge's younger sister. And as Hal's college friend, the producers picked a young man fresh from Yale Drama School and started him on his career; his name was Paul Newman. Incidentally, Newman was a discovery of William Liebling, who saw Paul first at Yale.

It was the resolution of the play itself that caused the major problem. In Bill's original draft, in the third act, Hal leaves the small Kansas town on the run, deserting Madge. Should she stay, and face those wagging tongues that would jeer at her for the rest of her life, or should she pack a bag and run away to join him?

As the play went into rehearsal, Madge stayed.

Logan, who had worked closely with Inge throughout the play's preparation and contributed considerably to the rewrites —part of any good director's contribution to an author—became convinced the play's original ending was downbeat, ultimately too depressing for an audience to accept. He pressed Inge to change it, to have Madge go off to follow her man, no matter what the cost.

Audience reaction out of town was the deciding factor. People simply resented Inge's suggestion that Madge remained behind, and so Bill rewrote the ending. At the end of the third act, Madge went off after Hal. But still audiences were not satisfied. Nor were the critics. Even in St. Louis, Bill's own home base, *Picnic* did not get a warm reception.

Finally Logan stumbled onto what he believed was the answer to the audience's coldness. It lay in the play's hero, Hal, and his own personality. A loudmouth, a braggart, almost a bully, he possessed an animal magnetism, a machismo, true, strong enough to draw Madge to him—and yet was he the sort of hero figure with whom they could sympathize? Obviously not.

One night Logan found his answer. ". . . two men came up the aisle talking excitedly," he recalled in his book, "and I heard only two vehemently spoken words . . . *Some hero!*"

A speech was needed, one that was written, in which Hal's college friend, Alan—played by Paul Newman—tries to explain to Madge's mother that Hal's overbearing manner is merely a defense mechanism, spawned by his own insecurity; beneath all the bluster and bravado, Hal is truly a decent, likable guy.

The missing piece of character exposition was vital. It appeased the audiences, and from that point on, *Picnic* worked, and does to this day.

Picnic won for Bill the Critics Circle Award, as well as the Pulitzer Prize. The proceeds from the sale of the motion-picture rights were large enough to afford him financial security for years to come.

And yet, paradoxically, Bill refused to accept the audience's verdict as to his play's resolution. He never stopped believing that his original ending, in which Madge remains behind, bereft of Hal, in that small Kansas town, to live out her days as a figure of gossip and a pathetic town character, was truer to his own vision of his characters.

Years later, he rewrote *Picnic* and changed the ending. It was retitled *Summer Brave,* and it was Bill's way of proving he was right. Alas, he was wrong. Audiences preferred his play in its original form.

Summer Brave has come and gone, but *Picnic* remains, as strong and successful as it was all those years ago when Madge first ran off to follow her lover, Hal, to the applause of satisfied theatergoers.

Two years later, Bill had completed his next play, and it too would be a remarkably successful work. This time he had told the story of a third-rate nightclub singer who is catapulted into an impromptu romance with a somewhat tongue-tied cowboy during the course of a blizzard, in which both are marooned in a small café, once again in Kansas.

Bus Stop was produced by Robert Whitehead and Roger

Stevens, and directed by Harold Clurman. It opened on Broadway March 2, 1955. This time, there were no problems with Bill's plot or characters; audiences and critics responded warmly to his story. Later, Twentieth Century-Fox would buy the screen rights, and *Bus Stop* would become a smash-hit film starring the late Marilyn Monroe as Cherie, the little girl singer who is swept off her somewhat shaky feet by Bo Decker, the cowboy.

But on Broadway, our star was Kim Stanley, and that lady, who opened to tumultuous critical praise, developed serious personal problems early in the run of the play.

I've always felt Kim is one of the finest actresses we have. I'm certain she could have done almost anything on a stage and been triumphant, but she was hampered, nay, almost destroyed by her emotional difficulties.

I can remember evenings when Kim would go to the Music Box Theatre before her performance, would get made up and into her first-act costume, and then sit in her dressing room, paralyzed by inner turmoil, and announce that she couldn't find it in herself to go on that night. Some nights Bob Whitehead would talk to her, on others it would be Harold Clurman trying to provide her with enough self-assurance to face the ticket buyers.

Sometimes Kim made it and went on. Sometimes, she did not.

All of which was enormously sad.

Perhaps one day Kim will return to Broadway, and then again audiences will be treated to her rare talent.

Bill was working well in those days, and outwardly, at least, he seemed secure. Two years later, he had written another play, *The Dark at the Top of the Stairs.* Once again, he was dealing with the small-town background he understood so well, and the cast assembled by Arnold Saint Subber and Elia Kazan—he was also to direct the play—included such fine performers as Pat Hingle, Teresa Wright and Eileen Heckart.

The play was a hit, and I sold the screen rights to Warner Bros. for a film. But after that, Bill's career began to move in another direction, steadily away from success.

Things began to go downhill with his next play, *A Loss of Roses*. It was produced in 1959 by Lester Osterman and Saint Subber and directed by Danny Mann, who had been so successful in bringing *Sheba* to life almost ten years before.

I had made a preproduction deal for the screen rights with Twentieth Century-Fox before rehearsals began, and everything augured well. I represented Bill, of course, but I also had made the deal for Danny to direct, and since I had once again persuaded Shirley Booth, our star of *Sheba*, to play the lead in this play, I represented her as well. It was a serious mistake for me to be involved with all three areas of the play's production. As it turned out, no single agent, no matter how strong, could ever cope with the stresses and strains that developed.

They began almost immediately.

In the play the producers cast, opposite Miss Booth, an unknown young actor named Warren Beatty. This would be his first Broadway appearance, he was an alumnus of Lee Strasberg's well-known Actors Studio, and he was dreadfully uncertain of himself. Perhaps due to his Actors Studio training as a "method" actor, Warren's technique—or lack of it—involved a great deal of introspective questioning of his character in Bill's play. During rehearsals, he would interrupt matters with constant and interminable discussions in which he probed Danny Mann to explain his motivations in various scenes. Some of these discussions became quite acrimonious. Relations between Beatty and Mann were increasingly tense.

Meanwhile, the star, Miss Booth, was becoming very upset by all of this. She, who properly felt she was quite primary to the play, decided she was not getting her director's full attention. Since I represented her, and she had a run-of-the-play contract, I found myself caught in an outrageously difficult spot. It became much worse when she announced, during our out-of-town tryout, that unless certain changes were made by Bill for her in the script, and unless Mann would concentrate on her performance rather than spending so much time with Beatty's, she would not come into New York with the play.

Under such circumstances, what could anyone do? In the theater, what seems a rational solution often does not apply to the emotional problems of creative people. Certainly the producers could argue, and could go to Actors Equity and complain about this situation, but if their star did not want to play the leading role, no legal recourse would solve their problem.

I tried very hard to bring all the parties concerned together, but no matter how many different solutions I proposed on behalf of my clients, there was truly no single one that would satisfy Bill, Mann and Shirley at the same time. It was an outrageous position for me, totally a no-win affair, one that I have been careful never to permit to happen to me again.

There was one solution to the problem posed by Shirley Booth, and it happened. She withdrew by mutual agreement, and Betty Field, another fine actress, was brought in to replace her.

But the New York opening still lay ahead of us; things were not improving. I became increasingly certain *A Loss of Roses* could not succeed on Broadway in its present state. It would be better to cut our losses, roses or not.

I suggested to the producers that they close the play now, before it went to New York. Because of the money which Fox had paid for the screen rights, there would be no loss to them; actually there would be a profit. They agreed.

Then I went to Bill and said, "I really don't think the play should open. I urge you to agree."

He said, "Can I think about it?"

Since I have always followed a policy of letting my clients make the final decision, I said, "Of course, Bill, it's your play."

He came back the next day and said he'd decided to let the play open. And that was that. We went forward.

And so, against everyone else's better judgment (as it turned out), *A Loss of Roses* came to New York, got indifferent notices and played a painfully brief twenty-five performances.

Years later, Bill was interviewed by some magazine about his career, and he ironically said, when asked about *A Loss of Roses*, that what had happened was my fault. According to him, at that point, I should have been *firmer* with him.

Do I have to explain any further how difficult it is to be an agent?

Bill was that rarity among playwrights, a talented author who was able to write for the screen as well. He did the screenplay for *The Dark at the Top of the Stairs* and was successful in transferring his play to the screen, no mean feat. Countless other playwrights have tried and failed to accommodate their own dramas to the more complex demands of the screen.

In 1963, he wrote an original screenplay, *Splendor in the Grass,* for producer-director Elia Kazan, who made it into a highly successful film for Warner Bros. starring Natalie Wood and Warren Beatty. The picture won an Academy Award, and the kudos he received for that piece of work were most important for his own self-esteem.

But his first love was, and remained, the theater. That season, he was back on Broadway with another drama, *Natural Affection.* Tony Richardson directed; Kim Stanley starred.

It was an arresting play, one even now I am convinced would make a fine film, but sad to relate, it was a failure—not helped by opening in the midst of a newspaper strike.

By now, things were not going at all well with Bill. He had begun to be depressed by the downturn in his career, and emotionally he was finding it more and more difficult to cope with failure.

He decided to leave New York. He sold his lovely coop apartment and moved to California, from which he would not return. He even canceled his subscription to the New York *Times*—obviously a gesture aimed at its drama critic, who had savaged his recent work. He was that deeply wounded by the reviewers, who had, in truth, been quite cruel.

It is a strange phenomenon, but somehow or other, critics do take a sort of particular delight, consciously or not, in dragging down creative talents who have heretofore been successful. This is especially true for dramatists. No matter how well established the playwright's previous work, or how good the past body of produced plays, each opening night is yet another obstacle course, one that grows tougher, not one whit easier, to navigate. Instead of cherishing our talents and encouraging them, critics seem often to relish demolishing them.

There was no question that Bill was a deeply wounded man.

Things did not improve. *A Loss of Roses* was made into a film and retitled by Fox (for some dreadful reason) *The Stripper*. It was not a film to be remembered. When it was released in England, its title was changed to *A Woman of Summer*. That was some improvement, but the box-office results were not.

Bill went on to write other films, including *All Fall Down*, from James Leo Herlihy's novel, and his own *Bus Riley's Back in Town*.

And then, finally, having severed all of his other New York ties, he even decided to leave me. Perhaps he felt that in some way, having been involved in his failures, I was somehow responsible. But if such were his wishes, I would not stand in his way. He stayed with the agency I now worked with, International Famous, but he placed his affairs in the hands of Bridget Aschenberg, one of my talented associates.

A couple of years passed, and we had no direct communication whatsoever. And then, without warning, one morning my phone rang. It was Bill, in California. He said, "Audrey?" and I said, "Yes, Bill?"

He said, "I've decided I want to come back to your family."

Then I said something I was happy to say, which was, quite spontaneously, "Bill, you know I never left you."

There was a long silence from the other end, and I could tell he was close to tears. Finally he spoke. "I'll tell Bridget," he said, "because she has been very kind to me."

I said, "No, no, I'll do it. Don't you worry, I'll take care of it all."

"But she may be upset," he said, softly.

I assured him she would not be, and told him I'd call him back soon.

Then, when I spoke to Bridget, she said, "Oh, Bill has already called me to tell me about it. I asked him, 'Exactly when did you arrive at this decision, Bill?' And he said, 'This morning, when I woke up.'"

"Well," I told Bridget, "a couple of days may change all this."

But I promptly wrote him a note, with my tongue in cheek, in which I said, "Dear Bill, if you still feel the way you felt this morning, I am enclosing agency contracts."

He didn't change his mind, I'm happy to say. He signed them and for the last few years of his life he was again with me.

We talked a good deal, and we tried. He continued to work, but it wasn't easy. Producers weren't interested in his newest plays. True, there were revivals of his earlier successes, but his latest plays, *Where's Daddy?* and *The Last Pad*, were not successful.

Leland Hayward attempted a production of *Picnic* as a musical, but it did not succeed. It closed out of town.

Meanwhile, I'd gone to California and seen him out there. I was shocked at what I saw. Bill had fallen off the wagon again, and the alcohol had caused him to become grossly fat. He told me he'd been going to a psychoanalyst out there, but he'd decided it was no help, and he'd left the doctor. Then he had been put into a hospital for treatment, but had walked out of it. It was painfully obvious that Bill was on a self-destructive path, one which could have drastic consequences.

He had done another rewrite of *Picnic*, that same version in which he'd revised the ending to satisfy his own taste. It was now called *Summer Brave*, and I had arranged for a tryout production of it to be played by the company at the summer theater in Stockbridge, Massachusetts. Since, at one time, Bill had been a patient there, at the Riggs Sanitarium, I reasoned it would be extremely fortuitous if we could get him out of Southern California and to Stockbridge; he could be there while his play was being produced, and probably return to Riggs, where there were competent people to care for him. And if the tryout was successful it might go a long way toward restoring Bill's self-confidence.

Bill agreed, and he got in touch with the people at Riggs, but as it turned out, sadly, they didn't have room for him at that time. And he did not come East to be there for the run of the play in Stockbridge.

I've always felt that perhaps if he'd seen *Summer Brave*, and become involved in the production at Stockbridge, gone back to his first love, the theater, it might have helped him.

But this is a wistful reflection on my part. It was not long after this I received the dreadful news. Bill had succeeded in committing suicide.

It's now three decades since the wonderfully exciting Sunday night when *Come Back, Little Sheba* was given its first performance in Westport. Somehow or other, in the way this business operates, Bill Inge's work is considered by the professional carpers and tastemakers to have become somewhat passé, hopelessly old-fashioned, perhaps permanently out of date.

I refuse to accept such a judgment. Bill had his failures, true, but which of my clients has not? Only mediocrities are afraid to dare.

I am convinced the body of his work, those warm and sensitive dramas in which he brought to life the small-town Americans he knew and identified with so much, will survive. I have no doubt Bill will remain a permanent and important force in our literature of the theater.

14

*A Prologue, a Trilogy
and an Epilogue*

In January 1980, I had a long-distance call from California, from David Rintels. He is a gentleman who's been involved in the theater and in television, both as a dramatist and a producer.

He told me he was coming to New York shortly, and would be bringing with him Ethel Winant, one of the vice-presidents of NBC Television, with whom Rintels is also associated. "We would like to have lunch with you and discuss a project we have in mind," he said.

We agreed on a date. And when we met, Rintels explained what our meeting was about. In conjunction with NBC, he had developed a concept for television which consisted of a series of dramatic productions that would be done live from local theaters around the country.

Since 1962, most television production has been produced either on film or on videotape. "I believe we've lost a very essential ingredient that way," he explained. "There's an excitement for an audience in watching a performance as it actually happens—the way opera is being produced on PBS. We'd like to try the same technique on drama. It worked before, in the early days of television; there's no reason why it couldn't be done again."

It seemed that he and Miss Winant had decided on the play they would like to produce as the first of this new series of live ventures. "It's one which you represent," he told me. "It's the last play in *The Texas Trilogy* by Preston Jones, *The Oldest Living Graduate.*"

Mr. Rintels had recently completed a television film which starred Henry Fonda. It was an adaptation of the book *Gideon's Trumpet,* and it was due to be seen shortly. He and Fonda had worked well together in the past, and he was eager to do another show with that superb actor. He'd discussed *The Oldest Living Graduate* with Fonda, and was pleased to report that Fonda was most interested in playing the leading role.

"We are thinking of doing it down in Dallas, where it was originally performed," said Mr. Rintels. "It would star Fonda and a good supporting cast, and hopefully in the Dallas Theater Center, where it had its premiere. We'd have a two-hour prime-time period on NBC, and that means that Preston Jones's play will be seen by millions of home viewers for the first time. Don't you think that's an exciting idea?"

"I think it's marvelous," I said. I was truly thrilled. "When will you start?"

"We'd like to schedule this performance for the night of the seventh of April," he said. "That would have been Preston Jones's forty-fourth birthday."

That made it a very tight schedule.

"Can we go back to your office and discuss a deal?" he asked.

"We don't have to wait that long," I said. "We can start right now."

Trilogy

After all these years it's become something of a reflex. I can pick up a new playscript by an author with whose work I'm unfamiliar, and my radar can usually sense, within the first ten

pages or so, whether or not I'm reading the work of someone
with talent.

And I'm reporting no trade secret if I report that out of all
those scripts I bring home each night and on the weekend, it's
rare when I turn up, from beneath the haystack of typed pages,
that shining needle.

But one keeps on reading, and hoping. And then, when one
discovers *three* plays—all by the same author—all of them cen-
tered on the same dusty West Texas town, written with a true
dramatist's gift, each play brimming with life and warmth and
sympathy for the lives of one's fellowman—ah, my friends, that
is indeed a rare and wonderful experience.

In my life, it only happened once.

And I did not read the plays. I saw them first on a stage,
down in Dallas.

As I've said before, when I fall in love with a talent, I fall
headlong. In the case of *The Texas Trilogy,* those three fine plays
I'll tell you about, I not only became involved with them as the
author's agent, but I also fell in love with their author, a greatly
talented and remarkable man, a true "natural" (as they say on
the sports pages), Mr. Preston Jones.

If it had not been for Kay Brown, I might not have gone
down to Dallas in the first place.

Kay had been asked to go down to Dallas to attend a sort of
"play market," at the Dallas Theater Center, a year-round regional company operated by a very capable man named Paul
Baker. Each year, Baker's company would perform new plays by
local authors, and in essence display their wares for potential
producers and interested theatrical people.

Kay said, "Audrey, I do think you should come down with
me," and after I'd thought that over, I agreed with her. So I
called Mr. Baker down in Dallas, and he promptly invited me.
Kay and I went down together.

We saw several plays, and then the curtain rose on a performance of a new play called *The Last Meeting of the Knights of
the White Magnolias.*

By the time the third act ended, I knew I'd encountered a remarkable piece of original playwriting.

Then I met the author, Preston Jones. He was a large, amiable, broad-shouldered gentleman, totally dissimilar to most playwrights I'd ever met. He wore a Western sombrero and a zip-up jacket, and seemed to have stepped right out of the cast of his own play. Which he did, for as an actor with Paul Baker's company, Preston had performed in his own play that night. In fact, I discovered Preston had been involved with the Dallas Theater Center as an actor for the past eighteen years. It was during that time he'd met and courted his wife, an actress-director named Mary Sue Jones, a lovely, sensitive lady.

Between puffs on his pipe, Preston explained to me what had inspired him to begin writing plays. He'd been assigned to read scripts submitted by hopeful authors to Paul Baker. "I didn't think any of 'em were any good," he drawled, "and so I decided to try to write a few myself."

Later, he enlarged on the subject. "I'll tell you," he told an interviewer, "the play that really affected me, turned everything around for me, was *Our Town,* which we did a few years ago. I played the stage manager. And I remember thinking while we were working on it that if I could write a play as beautiful as that, well, I'd quit acting."

I was tremendously impressed by what I'd seen. It was clear that Preston Jones, of Dallas, had achieved something that no other contemporary American playwright I can think of has accomplished. *The Last Meeting* was the first play of a trilogy, based on the same West Texas town. Three interconnected plays —a mammoth undertaking. The only other author I can think of in these days who has pulled it off successfully is Alan Ayckbourn, a prolific Englishman, who created the comedic trilogy, *The Norman Conquests,* several years ago.

What this actor-turned-writer had done was to take a broad canvas—Bradleyville, Texas—and populated all three plays with a frieze of characters, all townspeople. Skillfully interwoven, at different stages of their lives, some of them appeared in one play, or two, some in all three. *The Last Meeting* deals with the brethren of a moribund local fraternal group, on the night in which their tired organization finally comes apart. *Lu Ann Hampton Laverty Oberlander* is a sensitively drawn portrait of a young blond cheerleader. In the course of three acts, we learn a great deal about her boring and depressing post-high-school life, and her two unfortunate marriages. Lu Ann wanders through life a victim, and yet the ultimate irony is she will never know this.

And finally, there is *The Oldest Living Graduate,* a deeply moving play about the twilight days of Colonel J. C. Kinkaid, a graduate of the Mirabeau B. Lamar Military Academy and a World War I veteran, who returned home shell-shocked, and lives out his life in a semi-fantasy world.

In the published version of *The Texas Trilogy,* Preston would later describe the town: ". . . Bradleyville, Texas—population 6,000—a small, dead West Texas town in the middle of a big, dead West Texas prairie between Abilene and San Angelo. The new highway has bypassed it, and now the world is trying to."

That first night, I told Preston I would be very interested in trying to do what I could to get his trilogy a Broadway production, even though I was far from certain that I could arrange that. As a matter of fact, someone heard me say, later, "I never thought at my age I'd take on a trilogy."

But it seemed to me he was the sort of playwright that our theater desperately needs, an authentic American voice. I told him if he wished to have me represent him, I'd send him a contract when I returned to New York.

Obviously pleased, he told me that would be just fine with him.

(Later, Preston's sister confided to me that when the agency contracts arrived from my office in his mail for his signature, Preston dashed over to her house, waved them happily at her, chortling, "Look here—I got me an *agent!*")

The second of Preston's plays, *Lu Ann Hampton Laverty Oberlander,* was given its first performance at the Dallas Theater Center by Paul Baker's company in February 1974, and in November 1974, *The Oldest Living Graduate* was produced. All three plays were eventually moved from the Down Center Stage of the Dallas Theater Center up to the main stage, the Kalita

Humphreys Theater, where they became a repertory bill, all three plays being performed in sequence, on successive nights.

It was not until just before New Year's in 1975 that I was to see all three plays of *The Texas Trilogy*. Mr. Baker decided to have them all performed, all three in *one* evening, and down I went to Dallas again.

That was truly a marathon of an evening. The first curtain went up at 7 P.M. At around 10 P.M., there was an intermission during which the audience was served a delicious Texas barbecue supper in the lobby.

In another interview, Preston recalled, "One ol' boy from West Texas was in the lobby, and he was just poppin' corks and slurpin' champagne and saying over and over 'God bless Colorado City! God bless Colorado City!' "

Which turns out to be the "Bradleyville," of Preston's work. Preston was from New Mexico, but during the fifties, he had spent several years in the town.

After the barbecue, we returned to the theater. The final curtain did not fall on *The Oldest Living Graduate* until nearly 2 A.M.

So I left Dallas and returned to New York with a trilogy in my briefcase, three new plays by a very talented regional playwright.

Now came a major problem.

How was I to get them produced on Broadway?

Thinking about it on the plane coming back, I decided that it would be totally impractical to attempt *The Texas Trilogy* Dallas style, in one sitting, in New York. New Yorkers weren't accustomed to sitting that long in one theater seat. Nobody in Manhattan would serve an audience a Texas barbecue and champagne between the plays. And if the curtain came down at 2 A.M., where would the cabs be, to take the audience safely home?

No, I was certain I had to find a producer who would take on all three plays and put them into a theater, to be run in three successive performances.

Far from an easy problem to solve.

To begin with, there are now few knowledgeable producers in the so-called Broadway theater. In those years when I first began to sell plays, I could run down a list of thirty to forty potential buyers, all of them year-round entrepreneurs, in business fifty-two weeks of the year. Offices run by people with proven track records, such as George Abbott, Max Gordon, Brock Pemberton and Antoinette Perry, the Theatre Guild, Howard Lindsay and Russel Crouse, Cheryl Crawford, Kermit Bloomgarden, David Merrick and Leland Hayward, who had regular schedules of theatrical productions planned and executed each season. These days, one can count such full-time producers left in New York on the fingers of both hands—and have several fingers left over. Most so-called producers today have little or no theatrical background, and really aren't in the business on a permanent basis. Creative considerations cannot mean much to the impromptu syndicates which are brought together to finance single productions these days. And costs are so high, the expense of running a show each week so enormous, that the box office has, with few exceptions, taken complete precedence over art.

Which is why, most often, I prefer to start a project with a production somewhere in a regional theater. There, free from most of the high-tension cost-induced stresses of the Broadway scene, creative people can function on a less make-or-break level. It is only out in the hinterlands (as George Burns is so fond of pointing out) that we have a place where aspiring talent has the necessary room to be lousy.

But *The Texas Trilogy* had already succeeded in a regional theater, and it was a fine piece of work. It had no place to go except to New York. Who would take it on?

I had an author hitherto inexperienced. Pure, kind and gentle. I wanted to find him a producer of the same ilk.

That made it even harder.

The word had already gotten out about *The Texas Trilogy*. Two prospective producers were already pursuing me. Before I could make any decision of my own, I heard from Alexander H.

l Brynner congratulating Shirley Booth
the night when both of them received
onys for their performances, he as the
ing of Siam, she in the musical *A Tree
rows in Brooklyn*.

Karl Malden, one of Liebling's clients in
the days before Karl rescued travelers
from their foreign fiscal problems.

Eli Wallach, costarring in Tennessee
lovely play *The Rose Tattoo*.

Pat Hingle, a client of long standing with
Liebling.

ul Newman and Geraldine Page in *Sweet Bird of Youth*. (COURTESY OF THE WALTER
AMPDEN–EDWIN BOOTH THEATRE COLLECTION AND LIBRARY AT THE PLAYERS CLUB).

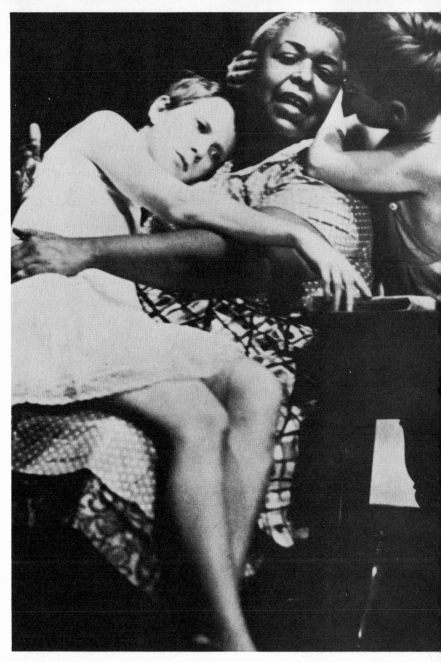

Ethel Waters, Julie Harris and Brandon deWilde in Carson McCullers' *Member of the
Wedding*. (COURTESY OF THE WALTER HAMPDEN–EDWIN BOOTH THEATRE COLLECTION AND
LIBRARY AT THE PLAYERS CLUB).

Cohen, who indicated in no uncertain terms that he was interested in Preston's plays, and was ready to produce them.

Somehow, I didn't think Mr. Cohen was the right producer, not for Preston. I'm still enough of an altruist to believe that when one produces a play, it is because one has fallen in love. If you haven't fallen in love with that play, then you shouldn't begin. Preston, and his plays, needed someone who was totally in love with *The Texas Trilogy*. I told Mr. Cohen I was afraid he was not the right man.

Mr. Cohen did not agree with me. He called and insisted he wished to produce the plays. Again, I tried to talk him out of doing them. He became angry, and after the call he proceeded to write a letter to Marvin Josephson, the head of ICM, and my boss. In his letter Mr. Cohen accused me of having been dishonest and unethical and having behaved in a most improper fashion in my efforts to keep him from optioning the rights to Preston's work.

Mr. Josephson showed me the letter. I explained my position. He said, "Audrey, in this matter, you are in total charge. We will back you up completely."

I then proceeded to write a letter to Mr. Cohen in which I tried again to explain my reasoning. I said I felt Preston Jones needed a different sort of a producer, and as his agent, acting on his behalf, I felt I had to make the final judgment.

Mr. Cohen wrote an even angrier letter in response.

Mr. Josephson advised me to drop the matter. I did so.

Meanwhile, without any warning, or discussion, out of the mail came a contract, drawn by Joseph Papp, of the Public Theater, downtown, calling for a production of *The Texas Trilogy* there. The contract was signed, as if it were a fait accompli.

I called Mr. Papp's assistant, Bernard Gersten, and said I was sorry, but in my opinion this was not the way to treat a new gifted playwright. One simply could not assume that because one had decided one wanted to produce the plays, one automatically had them.

When this message was delivered to him, Mr. Papp became very annoyed with me. Mr. Gersten called and asked for the contracts to be returned forthwith.

For some time after that, I heard absolutely nothing from Mr. Papp. Then, a year or so later, he called my office.

"Audrey," he announced, "this is Joe Papp. I just called up to tell you I'm talking to you again."

Meekly I accepted this bulletin.

(Only later, alas, did I think of what I should have told him, which would have been, "Why, Joe, *I* didn't know we weren't talking.")

A week or so later, there was a reading scheduled at the Public Theater, downtown, of a new play by one of my young playwrights, *G.R. Point*, by David Berry. I called up Joe, and very sweetly explained that he was my client. "May I come to the reading, Joe?" I asked.

"Why, of course, Audrey," he replied.

But after the reading, there was a postperformance conference, upstairs in Mr. Papp's office, to which I was not invited.

Preston needed a proper theatrical home. I still didn't have one for him.

One must use all sorts of techniques in order to place a new play with the right producer. Each submission calls for a new scenario.

Which, I suppose, is what makes each day in my office so interesting.

And then I thought of Robert Whitehead.

I'd worked with that gentleman before; he'd been involved with Carson McCullers' *The Member of the Wedding*, and Bill Inge's *Bus Stop*, as well as many other excellent productions. I decided that from the standpoint of temperament he would be very good for Preston. I also was certain he would give *The Texas Trilogy* the care and attention so necessary to Preston's first commercial production.

I called Bob. He'd heard of the three plays, of course, but he had no idea what they were about. I'm afraid I was very arbitrary with him. I told him, "Robert, I want you to read these three plays over the weekend, and then I want you to call me Monday morning and tell me if you want to produce them."

I didn't have many copies, and I arranged to leave one precious set at the Royalton Hotel desk for him to pick up. He was staying in New York, and I'd be going up to Westport for the weekend. Up there, for the next forty-eight hours, I tried not to think about whether or not Bob was falling in love with what he was reading.

He called Monday morning, and to my utter delight, he said, "Audrey, you're right. I would like to produce these plays."

We drew up the contracts.

Having been partnered previously with our mutual friend Roger L. Stevens, the director of the Kennedy Center, in Washington, D.C., Bob decided to join forces with him again. And thus, under proper auspices at last, the production of *The Texas Trilogy* for Broadway got under way.

Alan Schneider was hired as the director.

Preston had had so much experience in the theater that I discovered he was inclined to let a director he trusted simply proceed. But I called him and said, "Now, Preston, this New York opening is going to be terribly important, and you *must* be there to keep an eye on casting." And then I had the funniest feeling perhaps he'd never been to New York, ever, at all, so I asked him. Ah, but it turned out that yes, he had. He said, "Sure, Miss Wood," in that cowboy drawl. "I was there in 1962 for two days. Nice town. I liked it."

The arrangements were made for him to come up.

I called him down in Texas, to check on his arrival date, and then he said, "Miss Wood, where do you think I'm gonna stay? At the Algon-*queen* Hotel."

"Oh, that's marvelous, Preston," I replied. "I live right across the street, and we can see each other often."

There was a pause, and then he said, "Do you know what's at the Algon-*queen*? The Round Table." He said it with such reverence. "Miss Wood," he asked, "do you think it's still there?"

So I told him, "Well, Preston, perhaps the table's there, but I don't know whether any of those people who *sat* at it are still there."

He seemed rather disappointed. I suppose he'd been looking forward to seeing all those literary and theatrical luminaries who had once populated the Algonquin. From all those miles away, in the Southwest, where he'd grown up, they all must have seemed still very much alive.

So he came to New York alone. His wife was to join him later, and now he was across the street, at the Algonquin. The casting for *The Texas Trilogy* had begun, and one day we met for a drink, to discuss the way things were going.

There sat my displaced Texan playwright, in his zip-up jacket and sombrero, puffing on his pipe. He was very much in awe of his surroundings. Manhattan was a very big change for him.

"Do you know what I did last night?" he inquired.

I said I didn't.

"Well," drawled Preston, "I walked down the street, and I saw a sign pointin' upstairs, and it said TOPLESS GIRLS, and I decided I'd go up there and see what that was all about."

"And what was it all about?" I asked.

He said, "Well, ma'am, I walked through the door, and up the stairs, and I got me a drink, and you know, Miss Wood, they weren't topless, they were plumb naked!"

"Oh, my, Preston," I said, "what did you do?"

He said "I finished my drink and I left, that's what!"

It wasn't exactly the Round Table.

Finally the day came when the three plays he'd written were due to go into rehearsal.

In celebration, I asked Preston to join me at the Algonquin for lunch. I came in, and there he was, sitting at the table, waiting for me, still in his zip-up jacket. I asked him what he'd like to drink, and he ordered a Bloody Mary. When we'd finished our drinks, I asked him what he'd like to eat.

"I believe I'd like another Bloody Mary," he told me, and then he began to tell me a long, rambling story about where he'd been the night before, where he'd eaten, what the food had been, and how today his stomach wasn't very happy about it all.

Then, this big man, this broad-shouldered Texan, so warm and placid and jovial most of the time, looked at me and said softly, "You know, Miss Wood, I'm *scared.*"

Of course he was. I understood perfectly.

Imagine, coming up from Dallas, having never been produced on a Broadway stage, and having *three* of your plays going into rehearsal—knowing that it meant facing, a few weeks from now, those big-town New York critics . . .

Who wouldn't have been frightened?

After our lunch, we walked across town to the first rehearsal, which was held at the Little Theatre, on West Forty-fourth Street. And I, who came up to Preston's waist—he was so much taller than I—held his hand all the way to the stage door.

Then the rehearsals began. I sat beside him in the dark empty row, trying to give him some support during this difficult period. My client was being thrown headlong into the pressure cooker that is the commercial Broadway theater. I'd seen those same pressures destroy many other talents, some of them much stronger than Preston. My most urgent wish was that this amiable man, so gifted, would survive.

Sometime during that first day, there came a point when Alan Schneider was putting his actors through the scenes of *The Oldest Living Graduate.* Colonel Kinkaid, who was played by a fine actor, Fred Gwynne, has a highly emotional scene at the end of the play, where, approaching his own death, the old veteran turns over a piece of real estate, land which he's always cherished and protected, to his son, who wants to turn it into a lakefront development.

Suddenly, as the actors were going through their lines, I became conscious of Preston, in the darkened theater. His head was down, resting on the back of the seat in front of him, and he was crying, very softly.

That's when I realized that all these characters he'd written about were people he'd known. Obviously "Colonel Kinkaid" was someone he'd been very close to and loved, perhaps even a member of his family.

Finally, the rehearsal period ended, and *The Texas Trilogy* company went down to Washington, to prepare for the opening at the Kennedy Center.

I went down for the opening.

Everything seemed to be in order. Preston was holding up very well under the constant tension. Only once did he reveal the depth of his urgent emotion that was masked by his jovial exterior. We were seated in the Eisenhower Theatre, watching the final run-through. Suddenly, Preston turned away from the stage, leaned over to me and said, "God, it's so important to me to have a hit!"

For a while there, it seemed as if he did.

The Washington critics gave *The Texas Trilogy* marvelous reviews. There were raves for the acting, for the direction, and huzzas for the newly discovered playwright from Texas. Business was marvelous as well.

Paradoxically, it was this wildly enthusiastic reception which became our biggest problem.

Preston Jones was the talk of Washington, and that talk found its way back to New York. Gossip columnists picked up on the success of *The Texas Trilogy*. The media latched on to him; a week before we were due to come to New York, *Saturday Review* had a long article on Preston, with his picture in color on the cover, and beneath it the caption "Has Texas Spawned a New O'Neill?"

When I saw that, I was terrified.

I knew how dangerous this could be for Preston. With all of this out-of-town hoopla going on, he was being put into a terribly vulnerable position with those New York critics, whom he still had to face.

Long ago, I'd learned one basic lesson. New Yorkers do not

like to be told by out-of-town critics how good something is. It puts their teeth on edge; they feel challenged. If there is discovering to be done, it will be done here in New York, thank you . . .

I tried to explain this to Preston. "Please, believe me," I told him, "we're not there yet. It's wonderful we've done so well here in Washington, but this does not mean the same will happen in New York."

And it didn't happen in New York.

The town's leading critic, in 1977, was Clive Barnes, of the New York *Times*. When he reviewed *The Texas Trilogy*, it certainly seemed as if his teeth were on edge, and he did indeed feel challenged.

He was most unimpressed by Preston's limning of Bradleyville, and its inhabitants. West Texas was certainly foreign territory for Mr. Barnes, an Englishman whose background for dramatic criticism had consisted for some years in ballet criticism.

He seemed confused by what he saw. In his review of the second play, *Lu Ann Hampton Laverty Oberlander*, he made the statement that it had only begun to dawn on him now that all three of these plays were taking place in the same town.

How he could have been that obtuse about *The Texas Trilogy* remains, to this day, beyond my comprehension. Certainly he'd been exposed to the out-of-town reviews and articles; he must have known Preston was writing about one specific place.

In retrospect, I've thought it was a great mistake on our part not to have invited Mr. Barnes down to Washington, so he might have been in on the discovery taking place there in those successful weeks at the Kennedy Center. I don't know whether or not he would have come, but if he had he might not have been so obviously hostile to the plays when they arrived in New York.

But then again, this is the same critic who, after the death of my client Bill Inge, wrote a review of one of Bill's plays that had been revived, one which took place in Kansas, which Barnes had never seen before, and referred to Bill as "a writer of soap operas."

If a critic from England could not understand Kansas, how could one expect him to relate to West Texas?

After each of the opening nights of the three plays, Bob Whitehead and Roger Stevens gave a party. Preston, now wearing a dinner jacket—quite a change of costume for him—stood there, having a few drinks, when somebody brought in that peculiar review from Clive Barnes.

"Well," said Preston, "if he doesn't understand this one, I'll write another. If he doesn't understand *that*, I'll write another, damn it!"

There were other New York reviews that were much more affirmative. But, as anyone who's been around this business will agree, without a good review from the New York *Times*, you have a serious problem. Your play may not be terminal, but you're not healthy.

The Texas Trilogy had a respectable Broadway run, but when it closed it was far from a commercial success.

Outwardly, Preston took the closing well. That he was disappointed was obvious. But none of us knew how deeply he'd been hurt by those reviews.

He did what any good writer must do in order to survive such a failure. The rider who's been thrown gets back on his horse. The writer goes back to work.

He returned to Dallas and continued to act and write at the Dallas Theater Center. His experience as an actor had taught him a great deal about playwriting.

To an interviewer, Preston said, "I think my acting experience has taught me to use the actor as a story-teller. I think a lot of the time the actor can tell the offstage story better than the action can be shown onstage. And just in general—it's taught me to *trust* actors . . . the bits of business, the ad-libs they contribute, they're almost always right. And you'll find these scattered all through my plays. I take whatever I can get."

He had written another play, *A Place on the Magdalena Flats,* and it was given a production in the summer of 1979, at the University of Wisconsin.

The play deals with a section of New Mexico where there are tremendous dust storms, and again, he was writing about people close to him. When he'd finished the play he explained to an interviewer, ". . . I always said I'd write a play about my brother, and this is it. He more or less raised me, for better or for worse. The story is my own doing, but the central character is drawn right from life—from him. He was a Bataan veteran, one of those New Mexico National Guard boys who survived the goddamn Death March and sat out the war in a Japanese prison camp. Well, as you can imagine, it changed his whole life. He's still very bitter. And the play's about afterward—how it did change his life when he settled on this ranch he had."

A Place on the Magdalena Flats was well received. It is a very strong drama, a triangle between a husband and wife and the husband's younger brother. I did not feel it was right for a Broadway production, but I'm certain it will be produced at many regional theaters in years to come.

Between his acting jobs—he had returned to the Dallas Theater Center—Preston had written yet another play, this one called *Santa Fe Sunshine.* It was a much lighter work, done with warmth and humor, that dealt with a group of artistic types living in that New Mexico town. I went out to see a production in Santa Fe, too, and I thought it was a good job of work, but also not right for New York.

When I discussed it with him afterward, I said I didn't think we should try for a commercial producer. Preston didn't argue. He left such decisions to me. Once he assumed I was his agent, that was that. He went along with my suggestion that we try to sell the amateur rights to the play to the Dramatists Play Service. Which I did.

So often, a playwright whose work has not measured up to his own expectations, who is suffering from a bruised ego, will resist such advice. He'll insist that at least I should give his play a try, and send it around. Inevitably, we discover we were merely postponing the inevitable.

But that wasn't Preston's style. He was a thorough professional. He listened.

He wrote still another play, which is called *Remember*. Its title is based on that wonderful and wistful Irving Berlin ballad of the mid-twenties. In the summer of 1979, it had its first production down in Dallas, and I went to see it.

It's a poignant play. The story of a man, an actor, who returns to the small town where he used to live, where he grew up, it's about how he tries to find all his old buddies, and encounters the woman with whom he was once in love.

This man isn't a great actor, merely a member of a second-rate touring company, but although he's far from heroic, Preston has drawn a marvelous character by dramatizing all the man's warm remembrances of his past, brought together with the realities of his present.

There's obviously a great deal of autobiographical feeling in Preston's leading character. He's left all sorts of little clues scattered throughout the play. For instance, in the play, his lead was once a Jesuit. As a young man, so had been Preston. In the play, his lead comes to seek out a priest whom he remembers so fondly. He discovers the priest has left the order.

One day, I will find the right leading man for *Remember*. The part calls for someone as good as, say, Jack Lemmon. I'll keep on looking, and when I make the proper marriage between play and actor, with the blessing of a good producer, then we'll bring Preston Jones back to Broadway.

There were other assignments. A film producer decided *The Texas Trilogy* would be good material for the screen, and Preston sat down and developed a screenplay involving scenes and characters from all three plays. It's a fine job of work, and again is on the potential list.

One day in 1978, the New York *Times* called, and an editor inquired whether Preston might consider writing an article for the paper, dealing with his reminiscences of his childhood Thanksgiving in Texas. I put in a call to Preston and suggested he might want to take on such a job.

With absolutely no humor, Preston demurred. "Oh *no,* Miss Wood, I couldn't do that," he said. "I just *couldn't* write that."

"For heaven's sake, why not?" I asked.

"Well," he drawled, "'cause I was born in Albuquerque, New Mexico."

He finally gave in and the *Times* ran the piece on its Op Ed page.

In the season of 1979–80, Preston was rehearsing for a role in *A Man for All Seasons,* and he and his wife were scheduled to appear, later in the year, as George and Martha, in *Who's Afraid of Virginia Woolf?*

Then, one dreadful day in September, he was found unconscious by his friends, and rushed to St. Paul's Hospital, in Dallas. The diagnosis was bleeding ulcers, and he was immediately operated on. By the middle of that week, he seemed to be much better, and recovering.

I called him over the weekend, and he spoke to me from his hospital bed. "I'm *fine,* Miss Wood," he assured me. He sounded very cheerful and quite his old self, full of beans. "Gonna be up and out of here right away!"

But there were massive complications.

He died on September 19, 1979, two days later. He was forty-three years old.

I flew down to Dallas for the funeral. It was a moving ceremony. Everyone at the Dallas Theater Center collaborated on its rite, which consisted of readings from Preston's favorite authors.

It began with an excerpt from John Steinbeck's *Sweet Thursday,* a passage called "Lousy Wednesday," which quite adequately expressed how those of us who'd known and loved this man felt. Then there was a long passage from *Huckleberry Finn,* in which Mark Twain's two boys learn about acting the role of King Richard III from the Duke while floating down the river. There was a poem from Sir Philip Sidney called "Get Hence, Foul Grief," a reading from Thomas Wolfe's *You Can't Go Home Again,* and from *The Sea of Grass,* by Conrad Richter, a brief and moving excerpt about New Mexico, Preston's home state, by the American Indian author N. Scott Momaday, and finally, this quote from *Julius Caesar:*

> . . . His life was gentle, and the elements
> So mix'd in him that Nature might stand up
> And say to all the world, "This was a man!"

In Mel Gussow's obituary in the New York *Times*, Preston was quoted as having been interviewed about the failure of *The Texas Trilogy* in New York, two years before. When asked by a reporter how he'd felt about the disappointment, he is quoted as having said, "Hell, we were the longest running Texas trilogy in history!"

But when my good friend Roger Stevens, who'd gone through the whole experience as coproducer, called me up to commiserate with me on Preston's tragic death he said, "Audrey, do you know what killed Preston?"

"Bleeding ulcers," I said.

"No," said Roger. "It was the New York critics."

Epilogue

In early March 1980, I had another call from David Rintels, of NBC Television. For the past several months he'd been working on the forthcoming production, that two-hour live performance of Preston's play *The Oldest Living Graduate*, which was scheduled to be done on the night of April 7.

It would be quite a night. His cast, with Henry Fonda as the star, would include Cloris Leachman, George Grizzard, and John Lithgow. The director was Jack Hofsiss, who earlier had staged the smash-hit drama *The Elephant Man*.

"Everything is going very well," reported Mr. Rintels. "Would you consider flying down to Dallas for the weekend, as the guest of NBC, and being there for the telecast?"

Who could possibly say no to such an offer?

Friday afternoon, that first week in April, I was picked up at my office by a limousine and driven to Kennedy; I arrived in Dallas that night.

The next morning, I went over to the rehearsal.

The telecast would be taking place from the stage of the Southern Methodist University Theater. During the preparatory phases of this project, certain problems had arisen, most of them logistic. Eventually, instead of basing the performance at Paul Baker's Dallas Theater Group, Preston's home base for so many years, the NBC decision had been to use SMU's large physical plant. The entire affair was to be a benefit, the proceeds, at one hundred dollars per seat, to go to that theater. The house had been sold out weeks earlier.

When I walked into the theater, it proved to be quite a reunion. George Grizzard, an old friend, looked down from the stage where he was rehearsing, waved, and said "Audrey—you'd go *any*place to see a play, right?" Cloris Leachman, who'd been an aspiring ingenue, in the outer office waiting patiently all those years back, to see Liebling, embraced me. I had a lovely chat with Henry Fonda, whom I'd once represented, during those years when we were both part of MCA.

Everything seemed to be under control. No crises. Forty-eight hours from now, the red lights would glow in these TV cameras, and this cast would give a performance of *The Oldest Living Graduate* that would be shown in millions of American homes.

How ironic that Preston would not be there, to savor his evening of triumph.

I spent a good deal of time with Mary Sue, Preston's widow. She and Preston had been married for eighteen years; truly, it had been a fine marriage for both of them.

Sunday morning, she asked me if I'd like to go visit the cemetery where Preston was buried, and the two of us made the pilgrimage together.

When I'd arrived in Dallas, I found all sorts of flowers waiting for me in my hotel suite. I thought we should share them with Preston. So we brought them along.

He'd been buried in a beautiful little cemetery.

As we stood there, I noticed that nearby there was another new grave, and hanging above the new stone was a little birdhouse. Mary Sue explained to me it had been placed there by a gypsy family; the grave was of one of their number. In the birdhouse were placed cigarettes and other little dainties, bits of

candy and such, left there by the gypsies for the ghosts of other
gypsies who'd passed on.

Somehow, I felt Preston would have liked it very much. Actors and gypsies have always had an affinity.

Mary Sue agreed with me.

Monday morning, all the NBC brass began to assemble in
Dallas. This was truly to be a major programming event. In
newspapers all over the country, NBC took full-page adver-
tisements to announce tonight's performance.

Mr. Rintels called and asked me to come join him in his suite.

He said, "We've decided we would like to do something special to honor Preston tonight, and we'd like to put on a brief af-
terpiece at the end of the third act."

I thought this a fine idea. Even though it was very short notice, we all joined forces. I got in touch with Mary Sue, who
hurriedly provided Rintels with some photographs of Preston.
The local public TV station in Dallas had produced a documentary on Preston a year or so before. Unfortunately, the film had
not been shown outside of Texas. But the station management
was delighted to run it for Rintels. By midday, he'd seen it and
requested permission to show excerpts of the documentary that
night over NBC. Within four hours, the clearances had been
granted; the station was delighted to cooperate. Working with
remarkable speed and efficiency, Rintels and his production
crew were able to assemble the brief tribute to Preston. By the
end of the day, it was ready to show the TV audience. Henry
Fonda would do the live narration that night.

Shortly before we were due to go over to the theater for the
performance, I had a long-distance call from my old friend
Roger Stevens, in Washington. Roger had long since proved by
coproducing *The Texas Trilogy* that he is as much a devotee of
Preston's work as I am.

"Audrey," he asked, "what would you think of my moving this
whole production over here to the Kennedy Center?"

Roger is a man of rapid-fire decisions.

I told him I thought it would be a splendid project, except for
one practical consideration. "Tomorrow morning, once they've

finished their performance here, I'm certain all these marvelous people will be separating," I pointed out.

"Well, it's certainly worth thinking about," said Roger. "I won't be here at nine P.M., damn it, I've got another engagement, but I know what I'll do: I'll have a friend of mine do a videotape of it for me, and I'll see it tomorrow, and I'll call you back."

How can one do anything but encourage such a visionary?

On the way over to the theater, for the telecast, I reported to Rintels about Roger's call. "Isn't it amazing how these ideas occur to Roger?" I remarked. "Considering, of course, how improbable such a project could be . . ."

"Yes, indeed, very improbable," said Rintels.

It was a gala affair. The theater was absolutely full. All of the NBC production brass were there, Fred Silverman and his wife, Perry Lafferty, the entire crew from New York and Los Angeles, seated beside all the Dallas people.

At 9 P.M., the theater lights went down. The play was introduced, from the control booth, by Jane Fonda, and then the curtain rose on the stage, and a three-act play was performed, live, for the first time in eighteen years, for a vast American audience.

We in Dallas sat there and watched the action on a huge television screen which had been hung up above the theater proscenium. On it, magnified many times in size, we saw and heard Fonda as Colonel Kinkaid, Cloris, George, John and all the rest of the cast, as they gave a near-perfect performance of Preston's warm and touching drama.

Then, when the play ended, on came that documentary tribute to Preston. There, on what would have been his forty-fourth birthday, was my friend, large as life, smiling as he answered the interviewer's questions, throwing darts in his favorite local saloon, puffing on his pipe, bursting with enthusiasm.

Then we heard Henry Fonda, who quoted from Preston.

"Time," he said, "is not a clock. It is not a calendar. Time is an eroding, infinite mystery. Time is, in fact, a son of a bitch."

And then the program ended.

There was a party afterward, and Rintels came over to speak to me, obviously bursting with good news. He had checked with each member of the cast. Remarkably enough, none of the actors and actresses had any firm commitments for the next few weeks. "There's no problem in getting the play done in a theater," he said. "All that's needed is to find a producer who'll take the whole thing over."

When I got back to New York, I went to work on that possibility. Unfortunately, Roger Stevens wasn't able to arrange the dates to fit his busy schedule at the Kennedy Center, but another group of producers in California were able to do so.

On May 10, at the newly furbished Wilshire Theatre, in Beverly Hills, *The Oldest Living Graduate* opened for a six-week run. The reviews were excellent, and so was business at the Wilshire box office. Fonda, Cloris, George Grizzard and all the rest of that excellent cast Mr. Rintels had assembled repeating their moving production.

Their run is ended now, but there will be other productions of *The Texas Trilogy*.

Preston's nemesis, Clive Barnes, is no longer the drama critic for the New York *Times*. He has moved his typewriter over to the New York *Post*. In the past several seasons, his criticisms have become far less acerbic; he seems consciously to be trying to encourage, rather than destroy. That night in April, the New York *Post* assigned him to cover the live telecast from Dallas, to rereview *The Oldest Living Graduate*.

"It was probably the best of the trilogy," he wrote, the next day. ". . . but it was not . . . an outstandingly bad play. It was admired a great deal in Texas, and Washington, D.C., but like its partners, was received generously but far more coolly in New York."

Mr. Barnes' memory has failed him. His use of the word "generous" does not apply to those reviews he originally wrote.

The American theater has always maintained a tradition of regional playwrights. Some years back, there was a period when there were authors all over our country who drew on their native origins for their source material. We had such men as Lynn Riggs, of Oklahoma, Dan Totheroh, of the West, and Paul Green, of Chapel Hill in Carolina. Mr. Green's plays about his home ground and its history are classic. Lynn Riggs' play *Green*

Grow the Lilacs is the basis of the Rodgers and Hammerstein musical *Oklahoma!*

Later on, in the fifties, Bill Inge drew extensively on his home in Kansas for dramatic material. Currently, Paul Osborne's lovely comedy *Mornings at Seven*, which deals with his native Michigan, has been revived on Broadway, and is one of the season's biggest successes.

Preston Jones is very much a part of that tradition of regional American writers.

There's an old theatrical saying which showmen use to explain certain plays that develop an audience response despite adverse criticism.

It goes: *Nobody likes it but the people.*

New York critics or no, I am certain that *The Texas Trilogy* will—in fact, already has—become a major piece of American dramatic literature.

. . . And now I must get back to work, to find the right producer who will assemble the right cast for Preston's *Remember*.

15

Tea and Much More Than Sympathy

It was during the days of the British production of *The Glass Menagerie*, which was produced by "Binkie" Beaumont, then the leading London producer and operator of H. M. Tennant, Ltd. My phone rang the day before the opening, and Binkie said, "Audrey, darling, it's Binkie. . . . Tell me, what do you collect?"

"Ten per cent," I replied.

"*No*, dear," he said patiently. "I meant china, silver—or what?"

His was an opening-night question; my reply was the reflex of a lifetime.

On the wall above his desk, my client and friend Robert Anderson has a small sign, which perpetually warns REMEMBER NOBODY ASKED YOU TO BE A PLAYWRIGHT.

(To which he added, lately, "That's true, but the situation is still awful.")

The second sign, from Auguste Renoir, the painter, cautions, "First learn to be a good craftsman. That will not keep you from being a genius."

A third, from Edmund Burke, the great statesman, says, "Never despair, but if you do, work on in despair."

Finally, there is a quote from Georges Simenon, the French writer. "Writing is not a profession, but a vocation of unhappiness."

I leave these words of wisdom to serve as guideposts to all of you. Learn from Bob's wall—all of you out there who are hammering away at your second act and planning to make your future life's work in and around the theater.

John Gassner, a perceptive drama critic, once said of Bob, "He is a gentleman in an age of assassins."

I agree wholeheartedly.

In that frenetic, squirrel-cage maze which is sometimes whimsically referred to as "show business," any working relationship that continues on an even keel past, say, next Saturday, can be considered irrevocable. Bob has remained my client since 1946; we two have been around almost as long as *Oklahoma!* In fact, he once said to me, "You know, Audrey, we've been together for thirty-two years; that's longer than I spent with *both* my wives!"

I find it curious when something in one's life goes along as well as our experience together; one seems to permit it all to pass by placidly, sans any fuss. But in the words of Arthur Miller, another fine playwright, "Attention must be paid." Now, after thirty-five years, shouldn't Bob and I be waving a flag, or at the very least issue a commemorative stamp?

His first hit play was *Tea and Sympathy*, in 1953, but long before, for a decade at least, he was theater-struck. Young Bob first became involved, in the years before World War II, as a vocal student at a drama school in Boston, now gone, called the Erskine College.

One day the young singer was asked to audition for an acting role. When he entered the classroom where the auditions were being held, he met a talented young drama teacher and director named Phyllis Stohl. As he says now, "I met my life and my wife at the same time."

Phyllis, who went on to become a superb play agent, and was to work down the hall from me at MCA, was a graduate of the

Royal Academy of Dramatic Arts in London, and of the Yale
Drama School. Not only was she teaching at Erskine, she was
also directing student groups at nearby Radcliffe and Wellesley.

Bob took his M.A. at Erskine, and went on to work for his
Ph.D. He and Phyllis were married. Then he went off to serve in
the Navy during World War II. "I sometimes stayed on board
ship and wrote plays. I was worried about two things: that I
might be killed and leave the world no immortal play, and that I
might not be killed and would have to go back and finish my
Ph.D.," he later recalled.

One of Bob's plays won an Army-Navy award for the best
play written by a serviceman overseas. He wrote two more plays
before the war ended, and they earned for him a two-thousand-
dollar Rockefeller fellowship. "In those days," he comments,
"that was a great deal. So I didn't have to go back and finish my
Ph.D."

By this time, Phyllis had come to New York and gotten a job
working at ABC radio. Eventually, she joined the Theatre Guild,
where she became involved in the weekly production of that organization's prestigious hour-long radio show.

Phyllis had received Bob's prize-winning play, *Comes Marching Home,* by mail from the Pacific. She'd given it to a friend
who worked for the thriving theatrical production firm run by
Howard Lindsay and Russel Crouse, and eventually, the script,
highly recommended, came to me. I read it and thought it first-
rate. The drama of a returning serviceman and the problems he
encounters in civilian politics, *Comes Marching Home* seemed to
have the feeling of such a strong piece as Sinclair Lewis's *It
Can't Happen Here.*

I went to work to find Bob a producer, and he, home and in
civilian clothes, went to work to support himself and his wife.

Eventually I was able to secure the play a production, at the
Blackfriars' Guild, a Catholic drama group which had a small
theater on West Fifty-seventh Street. *Comes Marching Home*
was well received, and although it did not go anywhere else,
Bob was sufficiently encouraged to continue. The American
Theatre Wing asked him to teach playwriting in the Professional

Training Program, which took place in a small remodeled church in the West Forties.

"I've never taught playwriting," said Bob, dubiously.

"They said I had written plays, and I had done some teaching. *'Put them together.'* So I taught the class," he remembers, "and, incidentally, taught myself. If you want to learn something, teach it."

The young couple lived in a basement apartment in the same brownstone which housed the Theatre Guild. Upstairs, Phyllis labored for the radio department; downstairs, her husband pounded his typewriter. Eventually, the powers that be at the Guild deigned to give the young writer an opportunity to do an adaptation for radio. When TV drama began to flourish, he did scripts for "live" dramatic shows. But all the while, he continued to write for the theater.

In 1954, when our firm, Liebling-Wood, was purchased by MCA, the burgeoning entertainment agency, Phyllis also moved over from the Theatre Guild to become an agent there, specializing in the representation of young, unestablished playwrights. She took special delight in unearthing talent; she enthusiastically prodded and encouraged her various clients, cheering them on, ever helpful and sympathetic to their failures and frustrations. No fewer than eight produced plays—by her discoveries— wound up being dedicated to Phyllis Anderson.

When we found ourselves working together, one day I suggested she might wish to take on Bob's career. "Perhaps it would be better for you to represent your husband," I said.

Phyllis was appalled by my suggestion. "No, God, no, Audrey!" she exclaimed. "No, no—this is the way it should be. I don't want to represent my *husband!*"

. . . And so proudly I continued to represent Robert Anderson.

Several years passed, and Bob wrote another play, *The Eden Rose.* I was able to arrange for it to be tried out at a summer theater in Ridgefield, Connecticut. Although it was subsequently sold to a firm called Theatre, Inc., that organization was unable to cast the play properly for Broadway, and eventually the option lapsed. But Bob continued to write. (I suppose he had already placed those signs on his office wall.) He is a persistent man, and over the years, as I've said, I have come to believe that quality may be the most needed aspect of the playwright's personality.

His next play, *Love Revisited*, was optioned by the Theatre Guild. It was on the first day of rehearsals, up at the Westport Country Playhouse, that he received the crushing news: his wife Phyllis had a form of incurable cancer.

After *Love Revisited* returned to the author's filing cabinet, he worked at an adaptation of a novel by Donald Wetzel. *The Wreath and the Curse* was eventually given a production down at the Arena Stage, in Washington, D.C., under the title *All Summer Long*. That script was retrieved from a discard pile in a producer's office by Alan Schneider, the director. Schneider liked it well enough to arrange for the Arena Stage people to read it. But again, its eventual run in New York, in 1954, would be short —sixty performances.

As Bob remembers, "My wife and I asked a young actress friend how she was bearing up in her first year in New York. She said, 'It's not so bad. It gets lonely, but my landlady has me down for tea and sympathy.' That phrase hit me. I went home and wrote it down. Each of us has a kind of built-in Geiger counter which reacts to material. . . . A few years later I wrote a play and used *Tea and Sympathy* for the title. When I thanked the actress for the title, she said she had never said it, and the landlady hadn't had her down for tea, let alone sympathy. But it was in my notebooks."

Tea and Sympathy was an extremely well written drama which dealt in a sensitive manner with the agony of a young adolescent in a boys' prep school, where his peer group comes to suspect him of being a homosexual.

It was the final scene of the play which became so famous. There, the headmaster's attractive wife, touched by the boy's anguish—he has been to visit a local prostitute in an effort to prove his manhood, and failed miserably in the attempt—

decides to relieve his agony by seducing him. Just before the curtain, she begins to unbutton her blouse, and then comes the legendary line—

"Years from now, when you talk about this—and you will—be kind."

A quarter of a century láter, it's difficult to explain how daring that scene was in the theater. We were still years away from the permissive sixties, in which four-letter words would begin echoing, like angry gunfire, across Broadway stages. Who could foresee the time when young females—and males—would appear, sans G-strings, or even pasties, for eight performances weekly? And as for sex, and the sexual act, hitherto a well-kept dramatic secret, barely referred to, all of it would emerge from the locked closet to such an extent that audiences, once titillated, now yawned. (Was it not that eminent American philosopher Miss Gypsy Rose Lee who had warned us, "Nothing is duller than bare flesh"?)

But in the preemancipated days of 1953, *Tea and Sympathy* was a tough sell. Producers shied away from it. One afternoon Bob came up to my office at Liebling-Wood and I regretfully told him I'd had no luck at all placing it with a producer. He'd given me five bound manuscripts. I had four, now well worn and somewhat tattered, to return to him. One copy was still out. "It's over at the Playwrights Company," I said. "Let's not give up hope until we hear from them."

I had no idea how good that advice would be. Several days later, I had a call from the Playwrights. Bob's play had been read, and that prestigious group wished to option it for a Broadway production!

(If a playwright had brought me that plot development in a script, I would have rejected it as being too fanciful.)

The Playwrights Company was a unique organization, formed back in 1938 by Robert E. Sherwood, S. N. Behrman, Elmer Rice, Maxwell Anderson and Sidney Howard, certainly five of the most talented and successful American authors ever known to the theater. Guided for many years by the astute legal and managerial advice of the legendary John F. Wharton, these men had bonded together to produce their own plays. Ever since, the Playwrights Company had brought to Broadway a number of highly prestigious—if not always profitable—productions.

For a variety of logistic reasons, by the early fifties, the Playwrights had branched out into the productions of plays by other dramatists; some ventures that would succeed, others respectable failures. *Tea and Sympathy,* which was produced in association with Mary Frank, would prove to be one of the firm's most lucrative hits. Bob himself would become one of the managing partners in the Playwrights, and he would lend his considerable skills to its operation.

But all of that lay in the future, still. First came the complicated process of producing *Tea and Sympathy,* with that third-act curtain scene which would cause such controversy.

The director would be the talented Gadge Kazan, and Deborah Kerr was cast as the headmaster's sympathetic wife. Young John Kerr—no relation—would play the tortured student.

The play opened at the Shubert, in New Haven, in September 1953.

When the curtain fell on the final scene, with Deborah slowly unbuttoning her pink blouse, there was silence. Finally, there came applause. It was clear that the New Haven audience, while impressed with the play, had been caught completely off base by the sudden emergence—in the flesh, so to speak—of dat ol' debbil s-x, which had hitherto been merely hinted at, or mentioned by musical-comedy comedians on the Shubert stage.

Afterward, there was the usual postmortem meeting at the Taft Hotel. All the members of the Playwrights were there, along with Bob, Gadge, Liebling and myself. Someone suggested that the final scene was far too bold and literal, and that to avoid future tangles with the censors, it should be toned down, perhaps eliminated completely. It was suggested that the scene might offend, didn't work, and something must be done.

I remember well Kazan leaving the hotel suite living room and stalking into an adjoining bedroom. "Over my dead body," he said. "If it's cut, I shall leave the play."

At no time was there such a possibility; we would have fought it. The Playwrights decided to leave things as they were; the play was in good shape, and there would be no tampering. *Tea and Sympathy* went on to the Ethel Barrymore Theatre in New York and became a smash hit.

Throughout the long and successful run, I never sat through the final scene without an audience being held, totally. During those moments, nobody ever moved, coughed or whispered. Deborah and John played it with such sensitivity, and it was so well written and directed, how could anyone have been offended?

A year or so later, Bob and Phyllis gave me a dogwood tree which I had planted outside our Westport house. Every spring it blooms, wonderful light pink in its blossoms, the same shade as the blouse Deborah wore in her final scene. It always reminds me of that electric theatrical moment.

Bob was now established as a major playwright, but his next few years would be disastrous.

Phyllis, brave lady, was carrying on with her work, but with declining strength.

And then, Bob was hit with a plagiarism suit.

John Wharton, whose autobiography *Life Among the Playwrights* is an insightful memoir of those days, wrote: "If you ever have the good fortune to write a successful play and the bad fortune to be sued for plagiarism, you will be surprised by the amount of shock it produces. For willful plagiarism is a form of stealing—theft of another person's creative work—and to be *charged* with theft does something to the nervous system that is hard to describe. There have been people who were never able to write again after going through a plagiarism suit. . . . In Bob Anderson's case it was particularly shattering because his wife was drawn into it. And if ever there was a completely honorable woman, one who could really qualify in every way as Caesar's wife—it was Phyllis. No wonder he was temporarily stopped short in the field of creative writing."

The plaintiffs in the case alleged that they had submitted a play to Phyllis, at MCA, and that she, in what is known legally as "breach of trust," had given it to her husband to read. Subsequently, they alleged he had copied *Tea and Sympathy* from their manuscript.

The irrefutable fact, which would later be proved in court, was that *Tea and Sympathy* had been written *before* Phyllis ever saw the other script. The plaintiffs, confronted with this evidence, withdrew their suit, but, needless to observe, not before Bob—and the Playwrights Company—had paid over considerable legal fees.

I sold *Tea and Sympathy* to MGM for a whopping sum. While we'd had no censorship problems in New York, other productions did cause Bob trouble. When the play was done in London, Bob had to go over to make certain changes to satisfy the Lord Chamberlain. He went to Paris, where Ingrid Bergman played the leading role. In that enlightened city, there were no problems. The French seemed quite well adjusted to adultery. But when the time came for the film version, it was a long and complicated problem to get *Tea and Sympathy* past the still-potent Legion of Decency.

As Bob later recalled, "They told me at MGM, 'Of course you can't write the screenplay because movies are a totally different medium.' But they let me write a first draft to try to lick censorship problems. They decided it was all right—and so I became a film writer."

That was in 1956, the year Phyllis was to die.

Forty-eight hours before she died, she called Kay Brown, who'd been working with her at MCA, and asked if Kay and I would come over to see her at the hospital.

She lay in bed, pale and dreadfully ill, but this was not to be an occasion for sympathy. Phyllis, as always, was concerned, not about herself, but for her "brood"—her clients, those young hopefuls she handled. She had the list of their names, and she wanted us to take over their future affairs and see to it that they were properly represented. One by one, she went through their names, to tell us about each of her particular hopefuls. This one was gifted with a good story sense, but not so good at dialogue.

That one had problems with plot development. Another was financially strapped, and would we please help him to get work to sustain him? And this author had a fine comedic sense, and possibly could develop it for a Broadway audience . . .

She could not rest until she had made certain her chicks were resting in hands as capable as her own.

John Gassner once inscribed a book to Phyllis: "To Phyllis, who led a whole new generation of playwrights into the theatre." His statement and the legitimate theater which was subsequently named for her in Manhattan are a fitting but somehow less than adequate tribute to a remarkable spirit.

It took Bob some time to recover from such a loss, but he literally wrote his way out of his grief. He had developed a skill which resulted in his doing a script for MGM, *Until They Sail,* and when director Fred Zinnemann offered him the job of adapting *The Nun's Story* for the screen, he went to work on the project. With Audrey Hepburn as the star, the picture became a great success.

By 1958, Bob was back at playwriting, and finished a new play, *Silent Night, Lonely Night.* It was a gentle love story dealing with two lonely people who accidentally came together on Christmas Eve in a small New England inn.

The script was read by Henry Fonda, who was instantly taken with the male lead. Fonda told Bob he would agree to do the play, he would tour with it; he was so enthusiastic about its potential that he even suggested Bob direct it.

Word that Fonda had fallen in love with *Silent Night, Lonely Night* spread quickly; he himself let it be known how enthusiastic he was about starring in it. With Peter Glenville directing, the Playwrights Company production was planned; Barbara Bel Geddes was signed to play opposite Fonda.

So great was the advance word of mouth on the play that a major film company got in touch with me. Their representative offered a preproduction deal before rehearsals began. In 1959 the movie business was suffering deep wounds from the inroads of TV. Such preproduction deals were not easily gained.

But the proposed deal had one proviso. The film would not star Fonda. The studio reserved the right to do its own casting.

When Bob so informed Fonda, the news caused quite a ruckus. Fonda felt betrayed. So great was his faith in the play he had always envisioned himself in it on the screen. If it were to be sold out from under him, he let it be known he would consider it a breach of faith.

There was only one ethical way for us to proceed. We gave Fonda an opportunity to try to make a deal for the screen rights to the play in a "package," that would include his services as star. He agreed, and promptly presented the project as a proposed film to Universal, where he'd previously made such deals.

We waited to hear from Fonda. Sad to relate, Universal was not interested. They passed. Bob's new play went into rehearsal for Broadway, minus any film deal. Half a million dollars had swiftly vanished into the silent night.

Three days into rehearsal, our star underwent a strange metamorphosis. He literally fell out of love with *Silent Night, Lonely Night*. He continued to rehearse, to play his part, to do his best; Fonda is far too great a trouper ever to lay down on the job in any sense. But somehow, the performance he gave, during the tryout and then on Broadway, was not imbued with the same enthusiasm he'd felt before. His lack of excitement could not help but be communicated to his costar, Miss Bel Geddes, and since Bob's play was essentially a star vehicle for its two major performers, *Silent Night, Lonely Night,* was half a success. That vital spark needed to stir the audience, to dynamize its reaction, simply wasn't there. The play received indifferent notices, and ran a brief 124 performances before it closed.

Eventually the screen rights were sold—years later—and a film version was made, modestly enough, with a price far below that original six-figure offer. Starring Shirley Jones and Lloyd Bridges, it became a two-hour film for TV, and was shown at the appropriate time of year, just prior to the Christmas holidays.

Silent Night, Lonely Night proved to be such a success with TV audiences it turns up regularly in prime time year after year, usually at Yuletide. Ironically, Bob does not receive any further payment; the rerun fees have long since ended. Bob called me last year, over the holidays, and said ruefully, "Audrey, if I ever decide to write a film about the Easter Bunny, promise me we'll keep a large piece of it?"

Although he's far from sober and serious, and is blessed with a sense of humor permitting him to laugh at his own foibles, Bob had not yet tried his hand at writing a comedy.

The manner in which he set about doing so is indicative of how a shrewd teacher does his research—in this case, on you, his audience.

By that time, Bob had met and fallen in love with the lovely actress Teresa Wright. After they'd married, he came and told me he had decided to write something—"For Saturday-night audiences," he explained.

I asked what he meant by that, and he explained. "Somehow, on Saturday nights in the theater, there's always a letdown with my plays. I've noticed that ever since *Tea and Sympathy*. Deborah Kerr hated playing that night; she said the audience was totally different from the rest of the week.

"Perhaps it's because I am too much of a gentleman, and on Saturday night, you don't want to go out with a gentleman. Saturday nights are when you go out to have a real wide-open good time. Hank Fonda used to remark on the same thing—those Saturday people. I guess it's because they don't want anything serious. So I've decided to write something that will not only work during the week, but will keep the Saturday night crowd happy."

That "something" turned out to be not one but four plays—of various lengths, to be played on one bill—and they dealt with subjects Bob had never before tackled.

The first, a broad farce, dealt with an actor being interviewed by a producer who wished to know whether or not the actor would tackle a part which called for him to appear naked onstage. There were three others, a short drama and two comedies. The title of this bill would be *You Know I Can't Hear You When the Water's Running*.

"What do you think?" he asked.

"One thing's sure," I said. "You've certainly written a different sort of 'something.'"

The individual plays were fine. But would an audience accept such a fragmented evening?

"These are for the Saturday-nighters," he insisted.

"Hopefully they'll come for the other five nights as well," I said.

First, we needed a producer. I submitted the script to many established producers. No takers.

Then, one day, a pair of young men came into my office. With no prior experience in production, they wished to find a property to do on Broadway. One was Gilbert Cates, who'd had a good deal of experience in commercial TV, and the other was his partner, Jack Farren.

As theater producers they were an unknown quantity. But they were talented and enthusiastic.

I called Bob. "Shall we try them?" I asked. "Remember—they've never produced before."

Ever the pragmatist, Bob said, "What have we got to lose?"

Nothing at all, and as it turned out, in this remarkable gambling house of a business, a great deal to gain.

Gil and Jack optioned the plays, engaged Alan Schneider as director, cast them and produced them on Broadway. The critics were entertained and wrote hit notices. *You Know I Can't Hear You When the Water's Running* became a smash.

The Saturday-nighters justified Bob's research—in spades. They showed up for many, many weeks—every night.

There's an interesting footnote to the genesis of *I'm Herbert*, the hilarious two-character play which closes that four-part bill. It's a scene, sharply observed, between two old people, a man and his wife, who rock back and forth in their chairs on a porch and exchange conversation. Age has somewhat dimmed their memories, and they are constantly confusing each other with their questions and answers about time, place and themselves.

I wondered how the original notion for such a sharp piece of character study had come to Bob, and he grinned. "Oh, that one," he said. "That's actually Teresa and me.

"We were discussing taking a trip out West one night," he said, "and we mentioned stopping in Denver. Teresa was delighted. 'Oh, yes, let's go back there!' she said. 'That was where we spent that wonderful night in the hotel room, remember, darling?'

"I stared blankly at her, and then I finally said, 'Teresa, I'm sorry, but I've never been in Denver in my life.'

"She stared back, and finally, she asked, 'Are you sure?' I shook my head. Then suddenly, she burst out laughing, and said, 'Of course! It wasn't you at all, dear, was it? . . . But it *was* a wonderful night.'

"That gave me the idea—because I realized as I'd gotten older, I was doing the same thing—confusing places I'd been with others, mixing up people and events and dates. And that's where *I'm Herbert* came from."

Bob's next was a moving drama, *I Never Sang for My Father*, which Gil Cates produced and directed on Broadway, in 1969. There's a strong autobiographical cast to this play, which deals with the classic relationship between a strong father, now aging, and the son who has felt all his life he has somehow been inadequate in his father's judgment. The first and last line of the play is, "Death ends a life but it does not end a relationship, which struggles on in the survivor's mind towards some resolution which it may never find." Obviously autobiographical, the play dealt with a universal problem. I found it very touching, and I had high hopes for it.

Somehow, the play did not please Clive Barnes, then the major critic, on the New York *Times*. He found the play maudlin, and dismissed it with a lukewarm notice.

How ironic it was, the following day, when Bob, still smarting from this review, went to Sardi's for lunch and was somehow seated at a table next to Barnes himself! A friend of ours, Lewis Funke, then in the *Times* drama department, told me he met Bob in the lobby at Sardi's that day, and Bob, overwrought, said, "I don't know what to do! This man is a contemporary of mine, and he doesn't like my work, nor me—and after all these years in the theater, I don't know how to cope with it!"

It was one of the few times—very few over the years—that Bob had lost control.

But, professional to his fingertips, he came back off the ropes. Perhaps it is his sense of humor that sustains him. A year or so later, Gil Cates produced and directed a fine film version of *I Never Sang for My Father,* which starred Melvyn Douglas and Gene Hackman, and the film was very well received. It has since become something of a perennial, a minor classic playing regularly in art houses and film societies.

Since then, Bob has continued to write for the theater: he did an interesting bill of two plays in 1973 titled *Solitaire, Double Solitaire.* He has also written two novels—*After* and *Getting Up and Going Home.* In between, he writes for film and televison. Able to adapt his considerable talent to the various media, each of which calls for such different skills, he is a remarkable example of a professional, and I use that word in its best sense.

Bob has also given a great deal of his valuable time to helping others. Not only has he served as president of the Dramatists Guild, but he has also worked closely with the New Dramatists Committee, that remarkable group here in New York; he was one of the very first playwrights chosen to be in its pilot group back in 1949 when Howard Lindsay began this project, and over the years Bob has assisted the New Dramatists, which continues to do so much to encourage and foster new playwriting talent.

Several months ago, he delivered the manuscript of his latest play to me.

In my opinion, it could certainly rank as his best work. But with the commercial theater in the haphazard state that it is, it's taken time to find Bob's new play the appropriate producer. Fortunately, we have now "cast" the right man for the task. Roger L. Stevens has the play under option, and plans a production to open in the fall of 1981 at the Kennedy Center in Washington. Its title is *Free and Clear.*

Not too long ago, Bob gave a talk to a group of interested playwrights at the Dramatists Guild, and he closed his remarks by saying, "In the middle ages, the mapmakers drew in the world as far as they knew it, and around the edges of the known world, they wrote, in big letters, BEYOND HERE ARE MONSTERS. Well, playwrights are always venturing into that world of monsters . . . personal monsters, to find out what they didn't know they knew, and often what they didn't know they felt. That can be frightening, and healthy, for playwrights."

I suggest you playwrights would do well to tack this one above your writing desk as well.

16

Arthur

I've never thought of myself as particularly imposing or over-bearing. As a matter of fact, some years ago, writer William Goyen wrote, "In a tough profession, dominated by female brigands who throw stink-bombs over the literary sandbags behind which they crouch, Audrey Wood is not only a notable literary agent but a *woman*, and not your mother." (Those are his italics.)

But about twenty years back, a young Harvard graduate showed up in my office, and his visit forced me to reappraise my self-image.

His name was Arthur Kopit, and he's been my client ever since. But that earliest stage of our acquaintanceship was marked with a massive misunderstanding. It was mutual. I couldn't tell he wanted me for his agent, while he was too much in awe of me to ask.

We desperately needed our own John Alden, some messenger to bridge the verbal gap. Luckily, one finally came along.

Arthur is a lanky, cheerful man who has a great sense of humor—as anyone who is involved in playwriting will tell you, it is a godsend—and he has a total lack of pomposity. His is a constantly interesting mind, and he manages to communicate ideas to his theatrical audiences in dramatic visions that are at once original and arresting.

As a Harvard undergraduate, Arthur had begun writing short plays, staged by the Dramatic Club. Even then, so obvious was his talent that he won a traveling fellowship to Europe while still in his senior year.

In the summer of 1959, Arthur wrote a long one-act play—or so, at least, he'd originally conceived of it. The play's length, like Topsy, grew and grew. He finished writing it in Scandinavia, and submitted his manuscript to a playwriting contest being held by Adams House, at Harvard.

Arthur's play won, and while he was still abroad, enjoying his travels, a young Harvard classmate, Michael Ritchie, gave the play a production in Cambridge, at the Agassiz Theatre.

Arthur was far away. He and a group of friends were basking in the Spanish sun on the Torremolinos beaches. "I'd told my friends over and over the play was rotten," he remembers. "So we spent the evening drinking absinthe at the Bar Centrale with the owner, and I said at one point, 'I am so glad to be thousands of miles away from that disaster!'"

The following morning there was an urgent knocking at Kopit's door. A messenger was delivering a cable from one of his friends in Cambridge. The message read: "DO NOT SIGN WITH ANY-ONE. PLAY GREAT SUCCESS. REPEAT DO NOT SIGN!"

"My friends in Torremolinos were furious," says Arthur. "Why'd you tell us it stank?" they demanded.

"'Well,' I told them, 'we all make mistakes.'"

Young Michael Ritchie, who has since become a very success-ful film director, was even then aware of the value of publicity. He had persuaded the Boston newspaper critics to go far afield from their accustomed rounds to review this student production. All of them attended, and wrote excellent reviews. In fact, "The best play of the season," announced one critic, "is a play by a Harvard student!"

. . . Who had not yet seen his own work performed.

Naturally, the news traveled down from Boston, and raced through our business. People began talking about a play with a remarkable title—*Oh Dad, Poor Dad, Mama's Hung You in the Closet and I'm Feeling So Sad*. It was said to be funny, and at the same time had won its author some sort of prize for the longest title ever to grace a theater marquee.

Before he'd gone to Europe, Arthur had been introduced by mutual friends to Roger L. Stevens, the distinguished theatrical producer. Since Stevens had been impressed by the young man's talent, he went to see this new play in Cambridge and decided it might be a good bet for Broadway—all of this while Kopit was still far away, in Spain!

Stevens sent word to Kopit's parents that he would like to option the rights to their son's play as soon as he returned from Europe. And then, being the remarkable man he is, Roger suggested that Arthur must promptly get an agent. He refused to negotiate for Arthur's play until he could deal with someone who would properly protect Arthur's interests.

Who should that be? As it was later reported to me, Roger sent word to the Kopits: "I can't think of anybody better than Audrey Wood." And then he added a comment which I shall always cherish. "You must have her," he insisted, "because she's hell with producers, but great for playwrights."

Not only did he say it, but Roger, showman that he is, dramatized his remark. On his desk in Washington, he has a replica of a dinosaur bone, beneath which are clustered several small dinosaurs. Roger is fond of showing this to visitors. He refers to the display as "Audrey Wood protecting her young."

By the time the young absentee playwright had returned from his travels abroad, I had read *Oh Dad*. I thought it demonstrated remarkable talent. Here was a young man who had a superb sense of comedy, at times surrealistic, and a bizarre, original outlook on life; he had put them all together in this play. Yet . . . I had to wonder about its future. A hit in Cambridge, in those placid groves of academe on Brattle Street, yes . . . but would it work amid the jungles of Forty-fourth and Forty-fifth streets?

Our meeting was arranged. Arthur met me at a Fifty-seventh

Street restaurant and we lunched. By the time we'd met, I'd decided I wanted to represent him, not only for its future, but for whatever he would write.

We had a delightful lunch. He told me he was going back to Harvard and wanted time to make a decision as to whether or not I would be coming into his life. Among other things, he said he wasn't sure I had sufficient time to give him. As I look back now, I think perhaps Arthur didn't even believe I liked his play as much as I had said. He told me *Oh Dad* was to be produced again, a few weeks later, in February 1960, at the Loeb Theatre in Cambridge. I congratulated him, and wished him well.

He thanked me for the lunch, and left.

As far as I was concerned, nothing had been settled.

I suppose it was what sports writers call a stand-off.

Oh Dad went into rehearsal, and again, I began to get bulletins about it. Siobhan McKenna and Michael Wager, two good friends of mine who were acting in another play in Cambridge, had heard all about the play and this brilliant young writer; they were anxious to know if I'd heard of him and I told them indeed I had, in fact, I'd been in touch with him, and was waiting to hear back from him but had not.

On Arthur's opening night I sent him a wire in which I said something to the effect that I'd hoped I'd be the one who'd get the brass ring. Through the grapevine, I heard that quite a few of my competitors—other dramatic agents—had flocked up to Cambridge to attend that performance, and to woo Arthur.

Still, I heard nothing from him.

For weeks there was no communication between us, until one day I heard from Arthur in a most unique fashion. I had a call from Arthur Wang, whose publishing firm, Hill & Wang, seemed to be interested in printing the text of Kopit's play, even before any Broadway production.

"I'm sorry," I told Wang, "but I have nothing to do with that play, nor its author."

"That's strange," commented Wang. "I just spoke to Kopit up in Cambridge about publishing his play, and *he* said, 'Call Audrey Wood; she's my agent.'"

The logjam had finally broken. Arthur became my client, Wang became his publisher, and we've all three remained so ever since.

Those had to be heady days for Arthur. Barely out of college, he had a Dramatists Guild contract with a first-class producer, and a potential future as a professional playwright.

But it didn't prove all that easy.

When the time came to produce *Oh Dad* after that Cambridge success, Roger Stevens decided the play might do better with British audiences first. Experimental theater was thriving in England; it was the time of Samuel Beckett and Harold Pinter; we all agreed with his decision. Since Stevens had a close relationship with the British producer Binkie Beaumont, he made a partnership deal to mount the play in London.

Frank Corsaro was hired to direct, and to play the lead, the flamboyant Madame Rosepetal, the legendary Stella Adler was hired. Such casting was also a bold step: while Stella had been a powerful dramatic star years before, lately she'd retired and spent her time running a successful acting school. She herself was somewhat nervous about returning to the stage, but Stevens and Corsaro finally persuaded her to do so. I remember even her students urging her to do *Oh Dad*, so excited were they by the prospect of her taking the lead.

British Equity made a special dispensation and permitted Stella to work in that country. The rest of the cast was British. Liebling and I went to England to attend the opening performance of *Oh Dad*, which tried out in Cambridge.

The opening night audience was very enthusiastic; they loved Arthur's play and laughed a great deal. It all seemed to be going well. Both Liebling and I had other appointments to attend to, so we left England and returned to New York confident that *Oh Dad* would be a hit in London.

We were sadly mistaken. By the time the play arrived in London and opened at the Lyric Hammersmith, the performance was far from what the actors had played out of town. So was the audience reaction. Arthur called us to report the bad news. During the entire first act, there had not been a single laugh; the bemused London audience simply had no idea it was attending a comedy. The second act went somewhat better, but the opening night of *Oh Dad* was nothing at all like what we'd seen.

Arthur told me later that the late Kenneth Tynan, who was a fan of the play, spent the intermission on that disastrous night speaking to his fellow critics, insisting to them, "This is not a good production of this play!"

But it was no use. The London critics savaged *Oh Dad*. The following day, Binkie Beaumont called Arthur personally to warn him. "Don't," he told our young client, "go anywhere near the stage."

Things were that bad. *Oh Dad* closed shortly after.

Before the play had been produced in London, I had a call from Jerome Robbins, who was then a client of MCA, for whom I worked. He'd read the play and liked it and told me he wished to direct it. But such an arrangement was impossible: Frank Corsaro had already been signed for the job.

Much to my amazement, after the British disaster, Robbins called again, and informed me he'd still like to do *Oh Dad*—which, under the circumstances, seemed doubly courageous on his part.

It took time to assemble a proper cast. A deal was arranged between Roger Stevens and T. Edward Hambleton's Phoenix Theatre, up on Seventy-fourth Street, in a small off-Broadway theater. Jerry selected Jo Van Fleet to play Madame Rosepetal, young Austin Pendleton to play her son, and Barbara Harris to play his girlfriend.

Because *Oh Dad* was such a special play, Robbins told us he felt there should be a second play on the bill. Prudently enough, he was "buying insurance" in case the audience didn't go for the longer play.

Arthur had written a shorter play called *Sing to Me Through Open Windows,* and he brought it to Robbins, who agreed to make it the second play on the bill. He put it into rehearsal.

Since there were now two plays in rehearsal, that period before the opening lasted much longer than had been planned, but to Roger's credit he was very patient, and never complained about the extra costs.

Then came the problem of deciding in which order the two plays should be performed. Should *Oh Dad* be played before the other play, or after?

There were many run-throughs at the theater, in which Robbins tried the plays both ways, with no decision forthcoming. One night he tried *Oh Dad* first, the next night after.

Finally, the great mystery was solved. Everyone decided we didn't need *Sing to Me Through Open Windows* at all. It had become obvious that *Oh Dad* could play by itself!

It was the right decision. The critics loved Arthur's play, and it became a hit. It stayed up on Seventy-fourth Street for two years. Later, it would be sent on tour with Hermione Gingold playing the lead, and would then return to run in a Broadway theater.

With a solid hit running and weekly royalty checks arriving, with all the press accolades and the excitement *Oh Dad* had created, Arthur's career had gone into instant orbit. Here he was, pushing twenty-three, and by his own admission somewhat bedazzled by it all. "I'd always wanted to be a success, and in my own mind I'd given myself until the age of thirty to make it," he commented, later. "Here I was, eight years ahead of schedule —amazing!"

Under such circumstances, it would have been relatively simple—almost customary, in fact—for young Arthur to be seduced away from the legitimate theater. One phone call to California, one message to announce that Kopit was available, and the offers for my young client would have poured in. Even without such a call, there were constant inquiries from "the Coast." Film studios and TV companies beckoned, waving fat offers for his writing services. He was certainly the hottest of the hot.

Over the years I've been an agent, I've seen other authors, far too many, in fact, who've written a play, had it produced, and achieved success—and never written for the theater again. That first trip to California somehow always seems to become a one-way street. The legitimate theater can't compete with the weekly California payoff, and we here in New York, who deal so steadily in speculative futures, are always the losers. When those talented men and women do return to Manhattan, they talk wistfully of sitting down soon to their typewriters and "knocking out" that second play, or that original musical comedy libretto. Then, having seen the current plays, they fly back West, to their next well-paid assignment.

Since I felt Arthur's talents were truly unique, I knew the theater would be a difficult place for him to work in, but ultimately more rewarding. I was jealous of his talent. I wanted him to make full use of it. Since he was certainly young enough, he would have ample time in the future to move out to L.A. and work in films. Perhaps it was unbusinesslike of me to shield him from Hollywood, but I hoped he would stay on here, live on his royalties and write for the theater. I was pleased when he agreed with me.

In 1965, his curtain raiser, *Sing to Me Through Open Windows*, was produced off Broadway, along with another, longer play, *The Day the Whores Came Out to Play Tennis*. While the two works were respectfully received, they were not commercially successful. Undaunted, he went back to write other plays.

I was to discover that Arthur had his own methods of work. At one point he came to me to tell me he had an idea for a story which would deal with a murder taking place during the performance of an opera. I thought this was a promising start, and waited to see what would ensue.

I thought no more of it until a few nights later. Liebling and I had tickets to see *Aida* at the Metropolitan Opera. Imagine my astonishment when, during one of the crowd scenes, I spotted my young client Kopit, in costume, milling about in a crowd of operatic Egyptians!

"What were you doing in that opera last night?" I asked him the following day.

"Research," he told me.

Somehow, the opera project did not materialize, and he went on to another. Meanwhile, I'd sold the film rights to *Oh Dad*, and Paramount released the picture. It starred the late Rosalind Russell as Madame Rosepetal, with Bobby Morse and Barbara

Harris as her son and his girlfriend. In the somewhat startling title role, Oh Dad himself, Jonathan Winters made a brief appearance as an embalmed corpse. His character may have been symbolic of the entire venture, for somehow the film totally misfired. Satire is the most fragile of commodities, and faithful as it was to the structure of Arthur's play, *Oh Dad,* so consistently hilarious to theatergoers, did nothing to film-ticket buyers —what few there were. It remains one of those rare pictures which does not even show up on the Late Show.

But by that year, 1967, Arthur had brought me his next play, a full-length work called *Indians.* It represented a great step forward for him; it was a bold and important evocation of the tragic story of our frontiers—of that endless bloody struggle between the invading white man and the hapless native Americans. I was impressed with what he had written; I felt Arthur had written a major piece of theater, more than justifying my faith in him. I was delighted when I was able to arrange a production of it with the Royal Shakespeare Company in London.

I remember when Liebling and I were sailing over to London to see the first performance of *Indians* there, and he asked, "Audrey, how do you possibly expect the British can play all those very American roles?"

Well, the British did, and their production was marvelous. Arthur and I both felt this was a play which would have a better start in a country which did not have the long and anguished history of oppressing the American Indian. To play it first in London was a wise decision. Even with an all-British cast, the production captured the spirit beautifully. Audiences responded to it, as did the critics.

I proceeded to arrange for the American production.

Since *Indians* is a complex play which calls for a large cast, it seemed prudent to find a tributary theater where the production costs would not overwhelm the venture. Thus, the first American performance took place in Washington, D.C., at the Arena Stage. The Arena was then and still is under the direction of Zelda Fichandler, a capable lady who has guided many exciting dramatic works through their first productions.

One day in Westport I received a phone call from David

Susskind, the TV and film producer. He said he wanted to buy the film rights to *Indians* before it opened in New York. He made me an offer.

I told him I was sorry, but I didn't think his offer was sufficient to interest Kopit. Then I hung up.

Liebling heard my end of the conversation, and he asked "Audrey, what did he offer?"

I told him—$150,000.

My husband, always the pragmatist, asked, "Do you have any other interest in the picture rights?"

I admitted I did not.

He said, "Then don't you think it was rather rash of you to turn him off?"

"No," I said. "I'm sorry, but I think this property is worth much more."

"Tell him so," said Liebling.

He was absolutely right. I decided to pursue David's offer, and when we reopened the conversation, David and Arthur's lawyer, Frank Weisberg, agreed to discuss it further. David asked me if he might read Arthur's script.

The play had closed in Washington; it had not yet begun previewing in New York. I discussed Susskind's request with Arthur, and we both felt his play, so complicated on the typed page, would be difficult to read. Few people have the gift of being able to read a play script and to make a judgment on how it will seem when played on the stage. A good play is not meant to be read; its worth can be easily misjudged.

I worried that a reading of *Indians* might disconcert Susskind, and he might change his mind about buying it.

When I told him so, he offered to go to the theater and sit in on a rehearsal. I vetoed that suggestion. Then he offered to wait and see the first preview performance. I was very firm. I insisted that if he truly wished to buy *Indians* before it opened, he must sign a letter of intent immediately, agreeing to a specified price. I suggested a mammoth price for an unproduced play—$400,000 —plus a percentage of the film's eventual profits.

The letter of intent was drawn and sent over to David. While I waited for it to return to me, signed, I must say I was somewhat nervous. Such a price was truly huge, especially for a sight-unseen deal. Would David change his mind at the last minute and refuse to sign?

What I did not know at the time was David had already discussed this project with Paul Newman, who had strongly reacted to the idea of playing the lead in such a film, the legendary Buffalo Bill Cody. Reinforced with such a commitment from Newman and his partner, John Foreman, and certain in his mind to finance the picture would thus be no problem, David felt secure enough to sign my letter and return it.

Indians in its American production was far less successful than it had been in London. We were overproduced and over-sound-effected. The director, Gene Frankel, had decided the sound of horses' hooves was symbolic to the theme of the play; he wanted the hooves to be heard all over the theater, and he spent precious hours of rehearsal time listening to the pitch of the stereophonic effects, getting them exactly right, rather than trying to direct his actors. I can still remember the leading man, Stacy Keach, standing on the stage, patiently waiting for the sound effects to be tuned properly. It was not an easy time for him, nor for the rest of the large cast. Nor for the actors, nor for his agents.

Whatever the cause, mechanical or human, the flaws were glaring, and while *Indians* was an artistic success, it was not a commercial one.

And David, who'd paid over a huge sum before he'd ever seen or read the play, was not at all pleased by what he'd acquired.

A year or so later, he asked me to lunch, to discuss another matter—yes, we were still talking to each other—and he somewhat ruefully said "You know, Audrey, I will never, never forget what you did to me. You taught me a lesson. I will never prebuy a play."

I said, "David—*you* called *me*, remember?"

Eventually, Dino di Laurentiis and Susskind turned *Indians* into a film, and Paul Newman played Buffalo Bill. Robert Altman was hired to direct and, as he always does, took over the preparation of the screenplay and its production. He proceeded to revise Arthur's original play considerably; his version bore little, if any, relation to the stage play. Even the title was rewritten. It became *Buffalo Bill and the Indians*.

I was quite put off by what Altman had done. Arthur disagreed. "Even though there are only three lines of my original script on the screen," he said, "Bob Altman was completely faithful to the *spirit* of the play."

I respect Arthur's opinion. After all, he is the only person whose opinion matters. But *Buffalo Bill and the Indians (Or Sitting Bull's History Lesson)*, as it was finally titled, was released in 1976, to coincide with the Bicentennial celebration, and even with a cast that included Paul Newman, Burt Lancaster, Shelley Duvall, Joel Grey and Geraldine Chaplin, the picture was not a commercial success. Dyed-in-the-wool Altman fans may have enjoyed it; the customers did not. I'm told di Laurentiis himself was dismayed when he saw Altman's finished work. I feel sorry for him; I'm sure he felt that with such a title, he was to be the proud producer of an old-fashioned cowboys-and-Indians shoot-'em-up epic, so beloved of his Italian countrymen. What he finally saw was a strange, moody Altman vision—a Wild West show fashioned to serve as a parable of American history. A far cry from what *Variety* has always called Westerns—"oaters."

Opening nights are customarily harrowing, especially so for playwrights. Over the years I've sat by while many of them ran the gauntlet, each one responding to the ordeal in a different fashion. Such a talented titan as George S. Kaufman, who had more hits than most, was never secure on his opening nights. He could not bear to sit through them but paced dozens of miles, back and forth, into every nook and cranny of the rear of the theater. Bill Inge perched himself in the rear of the house, huddled on the steps going up to the balcony, hidden from sight. The ultimate worrier may have been Howard Lindsay, who refused to attend the premiere performance at all. He would sequester himself downtown at his club on Gramercy Park, the Players, where he would spend the evening at the billiard table. During the intermissions uptown, his collaborator, Buck Crouse, would dash to a pay phone in the theater lobby and keep Howard posted on how things were—or were not—going.

Tennessee Williams was an exception. On first nights, he always seated himself in the orchestra, in plain view of all, and usually enjoyed himself. Excepting perhaps for that one night, years back, in Boston, when *The Battle of Angels* opened, with smoke billowing from the stage, and anxious customers coughing and exiting angrily from the Wilbur. (Had anyone asked me that night if I represented the author of the play, I confess I would have found it very difficult to say, "Yes, I do.")

The Boston tryout in 1978, of Arthur's next play, *Wings*, of which I've written earlier, took place at that same Wilbur Theatre.

Arthur has no qualms about openings, at least no visible ones. On that night, he and his wife Leslie came down the aisle and were ushered to their seats in Row G. A moment or so later, just before the house lights began to dim, a tall white-haired gentleman was ushered into his seat in Row F, directly in front of Arthur. It was Elliot Norton, the dean of the Boston critics, a man whose opinion is quoted both there and in New York.

As the play went on, and Constance Cummings gave her stunning performance as Emily Stilson, the gallant lady struggling to recover from her stroke, how difficult it must have been for Arthur to sit and observe, at such close quarters, the "body language" of Boston's most important critic!

Norton left the theater impassively. We had to wait until the following day to read his verdict. Happily, he had loved the play, and told his readers *Wings* and Constance Cummings were an evening not to miss.

That night, we waited for the Boston reviews at the Ritz—that same hotel where I have sat through so many pre- and post-opening-night gatherings. Over the years I've been involved in many different scenes at the Ritz, some constructive, others far less so. There have been whimsical moments as well.

I remember one night there when I'd come up to Boston to attend the first performance of a play by one of my clients, Brian Friel. David Merrick was the producer. The play was *The Loves of Cass McGuire*. Weeks before, I'd sent him the Dramatists

Guild contracts that covered the production of my client's play, but for some reason known only to David, he'd never returned the signed copies to me or the Guild. That night we all attended the premiere, and as I recall, the play went well.

David hosted a post-opening party at the Ritz Hotel, and there we met. I said, "David, now that you've actually produced the play, why don't you go up to your room and bring me the contracts—*signed.*"

Without a word, David turned and left the party. He returned in a few minutes, bearing a small manila envelope. He smiled and handed it over.

The contracts had been signed, but for a while there, we had opened without them. And I have never been certain whether he'd signed before the opening—or after.

When the Boston notices came in at 2 A.M. for *Wings,* they were excellent. I got some sleep on that excellent Ritz bed, and left the following day for New York. I was cheered by the Boston notices, but my optimism was guarded: we still had a long way to go.

Wings moved on to the Kennedy Center, in Washington. There we encountered a different reaction. Richard Coe, the critic of the *Post,* wrote a review in which he said he thought *Wings* was too clinical. The other notices were good, but I began to get reports that the Washington audiences seemed puzzled, especially by the somewhat abrupt ending of Arthur's play.

I went down to see the play again. What was wrong? I did my best to analyze the audience confusion. Eventually, I began to know what it was. John Madden, the director, had opened the performance of *Wings* with no rising curtain. The lights came up full on Constance Cummings, as Emily Stilson, reading, alone in a chair, with a clock ticking beside her. Suddenly the clock and the lamp on the table disappear, the clock skips a beat, there is a crash and Emily has been struck down by the massive weight of a stroke.

At the play's end, when Emily, who was once a wing-walker in the early days of flying, soars off—free, on imagined wings—

in that imagery which Arthur had so brilliantly invented to indicate her death, there was again no curtain—merely a total blackout on the stage.

I sat through several performances, and finally I told Arthur what I'd discovered. I suggested he should sit in different locations around the theater instead of staying in the same seat each night. He asked why, and I told him: "In certain areas of the audience, I can see Constance Cummings walking off, in the darkness, after that blackout. Perhaps the audience does, too—and if so, that's why they don't know the play's ended. *I* do, so I begin applauding to get them started. That seems to work, but, unfortunately, I can't be here every night to clap."

"How do you think we should handle it?" he asked.

"Well," I said, "how about such an old-fashioned and radical idea as to bring down the curtain?"

At first this did not fit in with Arthur's creative concept. But he took my advice and saw the play from different seats. Before *Wings* came in to New York, to open at the Lyceum Theatre, he and John Madden had taken pains to hide Miss Cummings' final exit. The audiences were no longer, as it were, left in an uncertain dark.

Such are the sometimes peculiar functions which concern a playwright's agent.

Later, with a rueful smile, Arthur told me, "The reason I didn't want to change where I was sitting in the theater was because I was happy there. Who knows, in another seat, the play might have seemed lousy!"

There was little chance of that. For her superb performance in *Wings* Constance was awarded the Tony—the Antoinette Perry Award—for the Best Performance by a Leading Lady in 1979. The great French actress Madeline Renaud, did the play in Paris, and Constance recreated her performance in London, at the National Theatre. If the British critics did not seem as wildly enthusiastic about her and *Wings* as did their New York counterparts—Richard Eder of the New York *Times* said the play was "wise, magical and shattering"—it's perhaps because Londoners are a bit less impressed by great acting than we are; they seem to have so much more of it than we do here.

And Arthur is working on a new play. It is under option to Roger Stevens, the same man who has remained his producer ever since the days, twenty years or so ago, when he produced *Oh Dad,* his first work.

In the theater, a twenty-year association between a producer and a playwright has to stand as some sort of a record. And, may I add, it's not too bad a record for a playwright and his agent, either.

17

Studs' Place

Another of my clients is Studs Terkel. Studs is a Chicago boy who has written for the theater and also in the past done some acting. Years ago, he began his career as a disc jockey and radio sportscaster. If you're old enough, you probably remember him as the pivotal character in one of the earliest television shows to be shown on your mighty seven-inch screen; it was called "Studs' Place," and during that unique half hour the actors with Studs literally improvised their weekly show, sans any written script. They merely started out each week with an idea and let it happen. Studs felt it would be more interesting that way. While the show lasted, his audience agreed with him.

Early on, Studs developed his literary talents with the considerable assistance of a new invention, the tape recorder. It enabled him to let people talk while he listened. Studs has transformed the interview into high art. His technique is deceptively simple. On his reels and tape cassettes he has assembled American history.

He is not an ordinary reporter, interested primarily in the rich, the famous, the successful and powerful. No, Studs goes everywhere and lets everyone talk.

One of his books, *Hard Times: An Oral History of the Great Depression*, has become the source material for playwright Arthur Miller, in his latest play, *The American Clock*, which recently played on Broadway.

Studs' book *Working: People Talk About What They Do All Day—And How They Feel About What They Do* was the basis for a Broadway musical several seasons ago.

When Studs learned I was engaged in preparing my autobiography his first reaction was typical: enthusiasm. "Great idea!" he said. "Long overdue! But you mustn't write about *me*," he insisted. "You've got to let *me* talk about you."

Which accounts for the next few pages. Since Studs has spent twenty years or so interviewing other people, what follows is a reversal of the customary process.

It will be Studs himself, unedited. Not listening, for once, but talking.

STUDS: My first awareness of Audrey Wood came at Christmastime during the war, in Chicago, 1944. An unknown young playwright from St. Louis, Tennessee Williams, had a play called *The Glass Menagerie;* it opened there. It was bitter cold, midwinter, and I remember how Claudia Cassidy and Ashton Stevens, our two best critics, kept writing about it and helped it survive. With the magical Laurette Taylor playing the lead, I went to see it, at least a couple of times, and then I saw this woman. Tiny, all business, wearing a pillbox hat.

I had no idea who she was then, but she reminded me very much of an actress in films, Louise Closser Hale, who played dowager mothers and very high toned society types—a brisk lady, precise, gentle—that was Louise Closser Hale. That, I discovered, is also Audrey.

She has no time for nonsense, it's How are you, dear? Yes, dear, and we're meeting at two sharp, you be there, right? Boom. That's it. No good-byes; she has no time. She sticks only to the fundamentals and specifics.

Anyway, that's when I first heard of this celebrated agent Audrey Wood. I knew she was married to Bill Liebling. As I came to know them both I discovered the world they lived in was truly Thoreauvian: the theater is her entire world. Just as Thoreau's world was the yard outside his home and Walden Pond, so the theater world is what Audrey and Bill inhabited.

Later on, Lotte Lenya, whom I'd interviewed, liked my approach and told Audrey about me. I'd been up to the McDowell Colony writing my first play, and I'd finished. It was called *Amazing Grace*. It was about an earthy woman, very much like my mother, who ran a hotel. "Amazing Grace" and its theme of revelation was her hymn.

Audrey read it, she said, "I like it, we'll get it done. It needs work, dear, but the main thing is to get it on a stage."

She arranged a production up at Ann Arbor, at the University of Michigan in 1967—a professional theater company, first-rate people, produced and directed by Marcella Cisney. The casting wasn't right. Cathleen Nesbitt, who is an elegant actress—she's in her nineties now and still acting in the revival of *My Fair Lady*—played the lead but she was wrong for the part. Can you imagine the regal Cathleen Nesbitt doing a role meant for Maureen Stapleton? But the costarring role, her son, was played by Victor Buono, and he was magnificent. Cathleen later told me her big regret in their not going to New York was that the critics there never saw Victor. The critics who saw it in Ann Arbor blistered us, especially Dan Sullivan and *Variety*. None of that was Audrey's fault, it was mine; the play wasn't good enough!

That's where Audrey showed me what sort of an agent she was. She was always there, trying hard for me. She never gives up. "Well, dear, we'll try again." She kept after me to do another. "That's important."

We come to *Working*, years afterward, based on my book. It was tried out in Chicago, at the Goodman Theatre. The director was Stephen Schwartz, a very talented young composer. He'd written *Godspell*, a big hit, then the score for *Pippin*. Now he wanted to do a show which he controlled completely, from the very start. He had preconceived notions of how to do *Working* and that was it. Nobody else could tell him. We had two producers who were not theater men, they'd come into the business lately from some other line, investment consulting, where they'd made lots of money. I knew, going in, that this would be Schwartz's show, he was enthusiastic, I liked his ideas.

He went out and got together a group of other songwriters, very talented people, Susan Birkenhead, James Taylor, Micki Grant, Craig Cornelia, Mary Rodgers, all the bright young people of our time, and they wrote a marvelous score. So far, so good. Schwartz also contributed songs.

My book *Working* was all about ordinary everyday people, doing their jobs and talking to the audience about how they lived. Waitresses, truck drivers, steelworkers—the anonymous ones who keep our country going. Not an easy job to make into a Broadway show. No costume romance, no chorus lines, none of the usual glitter. I must say Schwartz respected my book and stayed close to the spirit of it, but perhaps the original mistake was that *Working* shouldn't have been a musical at all.

Or perhaps it was something else: Schwartz overproduced it with too much scenery, too many effects. I'm still not sure.

All through this, Audrey was there with me, nursing it along, watching it. We knew early in Chicago there was something wrong . . . something basically wrong with the concept. But it was exciting, and audiences liked it. One night, Dick Horner, who's a thoroughly theatrical guy, been around for years, came to see it in Chicago and said, "This could be one of two things— either a landmark in American theater, because it's a totally new thing, or it's not going to make it at all."

We went on, moved it to New York. One day we did an abbreviated version of *Working* for the theater-party ladies— they're very important. If they like a show, they buy whole performances for their clients—charities, church groups, temple sisterhoods, all the other organizations which use theatrical benefits to raise money. That afternoon there were three shows auditioning at a theater for those ladies: Mike Nichols had one, a musical version of *Alice in Wonderland,* done by an all-black cast— *Black Alice*—and Charles Strouse had another new show, also a musical, and then there was ours. Done very simply, Steve Schwartz talking and performing the score with three singers from our cast.

Steve was wonderful, the singers were exciting, the theater-party ladies loved it, just that way, simple, on a bare stage. *Working* worked. I went out afterward with Mike Nichols for a drink·and said, "I hope your thing goes."

He said, "No, it's *your* thing that's going to go."

I said, "It would go on one condition, that you'd direct it."

Well, no chance of that although, in retrospect, I realize I was right. Steve Schwartz is a very talented man, but his concept was wrong. Too much production. A stage that literally moved. There's nothing more beautiful than actors walking; he took away their feet. He was in love with Broadway, and bigness, and technology. The complete opposite of how I'd originally thought of the show.

Too late to stop it. It kept on growing the wrong way. We were dealing with ordinary people whom the audience would recognize—the waitress, the fireman, the supermarket checkout girl—but it was all snowballing, the show was becoming so big and so overproduced that the production overpowered the cast.

Back to Audrey. She's with me all through this, she's seen a lot of theater in her time, she's trying to fight for my concept but it's past that now. We're at rehearsals where the director is trying to get his cast to understand their roles, so hard now that he's saying to the girl who plays the waitress, "Go see a waitress at work," and the actress says, "But I've *seen* a waitress at work." And it's all going back and forth.

I say, "Just let them learn the lines and sing and *act*." No use. Poor Audrey is astounded by this, she's trying to get my points across for me, but no use. Nobody's listening. If I offer suggestions, nobody wants to hear them.

Finally Audrey says, "I've never seen anything like this before," and I said, "Audrey, you've done everything you can, maybe the best thing for you to do is to go up to Westport this weekend and rest."

It was a losing battle. By now the producers weren't in charge —not that they had any idea what it was about—it was strictly the director's game now; he was in complete control, running it his way. Perhaps, looking back, if we'd had a director like Hal

Prince or Nichols, one of those guys who can infuse a show with
his own magic . . .

We opened *Working* in New York. You've heard the old cliché
—"Audiences love it, critics hated it." In this case, literally so.
Bad notices, except for Harold Clurman. He saw what we were
after. Said it was a flawed show but it was one of the few moving pieces of theater on Broadway.

Every night we had audiences giving us standing ovations—
but without the notices, it was a losing battle. I don't want to
get into the trap of criticizing the critics. Of course, they
prevailed. They hit us for the wrong reasons.

Dick Horner was right. On opening night in New York, he
came up to me, shook his head and said, "No—sorry. It's not
going to make it."

All through this, Audrey had stayed with me. Every inch of
the way.

I'm sorry about Schwartz. In fairness to him, I should say he
wanted so much to succeed, and he wanted it to be so much his
own. Unfortunately he was rigid. The word director has a mean-
ing. You *direct* a show, and it's not accidental. There was no
sense of direction. It was anarchic.

The nice thing about *Working* is that it's been produced in
other theaters around the country since then, minus all that ex-
cess scenery and overproduction, and they report to me it's entirely different. The simpler concept really works. Maybe it will
be the kind of show that develops a life after it's flopped on
Broadway, who knows?

I think it must have been tougher for Audrey to go through
something like this than it was for me. She's been around a long
time, she's so knowledgeable about theater, and has a sense of
how things should be done professionally—from all those years
of experience operating with pros. Things in the theater have
changed so radically in the past few years. Instead of producers
who respect theater, we have all those financial people coming
in, guys who bring in the money but have no knowledge of the

theater at all. She has to deal with them, and that's tough. When
you see something being done, and you know it's being done
wrong, and you can't get producers to do what they're supposed
to do—to get a show back on the right track—how frustrating
that must be! Not only for the author, but for his agent as well.

Audrey sticks with her clients. Think about the faithfulness
she's shown all those years to her other clients. From Tennessee
Williams to Preston Jones, and to Bill Inge, and Kopit and Brian
Friel, the Irishman, and all the young ones—she sticks with
them all the way. She is endearingly tough. A little piece of
leather.

Just last summer, we went down to Charleston, Audrey and I
and Kay Brown, who's always been Arthur Miller's agent. There
was to be the first production of Miller's new play, *American
Clock*, here in the United States, which has some of my book
Hard Times in it.

I have to describe what happened to us down there, not just
with Miller's play, which I like, but with Audrey and Kay and
me one day out in a car. Kay Brown has a dear friend who went
to school with her years back, and she came around with her car
to take us all out for a drive, sightseeing. A big car, and we're all
in the back, and Kay's friend turns out to be a pretty wild
driver, and soon we're out on a main street and she's going
straight down the wrong lane, and there we are, weaving and
swaying in the back of the car, hanging on. Poor Kay says, "I
don't really know if we're doing this right," and her friend
laughs and keeps right on going. And Audrey, who's just as
scared as I am, pats me on the arm and says, "It's okay, dear
boy, it's okay, we'll survive this. Don't worry."

Which, in a way, sums up the whole story of our relationship,
doesn't it?

18

The View from the Sixth Floor

"There are more playwrights than people."

It's now the summer of 1981, and I'm as busy as ever. Still going up in the elevator each weekday morning directly to my office, without time to stop off at those art galleries on the floors below.

There's the customary pile of play scripts on my desk. For almost half a century now, they've arrived, those manuscripts bound in red, blue, yellow—typed, mimeographed, now often xeroxed. There may be fewer plays produced each year on Broadway, but there never seems to be a shortage of hopeful playwrights with their wares aimed at Forty-fifth Street. And even though the business—if one can call it that—gets tougher with each passing season, hardly a day passes without a call from other hopefuls who ask, "Miss Wood, have you a play I may read? I want to be a producer."

I can bring playwrights together with producers, and marry them together by contract. The trick is to make a marriage which will last past that first six-month option . . .

After we sold our firm in 1954 to MCA, Liebling did not wish to remain in the business of representing talent. He had always nurtured the dream of becoming a producer. Gradually, he withdrew from the daily activity involved with his acting clients. He kept one or two, such as Pat Hingle, but he began to occupy himself calling other play agents and suggesting that they send him scripts.

But as time passed, he could not seem to find a play which interested him sufficiently. Perhaps it was being married to me that hampered him. He was too professional to consider reading a script I was handling as an agent. How could other play agents not assume I wouldn't show my own husband a good script first? Ours is a business which feeds on such gossip. In fact, one day I heard a rumor that another agent had said she could not ever submit a script to Bill Liebling because obviously, if he wished to produce it, her client might very well end up becoming *my* client.

I was so hurt and angry by this malicious story that I went to her office and confronted her with it. I had it out with her then and there. "How dare you do this to my husband?" I demanded. "He sincerely wants to read plays and produce one. In all my life, have I ever touched a client of yours?"

She had to concede I hadn't.

But the truth was, being married to Audrey Wood, with all her playwriting clients, proved not very helpful to William Liebling as a potential producer.

I'd always wanted him to remain in his office, wherever that might be. But he resisted doing so—first at MCA, and then at Ashley Famous, Inc. Perhaps he somehow felt if he kept an office in a talent agency, he would inevitably be drawn back into being an actors' agent. And he'd had over forty years of that, quite enough.

For several years he continued looking for a play. But the old Broadway Liebling had known for all those years of the '20s and '30s had undergone great changes. Where once dozens of plays thrived each night, the theater district had shrunk in the '60s to a few short blocks where marquee lights still shone. Most of those active producers of his time had retired or quit, unable to compete with mounting financial pressures.

The problems of raising the money to get a play produced today are endless; costs have risen to such a dizzying peak one can only demonstrate them by citing actual figures. For example, in the days when Liebling-Wood was in business, say in 1943, a venturesome producer, Alfred de Liagre, could produce a hit play such as John Van Druten's *The Voice of the Turtle* for roughly ten thousand dollars. This week, in 1981, Mr. de Liagre has a play running called *Death Trap*. If his box office should not take in at least ten thousand dollars tonight, for *one* performance, the production will be in dire trouble. It will not have made this night's running expense. May I add that, in this particular instance, there is no such worry.

Eventually, Liebling gave up his producing ambition. He stayed in our hotel suite at the Royalton, where we'd lived since we'd first been married, and busied himself each day with various other matters. Being a man of action and a true patriot, he took to writing letters to congressmen and other members of the government, to speak out on the matters of politics and government he felt were important.

Politics, foreign affairs, economics—he was interested in all of these. Nothing escaped his attention. When Lynda Bird Johnson, the daughter of President Johnson, broke up her momentary romance with George Hamilton, Liebling wrote Mrs. Lady Bird Johnson a note telling her how happy he was to hear the news. "I must tell you, madame," he concluded, "actors are fun to know, but not to marry."

Back came a lovely note from the White House, with a personal thank-you from the somewhat relieved mother of the lady in question.

He also involved himself in charitable projects. After Castro took over the government of Cuba, many Cubans fled his regime. In 1959, many of them arrived here in New York, most of them bringing with them little more than the clothes on their backs. It was a cold winter. Liebling heard of the plight of the refugees. Touched by it, he began calling his friends to collect warm clothing for these unfortunates.

One morning he called our good friend Lou Schweitzer, the husband of the theatrical producer Lucille Lortel, and brought up the problem. Lou, a marvelously generous man, said, "I think I can be helpful. Meet me tomorrow and we'll see about it."

The following morning the two Good Samaritans met, and proceeded downtown.

They drove to a loft building off Fifth Avenue, in which a friend operated an overcoat factory. Once upstairs, Lou produced his checkbook, and wrote a check for five thousand dollars' worth of overcoats, to be turned over, through Liebling, to those Cuban refugees.

Liebling was a man of very strict morality. One night, a few years before he died, I asked him to accompany me to an off-Broadway production of a new play by a young author in whose work I was interested. As I recall, the play was being done in a store downtown, away from Broadway.

It was a play which dealt with an incestuous love affair between a brother and sister, one in which the sister becomes pregnant, by her brother, and the climax came when the poor pregnant lady, in crisis, needs a doctor—and the brother is unable to bring himself to leave their apartment to go find her help.

Finally, Liebling couldn't stand this any longer. He got up and stomped out, headed for the street, furious at what he'd seen. I followed him out and caught up with him. Before I could say anything, he turned and said, "Audrey Wood, what has become of you!"

I put out my hand to his arm, but he yanked it away, rigid. "No, no!" he insisted. He was so angry, he wouldn't allow me to *touch* him! He simply could not adjust to this new permissive era.

During the '60s, we began to spend more and more time in Sarasota, Florida, during the winters. Liebling's health was not being helped by those bitter Manhattan winds. When we'd first become aware he needed a more moderate climate, I went to Ted Ashley and suggested it was time for me to retire, and to spend my time with my husband.

"No, *no!*" insisted Ted. "You mustn't. You'll stay with us, keep your office and secretary, we'll pay your travel expenses, but you must continue to represent your clients."

His was good advice, for which I've always been grateful.

I went back and forth between Florida and New York. I was in constant touch with my office, and if there were plays to be covered in which my clients were involved, I would go up to Philadelphia or New Haven or Boston. I found other activities: one winter in Sarasota I ran a playwriting class at the nearby theater.

We moved into a large apartment there. One day Liebling had found the place, a building on Long Boat Key; he'd walked into a newly completed structure, and on impulse, signed a lease. Since I was busy in New York, he proceeded to furnish it completely, from scratch, and he did a superb job.

For those years, Sarasota seemed an answer. But then Liebling made another career decision. He had begun to be bored with the sedentary Florida life. Just as he had decided it was the proper time to sell Liebling-Wood, so now did he feel it was the propitious time for us to move, bag and baggage, to California.

Liebling explained his reasoning. The current state of the theater in the late '60s was rapidly changing, and in those tumultuous times, it was not for the better. He was anticipating the time when Los Angeles would become the future base, not only for film and TV but for whatever developments lay ahead in the entertainment business. Out there we had many friends, as well as clients. Should anything happen to him, this ever thoughtful man wished me to be surrounded by them. As always, he was planning for my future. So we must follow the instructions of Mr. Horace Greeley, and head West.

If dear Liebling had not died of a heart attack in late December 1969, we would have been on our way.

After his death, I did not choose to live in California.

Ever since, I have remained in Manhattan, unretired—thank God!

Liebling was a wonderful husband. One day, in my office, there arrived a huge bouquet of flowers. It was my birthday, and he'd remembered. Roberta Pryor, one of my associates, came in to ask where they'd come from, and I told her. Roberta remembers my saying to her, "It's wonderful to be married to a man who thinks you can do no wrong."

Which, in retrospect, is precisely the way I felt about him.

19

Are There Any Questions?

Do I believe in every play I sell? Yes, I do. Understand, there are certain plays which in my opinion have a very limited audience. There are certain plays that I feel will have a bigger audience if they're rightly produced, but as far as I'm concerned, I've always tried to work with writers whose quality of work I admire.

For example, I worked for years with a lady named Jane Bowles, on a beautiful play called *In the Summerhouse*, which Oliver Smith, the set designer, used to option each year for production. Jane was a short-story writer, a woman of enormous talent, and this was her only play—a very special one—and whenever Oliver Smith made any money from designing scenery, he would renew his option. Such was his deep faith in the play. This went on for years, and finally he got the play produced—in the season of 1953. It had a limited, distinguished run, with Dame Judith Anderson playing the lead; I believe Jean Stapleton (of "All in the Family") made her debut in it. Great notices, but it lasted only three months. Since then, another producer, a man named Hale Matthews, decided to make it into a film, and he kept on paying option money for the screen rights. It's a very special project. Perhaps one day it will be made into a film, perhaps not; but I shall keep on trying.

Each property has to find its proper niche. Sometimes it does, sometimes it doesn't; but one must keep on trying. Often, the timing is wrong. A great deal of theater history is made by *being there at the right moment, with the right people.*

Take the case of *Love Among the Ruins,* by my client James Costigan. Back in the early sixties, when Alfred Lunt and Lynne Fontanne made their TV debut, playing in *The Magnificent Yankee,* George Schaefer, the director, thought they could be lured into doing an original play for TV, and he discussed the project with Costigan. Costigan—who had written *Little Moon of Alban,* the award-winning play which starred Julie Harris, and had written a play called *Baby Want a Kiss,* which had a brief run with Paul Newman and Joanne Woodward—went to work and came up with a lovely story of a lady and a distinguished British barrister, involved in a breach-of-promise suit in the British courts.

The Lunts thought it would be a good idea, and Costigan went to work and completed a first draft, and then a rewrite. But then the Lunts turned it down. Perhaps it had something to do with the title; that word ruins did not appeal to two people of such advanced age.

The script sat in my office for years. I tried various ways to secure a production, but never did the pieces fall into place which would work properly. One day I had lunch with a TV producer and out of our conversation, I suggested the perfect leading lady—Katharine Hepburn. This was 1974, years later.

Miss Hepburn is a formidable lady. I called her up and said, "Miss Hepburn, I have a script I'd like you to read for TV."

Almost spitting, Miss Hepburn said, "Miss Wood, I don't do TV."

"But Miss Hepburn," I said, "you just did *The Glass Menagerie* on TV."

"Well," she conceded finally, "send it over."

I did. She read it. She invited me to tea in her house on Forty-ninth Street, and said she liked the part. "But we need a great *male* star," she told me.

Which I well knew. She proposed showing the script to her good friend, George Cukor, the director. She took it to L.A. and showed it to Cukor, who said he adored it, and he proposed taking it to London to show to Sir Laurence Olivier.

Then I received word from England, through Olivier's agent, Laurence Evans, that he was not interested. Once again, we were stymied.

Miraculously, Olivier's agent called again. Olivier had been under the impression we were proposing a film; if it were for TV, he *would* do *Love Among the Ruins!*

But we weren't yet set. There was a large impasse over billing: whose name would come first, Hepburn's or Olivier's?

That problem necessitated several more lengthy hassles, until finally Miss Hepburn herself proposed the solution: she would take top billing in the United States; Olivier could have top billing in England, his native land, and they would both divide up the rest of the world equally!

Eventually, all the pieces fell into place, and the production was shot in London—and almost ten years after Costigan had originally written the script, it was seen on television, in 1975, as a "spectacular."

Face it, all those years, the script sat in my office, and I kept on trying to find it the proper production. Perhaps, in the hands of another agent, it might never have been done at all; but I had faith in it, and finally it happened.

Who knows how many plays have died, unproduced, because it was simply too difficult to put the right pieces together?

What's ahead?

Robert Anderson's new play, *Free and Clear*, is under option to Roger Stevens, at the Kennedy Center. We're trying to arrange for the right director to take it on, and hopeful of finding one, so that casting can begin. It's a long process and a complex one, but it's necessary if a play is to be produced in 1981.

I've had two plays running out of town this fall. One of them is called *Rainbow Dancing*, and it's by one of my clients, Ed Graczyk. He's the author of a play which was produced off Broadway some seasons back, *Come Back to the Five and Dime, Jimmy Dean*. His new play deals with the dance halls of certain parts of Texas, where it seems married ladies whose husbands have gone to work, or whose children are off at school, can spend their daylight hours. The play opened in Columbus, Ohio, at a community theater. I think it is an interesting work, one which should find a home off Broadway, and I have found a producer who agrees with me.

The second play is called *Sweet Prince*, and it's by A. E. Hotchner. It was given an out-of-town production in St. Louis, at a theater called the Loretto Hilton. It was well received out there; if the producer decides to continue, *Sweet Prince* will be produced at a regional theater, or in New York.

There's also a gentleman in California who's been preparing a musical comedy version of William Inge's *Bus Stop*. People who've heard the score are very impressed. But we are merely beginning. Mr. Kevin Casselman, the hopeful producer, does not have a director, he has no backing yet, in fact, we do not even have a clearance for this project from Twentieth Century-Fox, which owns the rights to *Bus Stop*. However, it's quite possible that if we keep at it long enough, all the pieces will come together and there will be a production.

Each year, sixteen talented young writers are selected on the basis of their work to come to the National Playwrights Conference at the Eugene O'Neill Theatre Center in Waterford, Connecticut, and to have their plays given staged productions by professional actors. The process consists of three and a half days' rehearsals, after which the performance is given before an invited audience. Then comes a session of criticism, in which the author sits and answers questions from those who've seen his work in progress.

It's a grueling process, but an intensive learning one. Ever since 1964, when George White founded the O'Neill, and Lloyd Richards, the dean of the Yale Drama School, has run it, dozens of talented playwrights have been given invaluable experience. Lanford Wilson, Albert Innaurato, John Guare, Martin Sherman, David Berry and Christopher Durang, to name only a few, are all alumni of the O'Neill's summer sessions.

One of my clients who underwent the process this past year is Joseph Pintauro, who brought a new play called *The Snow Orchid*. The other is a young woman named Sybille Pearson, whose play is *Sally and Marsha*. In my opinion, both are extremely promising works. *The Snow Orchid* will be given a reading in New York at the off-Broadway Circle Repertory, and *Sally and Marsha* was done this past winter at the Yale Repertory Theater, in New Haven at its Winterfest. It is now headed for Broadway.

We shall see what happens to them after that.

By the time you read this, some, if not all, of the returns will be in.

And I shall by then be working on other play projects, some of which are still merely taking shape in playwrights' typewriters . . .

20

Coda

One of the things which bother me about the theater these days is the way sound is being used to amplify mechanically the voices of singers—and actors. I'll never forget going to see *Jesus Christ Superstar*. I almost went out of my mind with the noise, and I was so affronted by the sight of Jesus, *holding a mike*—and then the singer who played Jesus, kicking the cord with his foot every so often! The late Arnold Weissberger, the theatrical attorney, hadn't yet seen it, and he asked me one day, "Tell me, Audrey, is it really anti-Semitic?" And I said, "No, Arnold—it is merely antitaste."

I've always been proud of that.

I've been around long enough so that people tell me I have become a legend in my own time.

It's flattering to be so considered, but I've also been around long enough to know how rapidly, in this business, a legend can be displaced by next week's attraction.

Recently, I went to the opening night of a new play *The Tricks of the Trade*, by Sidney Michaels, starring George C.

Scott, produced and directed by my friend Gilbert Cates. When the curtain fell, at ten-fifteen, and the audience filed out of the Brooks Atkinson Theatre, none of us were yet aware we had been present at its one and only official Broadway performance. After reading the next morning's reviews, it was decided to close the play. Its opening night had been its closing night. According to *Variety,* that one-night run cost five hundred thousand dollars!

. . . So I have no illusions about permanence in the theater, for anyone—least of all myself.

But I must admit I am proud to have been a woman who's "made it" in what was once essentially a man's game. Today, there are numerous females in positions of power everywhere. Even in Hollywood, the head of production at Twentieth Century-Fox is now a woman, Sherry Lansing.

But in my youth, women were typists or answered phones. Or were decorative objects, up on the stage.

When I first started out, I never even thought about the obstacles which lay ahead of a young girl. I merely plunged in, went ahead, doing what I had to in order to survive. If there's one lesson I've learned, or may have been born knowing, it's that if you believe in yourself, you can do practically anything you set out to do.

I've been doubly blessed. Not only did I believe in myself, but I found a husband who believed in me fervently. If anyone had ever suggested I could be Queen of England, Liebling would have been the first to say, "She's absolutely right for the job!"

. . . And he would have meant it.

If you ask me what it is I do, up here on the sixth floor, even after all these pages, I can probably explain it best by saying, "I bring people together."

Even creative types who don't want or plan to be together.

And somehow, in this complex world of egos through which I travel daily, they must always feel this has happened without my guidance.

Several seasons ago I represented a play called *The Changing*

Room, by the British playwright David Storey. It had been a success in London, but it was a very special sort of work, one which dealt, on an allegorical basis, with the lives of a group of footballers in a small British club. Not an easy play to bring to New York.

Arvin Brown gave it a tryout production at Long Wharf, in New Haven, and Charles Bowden, a producer, became interested. But we still, even after rave reviews, had no New York production.

There were two ladies in my life then, both of whom had indicated that they were interested in producing. I went home, thought about the problem and decided to bring them together. Since Bowden had never met either of the ladies, I asked them all to come to my office. We were working against time, we had a limited run in New Haven and the obvious plan would be to move the show to New York. The two ladies represented enough money to capitalize the New York run.

It was like weaving a beautiful piece of golden cord together. When Bowden and the two ladies left my office, *The Changing Room* was on its way to New York and to critical success. That season it won the Critics Circle Award for Best Play.

But I always make sure everyone else thinks it's his or her own idea. It's a very subtle technique, but for me it's worked.

Being a small woman with a quiet voice also helps a good deal. I enjoy the idea of coming in with a group of creative types who are in the midst of a crisis—which occurs many times in the course of my day—and responding with grace and humor.

There are times when, believe me, it's tough.

I have a temper, too.

But I don't leave the room.

An agent cannot afford to lose her temper.

As Harry Truman's famous sign said, "If you can't stand the heat, get out of the kitchen."

I'm still in the kitchen, forty-odd years after the day I came up to William Liebling's office with some scripts in my briefcase, in response to his request to bring some plays he could read.

If I'd missed his original phone call, back then, who knows? My life might have been completely different.

Different, perhaps, but still involved with the theater. For, as I warned you early on during the exposition of my first act, Audrey Wood was, and will remain, hopelessly, constantly, on a twenty-four-hour daily basis, stagestruck.

A POSTSCRIPT

by Max Wilk

For the past three years I occupied a privileged status in Audrey's world. At her request, I was her Boswell, helping her with this autobiography.

With a total recall that is simply astonishing, with little or no recourse to reference books, she answered questions, supplied background material, and offered up incisive anecdotes by the hour. And I have laughed at her dry wit, empathized with her clients' triumphs, mourned their failures and sympathized as she described the incredibly patient work, long hours and constant faith and effort she lavished on those whose talent she admired. For all the years since she opened up the first manuscript and, as she described it to me, ". . . Somewhere a little light goes on, and you know—this one is worth working for."

I believe that is the key to Audrey Wood. It was always for others.

Right up to that night in April when she came home to the Royalton Hotel and started across the pavement to the apartment where she'd lived with Liebling since they'd first been married, back in 1938, and where she remained ever since, Audrey was hard at work, for others. And the only thing that could stop her forward motion was an accident even she couldn't cope with.

For after thousands of battles with producers and directors and actors on behalf of her clients, she had coped with everything else.

Monday and Tuesday of that week had been set aside for reading sessions of the final copyedited manuscript of *Represented by Audrey Wood*. Before it went to the printers, Audrey had insisted that she go through those 300-odd pages one more time. A career of negotiating legal documents and contracts had conditioned her to be hypercareful when it came to affixing her name to anything as vast as this bulky manuscript. Every *i* must be dotted, each *t* crossed.

Monday, I read through the pages without her. Then, as planned, Tuesday morning I went over to the Royalton Hotel to meet her at 9:45, to escort her crosstown to the Doubleday offices. I arrived at 9:43, and there stood Audrey, on the steps, waiting. Typical of her; always prompt, precise and available.

She spent that long Tuesday sitting in the conference room, neatly and succinctly responding to all of the red-ink queries. When it came to the mention of her birth, there was one note that caused her to chuckle aloud. It was a question pertaining to the exact date. "You may not want to answer that," I suggested. "Oh, why *not?*" replied Audrey. She wrote down the exact date in February 1905, and then added firmly, "It was a Sunday."

It was late Tuesday afternoon before she finally finished reading through the manuscript. We had a brief chat with the Doubleday editor; galley proofs would be back in early June. Audrey nodded. Should she set aside time then for reading the galleys in that month?

No, we told her, there was no need. In June she must plan a vacation, for in July, as always, she would spend a work week up in Waterford, Connecticut, at the Eugene O'Neill Conference, sitting with her promising playwrights and encouraging them to go forward. By August she would certainly have several productions headed for off- and on-Broadway, and in September there would be those customary out-of-town tryouts with all the assorted tensions and crises she has coped with all these years. Then, in October, there would be the publication of *Represented by Audrey Wood*. Certainly she would be interviewed, and promotion of the book would take a great deal of time.

So why should she not plan a June vacation, a cruise perhaps, a long quiet time at sea? "I've always loved that," she once confided. "I get aboard with a batch of books—all reading for pleasure, not commerce. No phones, no crises, no office, and if I so choose, the greatest luxury—I don't have to *talk* to anybody unless I want to."

Call the travel agent, we urged.

"It's a thought," said Audrey. "Now I really must get back to my office, where I'm sure there's been quite a lot happening while I've been sitting here, luxuriating in the past."

As usual, she was right. Up at 40 West 57th Street, on the sixth floor, there were dozens of phone messages of her to answer. Complex business affairs that needed her personal attention, and various dates to keep before she could sleep. . . .

Wednesday was another business day, a long one. After a hasty supper, she had a date to go to the theater, to see a play she'd already seen once. It wasn't pleasure; as usual, there was commerce involved. The evening continued at a Sardi table until nearly midnight.

"It was remarkable," reported producer Lester Osterman. "We were talking in all directions—nothing was being settled, and then Audrey took over. She chaired the meeting. Somehow, she literally turned everything around, and by the time we left Sardi's, we were all operating on the same wavelength."

That was Wednesday evening—or to be precise, early Thursday morning. By 11 A.M. that same day, Audrey was back in her ICM office, that cheerful corner room with its posters of the plays she'd represented hanging on the walls beside framed awards won over the years by those same works; with bookshelves crowded with books and scripts, the long sofa against the wall covered with stacks of more scripts; with framed photographs of friends and clients (in her case, the words often synonymous) everywhere.

When she returned home Thursday night at 9 P.M. to the Royalton, briefcase full of scripts in hand, she stepped out of her taxicab and collapsed on the sidewalk. Kind, concerned people inside the lobby hurried out to help her, got her to her suite, and called her doctor. Several hours later, she was taken to Mount Sinai Hospital. She had suffered a massive cerebral hemorrhage and had lapsed into a coma.

The years of hard work and effort on behalf of others, those endless late-night hours spent at out-of-town theaters, or in tiny off-Broadway lofts, or at midnight conferences in hotel suites—those weekends spent in reading plays, and the patient sessions of encouragement and ego-massage with her clients, past and present—they may go unrecorded, but all the results will not be. Not by those who were there with her.

"Audrey was a very special breed," said one Broadway veteran last week. "Most agents who represent a play show up on opening night. The rest of the time, you're lucky if you can get them on the phone. Not Audrey. When it was her client's play, she was with it all the way. It was her baby."

In the theater, curtains rise, lights come up and plays go on. If, by some remarkable alchemy, the play succeeds with critics and then audience, it will be repeated tomorrow night. Statistically, it probably won't. Compared to show business, quicksand is a permanent footing.

". . . No, it doesn't get any easier as one goes along," Audrey remarked once, somewhere in the midst of one of those conversations we have taped for the past several years. "In fact, I think it's much harder. It becomes tougher each season to find producers for the sort of play I'm interested in, and with costs going up so fast, I'm sometimes surprised when I can find one at all." She sighed. "There are times when I'm almost certain there's no place left in this so-called commercial Broadway theater for good writing or serious thought. We need playwrights so badly—but so few young people have the backbone to put up with all the constant obstacles in their path. And who can blame them for going to television? It worries me enormously. . . ."

But were they not the same obstacles that she, as the author's hardworking agent, continued to encounter, each and every day?

"Well, of course, but that's my *job*," said Audrey, smiling. "For which, through the peculiar lavishness of Mr. Marvin Josephson of ICM, I seem to be paid each week. Isn't it marvelous that, at my age, he considers it worthwhile to keep me on?"

"Since he's certainly not a philanthropist," I suggested, "you must be earning your keep."

She shrugged. "For which *I* should thank him," she said. "I enjoy it. But I do worry so about all those potential young people, huddled over their typewriters, scratching away, fighting for space, hoping to get the play written and produced, somewhere, somehow. Lord, how they all do need help. . . ."

They had been getting help from Audrey Wood Liebling, all the help she has been able to provide, right up until 9 P.M. on the night of April 30, 1981.

. . . Their loss is everyone's loss.

June 15, 1981

TRIBUTES

Robert Anderson

"Bob, I'm off to Seattle tomorrow to see a new play, but if you need me, call." . . . "I'm off of Louisville, but if you need me . . ."

Audrey Wood is at this moment lying in a coma in Mount Sinai Hospital, and I need her. I have needed her for the thirty-five years she has been my representative, and I shall go on needing her the rest of my writing life.

Audrey has traveled all over this country to find young playwrights. She found me in 1945 on a battleship in the Pacific. Armed with her letter of interest, I came to New York and started a new life. In that life Audrey has been my dear companion, caring as much for the well-being of the playwright as for the success of the plays.

The loss to her playwrights and all the playwrights she might have helped is incalculable.

Kitty Carlisle Hart

My friend Audrey Wood spent most of her long and busy career serving as trailblazer, nurse and mother to talented people. Playwrights and performers fortunate enough to have this extraordinary lady in their corners—and her client list is impressive indeed—can and will testify to Audrey's dedication. She has nurtured and cherished—brought into blazing triumph— a long list of the most important plays of our time. *Represented by Audrey Wood* is unique as a journal of accomplishment. Any reader, now and in the future, who has the slightest interest in how the American theater was and is, will derive knowledge and entertainment in joining Audrey through hundreds of opening and closing nights, on and off Broadway.

Katharine Houghton Hepburn

Audrey Wood was a tireless and imaginative caretaker for her writers—a mother—a tireless ear. She sent me James Costigan's *Love Among the Ruins* out of a clear sky—it had been written for the Lunts in the mid-sixties. It was always in her mind along with other works of other writers. Kate! she thought one day, and she acted and I liked it. And it was a boon to Larry Olivier, George Cukor and myself. Audrey was a real agent. There haven't been many.

Elia Kazan

I remember the forties and the fifties and they were good years. I remember that everytime we were trying out a play on the road, there she'd be, Audrey, as gentle as her name, and I remember her complexion, a delicate tint of orange it was and the the way she'd talk, always understanding, always supportive and so patient with the difficulties an embattled director might be having. She even understood that in certain cases what was finally there was about as much as could be done. I can't remember that she ever threw her weight around or, to be more accurate, the playwright's weight. Still, when the author needed help, a good deal for instance, yes, that too, she got it to support him through the years that were coming when the eight and a half by eleven was blank. I don't know if she was the best agent in the business, but I'm not sure I know what that phrase could possibly mean. This I know for sure, that when the best playwrights came by, they were with Audrey Wood and there was a reason.

Arthur Kopit

Audrey Wood had spread across the tabletops and desks of her office and home an extensive and lifelong collection of paperweights. I have often wondered about the lure to her of these objects. Most of them are smooth, finely painted stones. I have finally decided that somehow, and quite rightly, she perceived *herself* in them. She, like these smooth stones, held things together. Did so without fuss. Did not crumble under pressure. She was what we knew we could always count on. She was immutable.

Eva le Gallienne

It gives one a sense of pride to be able to say, "represented by Audrey Wood." For it is well known that Audrey Wood represented only people in whose talent she had faith. Since her judgment was highly regarded, this faith of hers was an accolade well worth receiving.

Audrey Wood's loyalty and integrity as an agent were unsurpassed. Her enthusiasm and her devotion to her clients was unlimited. Young playwrights found her immensely stimulating and encouraging in a constructive way, and through the years she discovered and fostered many, some of whom have, Tennessee Williams, for instance, become internationally famous.

As a friend, Audrey was a delight: wise, witty, tough and kind. We all respected and loved her and look forward to her book, which cannot help but reflect her unique personality, as well as give a fascinating picture of a memorable period in the theater in which she played such an active and constructive part.

Karl Malden

Audrey Wood—she was a playwrights' agent so I really never got to know her until I was cast in *A Streetcar Named Desire*. She was Tennessee Williams' agent. The first performance out of town she came backstage, stopped me and said, "You are Mitch. Thank you for a lovely performance."

Naturally she made a friend for life. She was quiet. Determined. And tough when she had to be. I know a few playwrights who are indebted to her, not only from a spiritual sense but from a monetary sense as well.

She was a great lady.

James Mason

I came to know Miss Wood only as recently as February 1979, when she introduced me to Brian Friel's play, *Faith Healer*.

During the brief initial career of that play in the United States, Miss Wood demonstrated an extraordinary devotion not only to her client's work, but also to José Quintero, Morton Gottlieb, my wife and myself.

In 1981, having occasion to become even more closely associated with her, we learned that her burning enthusiasm was something that had never cooled, that she was the kind of Guardian Agent without whom no professional in our line of business is complete, and that hers was a blood type that the American theater will always need.

Sidney Sheldon

Audrey Wood had a passionate love affair with the theater during nearly all her adult life. The theater is the richer for it, and so are we all.

Tennessee Williams

Thirty-one years is a long time for any kind of relationship to last between two very complex persons such as Audrey Wood and myself. I doubt that any writer has remained with a representative any longer than that. Slowly, painfully, most deep relationships wear out. Afterward, our understanding comes back slowly, and finally no bitterness remains.

I was a difficult client for Audrey from the beginning. The evening of the day when we first met in New York I remember that she and her husband, Bill Liebling, invited me to their suite at the Royalton Hotel. Sherry was served and Audrey raised her glass and said, "To us."

I don't know why I made this unintentional remark. To me it doesn't seem like me. I said, "Let's be honest and each of us drink to himself." She gave me a quick, probing look. Her looks were always probing. I suppose I blushed and smiled. Even then, the autumn of 1939, I was skeptical of sentimental gestures, and rara avis of honesty, sometimes above kindness. She understood. After we parted from each other, there were many people who thought I had been cruel to Audrey.

I recall an evening after the London revival of *Streetcar*. Miss Sue Mengers, a Hollywood agent, was seated beside me at dinner. Sue is inclined to plumpness and to an excessive appetite. I teased her by putting, out of her reach, everything she was served. I did it because I liked her, but she was not amused, and turning to the table at large, she exclaimed loudly, "How awful of Tennessee to have left Audrey."

I have a feeling that if Audrey had been there she would have said, "Sue, you don't understand." Audrey Wood's profession is one that has never been properly appreciated. Theatrical clients are often impossible people. No one understood them better than Audrey or knew so well that understanding was so essential to their existence.

June 15, 1981

Index